Integrated Research in GRID Computing

Integrated Research in GRID Computing

CoreGRID Integration Workshop 2005
(Selected Papers)
November 28-30, Pisa, Italy

edited by

Sergei Gorlatch
University of Münster
Germany

Marco Danelutto
University of Pisa
Italy

Springer

Sergei Gorlatch
Universität Münster
FB Mathematik und Informatik
Inst. f. Informatik
Einsteinstr. 62
48149 MÜNSTER
GERMANY
gorlatch@uni-muenster.de

Marco Danelutto
Dept. Computer Science
University of Pisa
Largo Pontecorvo, 3
56127 PISA
ITALY
marcod@di.unipi.it

INTEGRATED RESEARCH IN GRID COMPUTING
edited by Sergei Gorlatch and Marco Danelutto

ISBN 978-1-4419-4293-7

e-ISBN-13: 978-0-387-47658-2
e-ISBN-10: 0-387-47658-X

Printed on acid-free paper.

Printed in the United States of America.

9 8 7 6 5 4 3 2 1

springer.com

Contents

Foreword

This volume is a selection of best papers presented at the CoreGRID Integration Workshop 2005 (CGIW'2005), which took place on 28-30 November 2005 in Pisa, Italy.

The workshop was organised by the Network of Excellence CoreGRID funded by the European Commission under the sixth Framework Programme IST-2003-2.3.2.8 starting September 1st, 2004 for a duration of four years. CoreGRID aims at strengthening and advancing scientific and technological excellence in the area of Grid and Peer-to-Peer technologies. To achieve this objective, the network brings together a critical mass of well-established researchers (145 permanent researchers and 171 PhD students) from forty two institutions who have constructed an ambitious joint programme of activities.

The goal of the workshop is to promote the integration of the CoreGRID network and of the European research community in the area of Grid and P2P technologies, in order to overcome the current fragmentation and duplication of efforts in this area.

The list of topics of Grid research covered at the workshop included but was not limited to:

- knowledge & data management;
- programming models;
- system architecture;
- Grid information, resource and workflow monitoring services;
- resource management and scheduling;
- systems, tools and environments;
- trust and security issues on the Grid.

Priority at the workshop was given to work conducted in collaboration between partners from different research institutions and to promising research proposals that can foster such collaboration in the future.

The workshop was open to the participants of the CoreGRID network and also to the parties interested in cooperating with the network and/or, possibly joining the network in the future.

The Programme Committee who made the selection of papers included:
Sergei Gorlatch, University of Muenster, Chair
Marco Danelutto, University of Pisa
Domenico Laforenza, ISTI-CNR
Uwe Schwiegelshohn, University of Dortmund
Thierry Priol, INRIA/IRISA
Artur Andrzejak, ZIB
Vladimir Getov, University of Westminster
Ludek Matyska, Masaryk University Brno
Domenico Talia, University of Calabria
Ramin Yahyapour, University of Dortmund
Norbert Meyer, Poznan Supercomputing and Networking Center
Pierre Guisset, CETIC
Wolfgang Ziegler, Fraunhofer-Institute SCAI
Bruno Le Dantec, ERCIM
The Workshop Organising Committee included:
Marco Danelutto, University of Pisa
Martin Alt, University of Muenster
Sonia Campa, University of Pisa
Massimo Coppola, ISTI/CNR

All papers in this volume were additionally reviewed by the following external
reviewers whose help we gratefully acknowledge:
Ali Anjomshoaa
Rajkumar Buyya
Andrea Clematis
Massimo Coppola
Rubing Duan
Vincent Englebert
Eitan Frachtenberg
Dieter Kranzlmueller
Salvatore Orlando
Carles Pairot
Hans-Werner Pohl
Uwe Radetzki
Wolfgang Reisig
Michal Sajkowski
Volker Sander
Mumtaz Siddiqui
Anthony Sulistio
Hong-Linh Truong

We gratefully acknowledge the support from the members of the Scientific Advisory Board and Industrial Advisory Board of CoreGRID, and especially the invited speakers John Easton (IBM Grid Computing UK) and Uwe Schwiegelshohn (University of Dortmund). Special thanks are due to the authors of all submitted papers, the members of the Programme Committee and the Organising Committee, and to all reviewers, for their contribution to the success of this event. We are grateful to the University of Pisa for hosting the Workshop and publishing its preliminary proceedings.

Muenster and Pisa, July 2006

> Sergei Gorlatch and Marco Danelutto (workshop organizers)
> Thierry Priol (Scientific Coordinator of CoreGRID)

Contributing Authors

Marco Aldinucci   Department of Computer Science, University of Pisa, Largo Bruno Pontecorvo 3, 56127 Pisa, Italy (aldinuc@di.unipi.it)

Francoise André   IRISA / University of Rennes 1, Avenue du Général Leclerc, 35042 Rennes, France (fandre@irisa.fr)

Sergio Andreozzi   INFN-CNAF, Viale Berti Pichat 6/2, 40126 Bologna, Italy (sergio.andreozzi@cnaf.infn.it)

Demetres Antoniades   Institute of Computer Science, Foundation for Research and Technology-Hellas, P.O. Box 1385, 71110 Heraklion-Crete, Greece (danton@ics.forth.gr)

Elias Athanasopoulos   Institute of Computer Science, Foundation for Research and Technology-Hellas, P.O. Box 1385, 71110 Heraklion-Crete, Greece (elathan@ics.forth.gr)

Rosa M. Badia   Computer Architecture Department, Universitat Politècnica de Catalunya, Spain (rosab@ac.upc.edu)

Zoltán Balaton   Computer and Automation Research Institute, Hungarian Academy of Sciences (MTA-SZTAKI), P.O.Box 63, 1528 Budapest, Hungary (balaton@sztaki.hu)

Francoise Baude   INRIA, CNRS-I3S, University of Nice Sophia-Antipolis, France (Francoise.Baude@sophia.inria.fr)

Anne Benoit   LIP, Ecole Normale Supérieure de Lyon, 46 Allée d'Italie, 69364 Lyon Cedex 07, France (Anne.Benoit@ens-lyon.fr)

Jérémy Buisson   IRISA / University of Rennes 1, Avenue du Général Leclerc, 35042 Rennes, France (jbuisson@irisa.fr)

Sonia Campa   Department of Computer Science, University of Pisa, Largo Bruno Pontecorvo 3, 56127 Pisa, Italy (campa@di.unipi.it)

Augusto Ciuffoletti   INFN-CNAF, Viale Berti Pichat 6/2, 40126 Bologna, Italy (augusto@di.unipi.it)

Carmela Comito   DEIS, University of Calabria, Italy (ccomito@deis.unical.it)

Massimo Coppola   ISTI, Area della Ricerca CNR, 56124 Pisa, Italy (coppola@di.unipi.it)

Julita Corbalan   Computer Architecture Department, Universitat Politècnica de Catalunya, Spain (juli@ac.upc.edu)

Kevin Cristiano   École d'Ingénieurs et d'Architectes, 1705 Fribourg, Switzerland (kevin.cristiano@eif.ch)

Natalia Currle-Linde   High Performance Computing Center (HLRS), University of Stuttgart, Germany (linde@hlrs.de)

Marco Danelutto   Department of Computer Science, University of Pisa, Largo Bruno Pontecorvo 3, 56127 Pisa, Italy (marcod@di.unipi.it)

Jiří Denemark   Institute of Computer Science, Masaryk University, Botanická 68a, 60200 Brno, Czech Republic (jirka@ics.muni.cz)

Marios Dikaiakos   Department of Computer Science, University of Cyprus, P.O. Box 537, 1678 Nicosia, Cyprus (mdd@cs.ucy.ac.cy)

Piotr Domagalski   Poznań Supercomputing and Networking Center, Noskowskiego 10, 60688 Poznań, Poland (piotrdom@man.poznan.pl)

Jan Dünnweber University of Münster, Department of Mathematics and Computer Science, Einsteinstrasse 62, 48149 Münster, Germany (duennweb@uni-muenster.de)

Maciej Dyczkowski Wrocław Center for Networking and Supercomputing, Wrocław University of Technology (maciej.dyczkowski@pwr.wroc.pl)

Dick H.J. Epema Faculty of Electrical Engineering, Mathematics, and Computer Science, Delft University of Technology, Mekelweg 4, 2628 CD, Delft, The Netherlands (D.H.J.Epema@tudelft.nl)

Paraskevi Fragopoulou Institute of Computer Science, Foundation for Research and Technology-Hellas, P.O. Box 1385, 71110 Heraklion-Crete, Greece (fragopou@ics.forth.gr)

Antonia Ghiselli INFN-CNAF, Viale Berti Pichat 6/2, 40126 Bologna, Italy (antonia.ghiselli@cnaf.infn.it)

Gábor Gombás Computer and Automation Research Institute, Hungarian Academy of Sciences (MTA-SZTAKI), P.O.Box 63, 1528 Budapest, Hungary (gombasg@sztaki.hu)

Sergei Gorlatch University of Münster, Department of Mathematics and Computer Science, Einsteinstrasse 62, 48149 Münster, Germany (gorlatch@uni-muenster.de)

Anastasios Gounaris School of Computer Science, University of Manchester, UK (gounaris@cs.man.ac.uk)

William Groleau Institut National des Sciences Appliquées de Lyon (INSA), Lyon, France (william.groleau@insa-lyon.fr)

Ralf Gruber École Polytechnique Fédérale de Lausanne, 1015 Lausanne, Switzerland (ralf.gruber@epfl.ch)

Francesc Guim Computer Architecture Department, Universitat Politècnica de Catalunya, Spain (fguim@ac.upc.edu)

William Hoarau LRI-CNRS 8623 & INRIA Grand Large, Université Paris Sud XI, France (hoarau@lri.fr)

Alexandru Iosup Faculty of Electrical Engineering, Mathematics, and Computer Science, Delft University of Technology, Mekelweg 4, 2628 CD, Delft, The Netherlands (A.Iosup@tudelft.nl)

Michal Jankowski Poznań Supercomputing and Networking Center, Noskowskiego 10, 60688 Poznań, Poland (jankowsk@man.poznan.pl)

Péter Kacsuk Computer and Automation Research Institute, Hungarian Academy of Sciences (MTA-SZTAKI), P.O.Box 63, 1528 Budapest, Hungary (kacsuk@sztaki.hu)

Vincent Keller École Polytechnique Fédérale de Lausanne, 1015 Lausanne, Switzerland (vincent.keller@epfl.ch)

Thilo Kielmann Dept. of Computer Science, Vrije Universiteit, Amsterdam, The Netherlands (kielmann@cs.vu.nl)

Pierre Kuonen École d'Ingénieurs et d'Architectes, 1705 Fribourg, Switzerland (pierre.kuonen@eif.ch)

Krzysztof Kurowski Poznań Supercomputing and Networking Center, Noskowskiego 10, 60688 Poznań, Poland (krzysztof.kurowski@man.poznan.pl)

Agnieszka Kwiecień Wrocław Center for Networking and Supercomputing, Wrocław University of Technology (agnieszka.kwiecien@pwr.wroc.pl)

Jesus Labarta Computer Architecture Department, Universitat Politècnica de Catalunya, Spain (jesus@ac.upc.edu)

Alexandros Labrinidis Department of Computer Science, University of Pittsburgh, Pittsburgh 15260, USA (labrinid@cs.pitt.edu)

Sébastien Lacour IRISA/INRIA, Campus de Beaulieu, 35042 Rennes Cedex, France

Virginie Legrand   INRIA, CNRS-I3S, University of Nice Sophia-Antipolis, France (Virginie.Legrand@sophia.inria.fr)

Róbert Lovas   Computer and Automation Research Institute, Hungarian Academy of Sciences (MTA-SZTAKI), P.O.Box 63, 1528 Budapest, Hungary (rlovas@sztaki.hu)

Jason Maassen   Dept. of Computer Science, Vrije Universiteit, Amsterdam, The Netherlands (Jason@cs.vu.nl)

Sergio Maffioletti   Swiss National Supercomputer Centre, 1015 Manno, Switzerland (sergio.maffioletti@cscs.ch)

Evangelos P. Markatos   Institute of Computer Science, Foundation for Research and Technology-Hellas, P.O. Box 1385, 71110 Heraklion-Crete, Greece (markatos@ics.forth.gr)

Luděk Matyska   Institute of Computer Science, Masaryk University, Botanická 68a, 60200 Brno, Czech Republic (ludek@ics.muni.cz)

Norbert Meyer   Poznań Supercomputing and Networking Center, Noskowskiego 10, 60688 Poznań, Poland (meyer@man.poznan.pl)

Jarek Nabrzyski   Poznań Supercomputing and Networking Center, Noskowskiego 10, 60688 Poznań, Poland (naber@man.poznan.pl)

Nello Nellari   Swiss National Supercomputer Centre, 1015 Manno, Switzerland (nello.nellari@cscs.ch)

Rob van Nieuwpoort   Dept. of Computer Science, Vrije Universiteit, Amsterdam, The Netherlands (Rob@cs.vu.nl)

Ariel Oleksiak   Poznań Supercomputing and Networking Center, Noskowskiego 10, 60688 Poznań, Poland (ariel@man.poznan.pl)

Charis Papadakis   Institute of Computer Science, Foundation for Research and Technology-Hellas, P.O. Box 1385, 71110 Heraklion-Crete, Greece (adanar@ics.forth.gr)

Nikos Parlavantzas Harrow School of Computer Science, University of Westminster, HA1 3TP, UK (N.Parlavantzas@westminster.ac.uk)

Marcelo Pasin Universidade Federal de Santa Maria, Santa Maria RS, Brasil (pasin@inf.ufsm.br)

Christian Pérez IRISA/INRIA, Campus de Beaulieu, 35042 Rennes Cedex, France (Christian.Perez@irisa.fr)

Josep M. Pérez Computer Architecture Department, Universitat Politècnica de Catalunya, Spain (perez@ac.upc.edu)

Michalis Polychronakis Institute of Computer Science, Foundation for Research and Technology-Hellas, P.O. Box 1385, 71110 Heraklion-Crete, Greece (mikepo@ics.forth.gr)

Konstantin Popov Swedish Institute of Computer Science (SICS), Kista, Sweden (kost@sics.se)

Thierry Priol IRISA/INRIA, Campus de Beaulieu, 35042 Rennes Cedex, France (Thierry.Priol@irisa.fr)

Michael Resch High Performance Computing Center (HLRS), University of Stuttgart, Germany (resch@hlrs.de)

Miroslav Ruda Institute of Computer Science, Masaryk University, Botanická 68a, 60200 Brno, Czech Republic (ruda@ics.muni.cz)

Rizos Sakellariou School of Computer Science, University of Manchester, UK (rizos@cs.man.ac.uk)

Marie-Christine Sawley Swiss National Supercomputer Centre, 1015 Manno, Switzerland (sawley@cscs.ch)

Luis Silva Dep. Engenharia Informatica, University of Coimbra, Polo II, 3030 Coimbra, Portugal (luis@dei.uc.pt)

Gergely Sipos Computer and Automation Research Institute, Hungarian Academy of Sciences (MTA-SZTAKI), P.O.Box 63, 1528 Budapest, Hungary (sipos@sztaki.hu)

Raül Sirvent Computer Architecture Department, Universitat Politècnica de Catalunya, Spain (rsirvent@ac.upc.edu)

Michela Spada École Polytechnique Fédérale de Lausanne, 1015 Lausanne, Switzerland (michela.spada@epfl.ch)

Domenico Talia DEIS, University of Calabria, Italy (talia@deis.unical.it)

Sébastien Tixeuil LRI-CNRS 8623 & INRIA Grand Large, Université Paris Sud XI, France (tixeuil@lri.fr)

Nicola Tonellotto ISTI, Area della Ricerca CNR, 56124 Pisa, Italy (nicola.tonellotto@isti.cnr.it)

Trach-Minh Tran École Polytechnique Fédérale de Lausanne, 1015 Lausanne, Switzerland (trach-minh.tran@epfl.ch)

Panos Trimintzios European Network and Information Security Agency, P.O. Box 1309, 71001 Heraklio, Greece (panagiotis.trimintzios@enisa.eu.int)

Eleni Tsiakkouri Department of Computer Science, University of Cyprus, P.O. Box 537, 1678 Nicosia, Cyprus (cstsiak@cs.ucy.ac.cy)

Vladimir Vlassov Royal Institute of Technology (KTH), Stockholm, Sweden (vlad@it.kth.se)

Oliver Wäldrich Institute SCAI, Fraunhofer Gesellschaft, 53754 St. Augustin, Germany (oliver.waeldrich@scai.fraunhofer.de)

Philipp Wieder Forschungszentrum Jülich GmbH, 52425 Jülich, Germany (ph.wieder@fz-juelich.de)

Marcin Wojtkiewicz   Wrocław Center for Networking and Supercomputing, Wrocław University of Technology (marcin.wojtkiewicz@pwr.wroc.pl)

Pawel Wolniewicz   Poznań Supercomputing and Networking Center, Noskowskiego 10, 60688 Poznań, Poland (pawelw@man.poznan.pl)

Gosia Wrzesiñska   Dept. of Computer Science, Vrije Universiteit, Amsterdam, The Netherlands (gosia@cs.vu.nl)

Ramin Yahyapour   Robotics Research Institute, University of Dortmund, 44221 Dortmund, Germany (ramin.yahyapour@udo.edu)

Henan Zhao   School of Computer Science, University of Manchester, UK (hzhao@cs.man.ac.uk)

Wolfgang Ziegler   Institute SCAI, Fraunhofer Gesellschaft, 53754 St. Augustin, Germany (wolfgang.ziegler@scai.fraunhofer.de)

Corrado Zoccolo   Department of Computer Science, University of Pisa, Largo Bruno Pontecorvo 3, 56127 Pisa, Italy (zoccolo@di.unipi.it)

DATA INTEGRATION AND QUERY REFORMULATION IN SERVICE-BASED GRIDS

Carmela Comito and Domenico Talia
DEIS, University of Calabria, Italy
ccomito@deis.unical.it
talia@deis.unical.it

Anastasios Gounaris and Rizos Sakellariou
School of Computer Science, University of Manchester, UK
gounaris@cs.man.ac.uk
rizos@cs.man.ac.uk

Abstract

This paper describes the XMAP data integration framework and query reformulation algorithm, provides insights into the performance of the algorithm, and about its use in implementing query processing services. Here we propose an approach for data integration-enabled distributed query processing on Grids by embedding the XMAP reformulation algorithm within the OGSA-DQP distributed query processor. To this aim we exploit the OGSA-DQP XML representation of relational schemas by applying the XMAP algorithm on them. Moreover, we introduce a technique to rewrite an XPath query into an equivalent OQL one. Finally, the paper presents a roadmap for the integration system implementation aiming at constructing an extended set of services that will allow users to submit queries over a single database and receive the results from multiple databases that are semantically correlated with the former one.

Keywords: XML databases, semantic data integration, schema mappings, distributed query processing, Grid services.

1.   Introduction

The Grid offers new opportunities and raises new challenges in data management that originate from the large scale, dynamic, autonomous, and distributed nature of data sources. A Grid can include related data resources maintained in different syntaxes, managed by different software systems, and accessible through different protocols and interfaces. Due to this diversity in data resources, one of the most demanding issues in managing data on Grids is reconciliation of data heterogeneity [11]. Therefore, in order to provide facilities for addressing requests over multiple heterogeneous data sources, it is necessary to provide data integration models and mechanisms.

Data integration is the flexible and managed federation, analysis, and processing of data from different distributed sources. In particular, the increase in availability of web-based data sources has led to new challenges in data integration systems for obtaining decentralized, wide-scale sharing of data, preserving semantics. These new needs in data integration systems are also felt in Grid settings. In a Grid, a centralized structure for coordinating all the nodes is not efficient because it can represent a bottleneck and, more importantly, it cannot accommodate the dynamic and distributed nature of Grid resources.

The Grid community is devoting great attention toward the management of structured and semi-structured data such as relational and XML data. Two significant examples of such efforts are the *OGSA Data Access and Integration* (OGSA-DAI) [3] and the *OGSA Distributed Query Processor* (OGSA-DQP) [2] projects. However, till today only few projects (e.g., [8, 6]) actually meet schema-integration requirements necessary for establishing semantic connections among heterogeneous data sources.

For these reasons, we propose the use of the *XMAP* framework [9] for integrating heterogeneous data sources distributed over a Grid. By means of this framework, we aim at developing a decentralized network of semantically related schemas that enables the formulation of distributed queries over heterogeneous data sources. We designed a method to combine and query XML documents through a decentralized point-to-point mediation process among the different data sources based on schema mappings. We offer a decentralized service-based architecture that exposes this XML integration formalism as an e-Service. The infrastructure proposed exploits the middleware provided by OGSA-DQP and OGSA-DAI, building on top of them schema-integration services.

The remainder of the paper is organized as follows. Section 2 presents a short analysis of data integration systems focusing on specific issues related to Grids. Section 3 presents the XMAP integration framework; the underlying integration model and the XMAP query reformulation algorithm are described. The OGSA-DQP and OGSA-DAI existing query processing services are outlined in Section

4. Section 5 presents an example of applying the XMAP algorithm to OGSA-DQP, whereas Section 6 introduces the approach proposed to rewrite an XPath query into an equivalent OQL one. Finally, Section 8 concludes the paper.

2. Data Integration in Grids

The goal of a data integration system is to combine heterogeneous data residing at different sites by providing a unified view of this data. The two main approaches to data integration are federated database management systems (FDBMSs) and traditional mediator/wrapper-based integration systems.

A federated database management system (FDBMS) [19] is a collection of cooperating but autonomous component database systems (DBSs). The DBMS of a component DBS, or component DBMS, can be a centralized or distributed DBMS or another FDBMS. The component DBMSs can differ in different aspects such as data models, query languages, and transaction management capabilities.

Traditional data integration systems [17] are characterized by an architecture based on one or more mediated schemas and a set of sources. Each source contains data, while every mediated schema provides a reconciled, integrated, and virtual view of the underlying sources. Moreover, the system includes a set of source descriptions that provide semantic mappings between the relations in the source schemas and the relations in the mediated schemas [18] .

Data integration on Grids presents a twofold characterization:

1 data integration is a key issue for exploiting the availability of large, heterogeneous, distributed and highly dynamic data volumes on Grids;

2 integration formalisms can benefit from an OGSA-based Grid infrastructure, since it facilitates dynamic discovery, allocation, access, and use of both data sources and computational resources, as required to support computationally demanding database operations such as query reformulation, compilation and evaluation.

Data integration on Grids has to deal with unpredictable, highly dynamic data volumes provided by unpredictable membership of nodes that happen to be participating at any given time. So, traditional approaches to data integration, such as FDBMS [19] and the use of mediator/wrapper middleware [18] , are not suitable in Grid settings.

The federation approach is a rather rigid configuration where resources allocation is static and optimization cannot take advantage of evolving circumstances in the execution environment. The design of mediator/wrapper integration systems must be done globally and the coordination of mediators has been done by a central administrator which is an obstacle to the exploitation of evolving characteristics of dynamic environments. As a consequence, data sources cannot change often and significantly, otherwise they might violate the mappings to the mediated schema.

The rise in availability of web-based data sources has led to new challenges in data integration systems in order to obtain decentralized, wide-scale sharing of semantically-related data. Recently, several works on data management in peer-to-peer (P2P) systems are pursuing this approach [4, 7, 13, 14, 15]. All these systems focus on an integration approach that excludes a global schema: each peer represents an autonomous information system, and data integration is achieved by establishing mappings among the various peers.

To the best of our knowledge, there are only few works designed to provide schema-integration in Grids. The most notable ones are *Hyper* [8] and *GDMS* [6] . Both systems are based on the same approach that we have used ourselves: building data integration services by extending the reference implementation of OGSA-DAI. However, the *Grid Data Mediation Service* (GDMS) uses a wrapper/mediator approach based on a global schema. GDMS presents heterogeneous, distributed data sources as one logical virtual data source in the form of an OGSA-DAI service. For its part, *Hyper* is a framework that integrates relational data in P2P systems built on Grid infrastructures. As in other P2P integration systems, the integration is achieved without using any hierarchical structure for establishing mappings among the autonomous peers. That framework uses a simple relational language for expressing both the schemas and the mappings. By comparison, our integration model follows, like Hyper, an approach not based on a hierarchical structure. However, differently from Hyper, it focuses on XML data sources and is based on schema-mappings that associate paths in different schemas.

3.   XMAP: A Decentralized XML Data Integration Framework

The primary design goal the XMAP framework is to develop a decentralized network of semantically related schemas that enables the formulation of queries over heterogeneous, distributed data sources. The environment is modeled as a system composed of a number of Grid nodes, where each node can hold one or more XML databases. These nodes are connected to each other through declarative mappings rules.

The XMAP integration [9] model is based on schema mappings to translate queries between different schemas. The goal of a schema mapping is to capture structural as well as terminological correspondences between schemas. Thus, in [9] , we propose a decentralized approach inspired by [14] where the mapping rules are established directly among source schemas without relying on a central mediator or a hierarchy of mediators. The specification of mappings is thus flexible and scalable: each source schema is directly connected to only a small number of other schemas. However, it remains reachable from all other schemas that belong to its transitive closure. In other words, the system supports two different kinds of mapping to connect schemas semantically: point-to-point mappings and transitive mappings. In transitive mappings, data sources are related through one or more "mediator schemas".

We address structural heterogeneity among XML data sources by associating paths in different schemas. Mappings are specified as path expressions that relate a specific element or attribute (together with its path) in the source schema to related elements or attributes in the destination schema.. The mapping rules are specified in XML documents called XMAP documents. Each source schema in the framework is associated to an XMAP document containing all the mapping rules related to it.

The key issue of the XMAP framework is the XPath reformulation algorithm: when a query is posed over the schema of a node, the system will utilize data from any node that is transitively connected by semantic mappings, by chaining mappings, and reformulate the given query expanding and translating it into appropriate queries over semantically related nodes. Every time the reformulation reaches a node that stores no redundant data, the appropriate query is posed on that node, and additional answers may be found. As a first step, we consider only a subset of the full XPath language.

We have implemented the XMAP reformulation algorithm in Java and evaluated its performance by executing a set of experiments. Our goals with these experiments are to demonstrate the feasibility of the XMAP integration model and to identify the key elements determining the behavior of the algorithm. The experiments discussed here have been performed to evaluate the execution time of the reformulation algorithm on the basis of some parameters like the *rank* of the semantic network, the *mapping topology*, and the *input query*. The rank corresponds to the average rank of a node in the network, i.e., the average number of mappings per node. A higher rank corresponds to a more interconnected network. The topology of the mappings is the way how mappings are established among the different nodes, it is the shape of the semantic network.

The experimental results were obtained by averaging the output of 1000 runs of a given configuration. Due to lacks of space here we report only few results of the performed evaluations .

Figure 1 shows the total reformulation time as function of the number of paths in the query for three different ranks. The main result showed in the figure is the low time needed to execute the algorithm that ranges from few milliseconds when a single path is involved to one second where a larger number of paths are to be considered. As should be noted from that figure, for a given rank value, the running times are lower when the mappings guarantee a uniform semantic connection This happens because some mappings provide better connectivity than others.

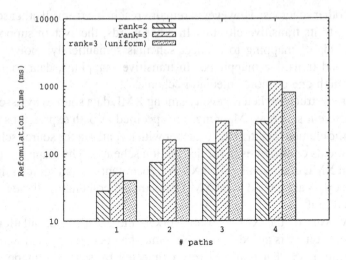

Figure 1. Total reformulation time as function of the number of paths in the query for three different ranks.

In another set of experiments in which we have used the mapping topology as a free variable (see Figure 2), we deduced that for large-scale, highly dynamic networks the best solution is to organize mappings in random topologies with a low average rank. A random topology produces smaller reformulation steps (that is, a smaller number of recursive invocations of the algorithms) that results in lower reformulation times so guaranteeing scalability, fault-tolerance, and flexibility.

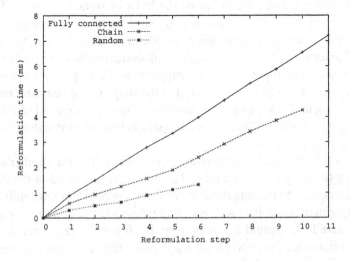

Figure 2. Time to first reformulation for the different topologies.

4. Introduction to Grid query processing services

The Grid community is devoting great attention toward the management of structured and semi-structured data such as relational and XML data. Two significant examples of such efforts are the *OGSA Data Access and Integration* (OGSA-DAI) [3] and the *OGSA Distributed Query Processor* (OGSA-DQP) projects [2].

OGSA-DAI provides uniform service interfaces for data access and integration via the Grid. Through the OGSA-DAI interfaces disparate, heterogeneous data resources can be accessed and controlled as though they were a single logical resource. OGSA-DAI components also offer the potential to be used as basic primitives in the creation of sophisticated higher-level services that offer the capabilities of data federation and distributed query processing within a Virtual Organization (VO).

OGSA-DAI can be considered logically as a number of co-operating Grid services. These Grid services act as proxies for the systems that actually hold the data that is relational databases (for example MySQL) and XML databases (for example Xindice). Clients requiring data held within such databases access the data via the OGSA-DAI Grid services. The Grid Data Service (GDS) is the primary OGSA-DAI service. GDSs provide access to data resources using a document-oriented model: a client submits a data retrieval or update request in the form of an XML document, the GDS executes the request and returns an XML document holding the results of the request.

OGSA-DQP is an open source service-based Distributed Query Processor that supports the evaluation of queries over collections of potentially remote data access and analysis services. Here query compilation, optimisation and evaluation are viewed (and implemented) as invocations of OGSA-compliant GSs. OGSA-DQP supports the evaluation of queries expressed in a declarative language over one or more existing services. These services are likely to include mainly database services, but may also include other computational services. As such, OGSA-DQP supports service orchestration and can be seen as complementary to other infrastructures for service orchestration, such as workflow languages.

OGSA-DQP uses Grid Data Services (GDSs) provided by OGSA-DAI to hide data source heterogeneities and ensure consistent access to data and metadata. Notably, it also adapts techniques from parallel databases to provide implicit parallelism for complex data-intensive requests. The current version of OGSA-DQP, OGSA-DQP 3.0, uses Globus Toolkit 4.0 for grid service creation and management. Thus OGSA-DQP builds upon an OGSA-DAI distribution that is based on the WSRF infrastructure. In addition, both GT4.0 and OGSA-

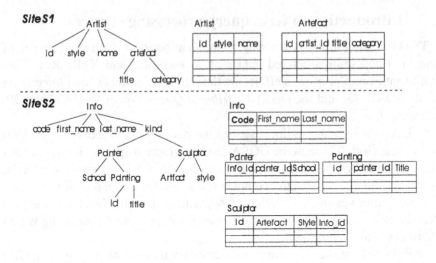

Figure 3.   The example schemas.

DAI require a web service container (e.g. Axis) and a web server (such as Apache Tomcat) below them.

OGSA-DQP provides two additional types of services, Grid Distributed Query Services (GDQSs) and Grid Query Evaluation Services (GQESs). The former are visible to end users through a GUI client, accept queries from them, construct and optimise the corresponding query plans and coordinate the query execution. GQESs implement the query engine, interact with other services (such as GDSs, ordinary Web Services and other instances of GQESs), and are responsible for the execution of the query plans created by GDQSs.

5.   Integrating the XMAP algorithm in service-based Grids: A walk-through example

The XMAP algorithm can be used for data integration-enabled query processing in OGSA-DQP. This example aims to show how the XMAP algorithm can be applied on top of the OGSA-DAI and OGSA-DQP services. In the example, we will assume that the underlying databases, of which the XML representation of the schema is processed by the XMAP algorithm, are, in fact, relational databases, like those supported by the current version of OGSA-DQP.

We assume that there are two sites, each holding a separate, autonomous database that contains information about artists and their works. Figure 3 presents two self-explanatory views: one hierarchical (for native XML databases), and one tabular (for object-relational DBMSs).

In OGSA-DQP, the table schemas are retrieved and exposed in the form of XML documents, as shown in Figure 4.

```
<databaseSchema dbname="S1">
    <table name="Artist">
        <column name="id" />
        <column name="style" />
        <column name="name" />
        <primaryKey>
            <columnName>id</columnName>
        </primaryKey>
    </table>
    <table name="Artefact">
        <column name="artist_id" />
        <column name="title" />
        <column name="category" />
    </table>
</databaseSchema>

<databaseSchema dbname="S2">
    <table name="Info">
        <column name="id" />
        <column name="code" />
        <column name="first_name" />
        <column name="last_name" />
        <column name="kind" />
        <primaryKey>
            <columnName>id</columnName>
        </primaryKey>
    </table>
    <table name="Painter">
        <column name="painter_id" />
        <column name="info_id" />
        <column name="school" />
        <primaryKey>
            <columnName>painter_id</columnName>
        </primaryKey>
    </table>
    <table name="Painting">
        <column name="painter_id" />
        <column name="title" />
        <primaryKey>
            <columnName>title</columnName>
        </primaryKey>
    </table>
    <table name="Sculptor">
        <column name="info_id" />
        <column name="artefact" />
        <column name="style" />
    </table>
</databaseSchema>
```

Figure 4.   The XML representation of the schemas of the example databases.

The XMAP mappings need to capture the semantic relationships between the data fields in different databases, including the primary and foreign keys. This can be done in two ways, which are illustrated in Figures 5 and 6, respectively. Both the ways seem to be feasible. However, the second one is slightly more comprehensible, and thus more desirable.

The actual query reformulation occurs exactly as described in [9]. Initially, users submit XPath queries that refer to a single physical database. E.g., the query /S1/Artist [style="Cubism"]/name extracts the names of the artists whose style is *Cubism* and their data is stored in the *S1* database. Similarly, the query /S1/Artefact/title returns the titles of the artifacts in the same database. When the XMAP algorithm is applied for the second query, two more XPath expressions will be created that refer to the *S2* database:

```
i)
databaseSchema[@dbname=S1]/table[@name=Artist]/column[@name=style]
->
    databaseSchema[@dbname=S2]/table[@name=Painter]/column[@name=school],
    databaseSchema[@dbname=S2]/table[@name=Sculptor]/column[@name=style]
ii)
databaseSchema[@dbname=S1]/table[@name=Artefact]/column[@name=title]
->
    databaseSchema[@dbname=S2]/table[@name=Painting]/column[@name=title],
    databaseSchema[@dbname=S2]/table[@name=Sculptor]/column[@name=artefact]

iii) databaseSchema[@dbname=S1]/table[@name=Artist/column[@name=id
->
    databaseSchema[@dbname=S2]/table[@name=Info/column[@name=id]

iv)
databaseSchema[@dbname=S1]/table[@name=Artefact]/column[@name=artist_id]
->
    databaseSchema[@dbname=S2]/table[@name=Painter]/column[@name=info_id],
    databaseSchema[@dbname=S2]/table[@name=Sculptor]/column[@name=info_id]
```

Figure 5. The XMAP mappings.

```
i) S1/Artist/style -> S2/Painter/school, S2/Sculptor/style

ii)S1/Artefact/title -> S2/Painting/title, S2/Sculptor/artefact

iii) S1/Artist/id -> S2/Info/id

iv) S1/Artefact/artist_id->S2/Painter/info_id,S2/Sculptor/info_id
```

Figure 6. A simpler form of the XMAP mappings.

/S2/Painting/Title and /S2/Sculptor/Artefact. At the back-end, the following queries will be submitted to the underlying databases (in SQL-like format):

    select title from Artefact;
    select title from Painting; and
    select Artefact from Sculptor;

Note that the mapping of simple XPath expressions to SQL/OQL is feasible [16].

6.   XPath to OQL mapping

OGSA-DQP through the *GDQS* service should be capable of accepting XPath queries, and of transforming these XPath queries to OQL before parsing, compiling, optimising and scheduling them. Such a transformation falls in an active research area (e.g., [12, 5]), and is implemented as an additional component within the query compiler. In general, the set of meaningful XPath queries over the XML representation of the schema of relational databases supported by OGSA-DQP fits into the following template:

$$/database\_A[predicate\_A]/table\_A[predicate\_B]/column\_A$$

where

$$predicate\_A ::= table\_pred\_A[column\_pred\_A = value\_pred\_A], \text{ and}$$

$$predicate\_B ::= column\_pred\_B = value\_pred\_B$$

As such, the mapping to the `select`, `from`, `where` clauses of OQL is straightforward. *column_A* defines the `select` attribute, whereas *table_A, table_pred_A* populate the `from` clause. If *column_pred_A=value_pred_A, column_pred_B=value_pred_B* exist, they go into the `where` field.

The approach above is simple but effective; nevertheless two important observations are: firstly, it does not benefit from the full expressiveness of the XPath queries supported by the XMAP framework, and secondly, it requires the join conditions between tables *table_A, table_pred_A* to be inserted in a post-processing step.

Apparently, this is not the only change envisaged to the current querying services, as these are provided by OGSA-DQP. An enumeration of such modifications appears in [10].

7. Implementation Roadmap: Service Interactions and System Design

In this section we will describe in brief the system design that we envisage along with the service interactions involved.

The XMAP query reformulation algorithm is deployed as a stand-alone service, called *Grid Data Integration service (GDI)*. The *GDI* is deployed at each site participating in a dynamic database federation and has a mechanism to load local mapping information. Following the Globus Toolkit 4 [1] terminology, it implements additional *portTypes*, among which the *Query Reformulation Algorithm (QRA)* portType, which accepts XPath expressions, applies the XMAP algorithm to them, and returns the results. A database can join the system as in OGSA-DQP: registering itself in a registry and informing the *GDQS*. The only difference is that, given the assumptions above, it should be associated with both a *GQES* and a *GDI*.

Also, there is one *GQES* per site to evaluate (sub)queries, and at least one *GDQS*. As in classical OGSA-DQP scenarios, the *GDQS* contains a view of the schemas of the participating data resources, and a list of the computational resources that are available. The users interact only with this service from a client application that need not be exposed as a service.

8.   Summary

The contribution of this work is the proposal of a framework and a methodology that combines a data integration approach with existing grid services (e.g., OGSA-DQP) for querying distributed databases. This way we provide an enhanced, data integration-enabled service middleware supporting distributed query processing.

The data integration approach is based upon the XMAP framework that takes into account the semantic and syntactic heterogeneity of different data sources, and provides a recursive query reformulation algorithm. The Grid services used as a basis are the outcome of the OGSA-DAI/DQP projects, which have paved the way towards uniform access and combination of distributed databases. In summary, in this paper (i) we provided an overview of XMAP and existing querying services, (ii) we showed how they can be used together through an example, (iii) we presented a service-oriented architecture to this end and (iv) we discussed how the proposed architecture will be implemented.

Acknowledgments

This research work was carried out jointly within the CoreGRID Network of Excellence founded by the European Commission's IST Programme under grant FP6-004265.

References

[1] The Globus toolkit, http://www.globus.org.

[2] M. Nedim Alpdemir, Arijit Mukherjee, Anastasios Gounaris, Norman W. Paton, Paul Watson, Alvaro A. A. Fernandes, and Desmond J. Fitzgerald. OGSA-DQP: A service for distributed querying on the grid. In *Advances in Database Technology - EDBT 2004, 9th International Conference on Extending Database Technology*, pages 858–861, March 2004.

[3] Mario Antonioletti and et al. OGSA-DAI: Two years on. In *Global Grid Forum 10 — Data Area Workshop*, March 2004.

[4] Philip A. Bernstein, Fausto Giunchiglia, Anastasios Kementsietsidis, John Mylopoulos, Luciano Serafini, and Ilya Zaihrayeu. Data management for peer-to-peer computing : A vision. In *Proceedings of the 5th International Workshop on the Web and Databases (WebDB 2002)*, pages 89–94, June 2002.

[5] Kevin S. Beyer, Roberta Cochrane, Vanja Josifovski, Jim Kleewein, George Lapis, Guy M. Lohman, Bob Lyle, Fatma Ozcan, Hamid Pirahesh, Norman Seemann, Tuong C. Truong, Bert Van der Linden, Brian Vickery, and Chun Zhang. System rx: One part relational, one part xml. In *SIGMOD Conference 2005*, pages 347–358, 2005.

[6] P. Brezany, A. Woehrer, and A. M. Tjoa. Novel mediator architectures for grid information systems. *Journal for Future Generation Computer Systems - Grid Computing: Theory, Methods and Applications.*, 21(1):107–114, 2005.

[7] Diego Calvanese, Elio Damaggio, Giuseppe De Giacomo, Maurizio Lenzerini, and Riccardo Rosati. Semantic data integration in P2P systems. In *Proceedings of the First*

International Workshop on Databases, Information Systems, and Peer-to-Peer Computing (DBISP2P), pages 77–90, September 2003.

[8] Diego Calvanese, Giuseppe De Giacomo, Maurizio Lenzerini, Riccardo Rosati, and Guido Vetere. Hyper: A framework for peer-to-peer data integration on grids. In *Proc. of the Int. Conference on Semantics of a Networked World: Semantics for Grid Databases (ICSNW 2004)*, volume 3226 of *Lecture Notes in Computer Science*, pages 144–157, 2004.

[9] C. Comito and D. Talia. Xml data integration in ogsa grids. In *Proc. of the First International Workshop on Data Management in Grids (DMG05). In conjuction with VLDB 2005*, volume 3836 of *Lecture Notes in Computer Science*, pages 4–15. Springer Verlag, September 2005.

[10] Carmela Comito, Domenico Talia, Anastasios Gounaris, and Rizos Sakellariou. Data integration and query reformulation in service-based grids: Architecture and roadmap. Technical Report CoreGrid TR-0013, Institute on Knowledge and Data Management, 2005.

[11] Karl Czajkowski and et al. The WS-resource framework version 1.0. The Globus Alliance, Draft, March 2004. http://www.globus.org/wsrf/specs/ws-wsrf.pdf.

[12] Wenfei Fan, Jeffrey Xu Yu, Hongjun Lu, and Jianhua Lu. Query translation from xpath to sql in the presence of recursive dtds. In *VLDB Conference 2005*, 2005.

[13] Enrico Franconi, Gabriel M. Kuper, Andrei Lopatenko, and Luciano Serafini. A robust logical and computational characterisation of peer-to-peer database systems. In *Proceedings of the First International Workshop on Databases, Information Systems, and Peer-to-Peer Computing (DBISP2P)*, pages 64–76, September 2003.

[14] Alon Y. Halevy, Dan Suciu, Igor Tatarinov, and Zachary G. Ives. Schema mediation in peer data management systems. In *Proceedings of the 19th International Conference on Data Engineering*, pages 505–516, March 2003.

[15] Anastasios Kementsietsidis, Marcelo Arenas, and Renée J. Miller. Mapping data in peer-to-peer systems: Semantics and algorithmic issues. In *Proceedings of the 2003 ACM SIGMOD International Conference on Management of Data*, pages 325–336, June 2003.

[16] George Lapis. Xml and relational storage - are they mutually exclusive? available at http://www.idealliance.org/proceedings/xtech05/papers/02-05-01/ (accessed in july 2005).

[17] Maurizio Lenzerini. Data integration: A theoretical perspective. In *Proceedings of the Twenty-first ACM SIGACT-SIGMOD-SIGART Symposium on Principles of Database Systems (PODS)*, pages 233–246, June 2002.

[18] Alon Y. Levy, Anand Rajaraman, and Joann J. Ordille. Querying heterogeneous information sources using source descriptions. In *Proceedings of 22th International Conference on Very Large Data Bases (VLDB'96)*, pages 251–262, September 1996.

[19] Amit P. Sheth and James A. Larson. Federated database systems for managing distributed, heterogeneous, and autonomous databases. *ACM Computing Surveys*, 22(3):183–236, 1990.

TOWARDS A COMMON DEPLOYMENT MODEL FOR GRID SYSTEMS

Massimo Coppola and Nicola Tonellotto
ISTI
Area della Ricerca CNR, 56124 Pisa
Italy
coppola@di.unipi.it
nicola.tonellotto@isti.cnr.it

Marco Danelutto and Corrado Zoccolo
Dept. of Computer Science, University of Pisa
L.go B. Pontecorvo, 3, 56127 Pisa
Italy
marcod@di.unipi.it
zoccolo@di.unipi.it

Sébastien Lacour and Christian Pérez and Thierry Priol
IRISA/INRIA
Campus de Beaulieu, 35042 Rennes Cedex
France
Christian.Perez@irisa.fr
Thierry.Priol@irisa.fr

Abstract   Deploying applications within a Grid infrastructure is an important aspect that has not yet been fully addressed. This is particularly true when high-level abstractions, like objects or components, are offered to the programmers. High-level applications are built on run-time supports that require the deployment process to span over and coordinate several middleware systems, in an application independent way. This paper addresses deployment by illustrating how it has been handled within two projects (ASSIST and GridCCM). As the result of the integration of the experience gained by researchers involved in these two projects, a common deployment process is presented.

Keywords: Grid computing, deployment, generic model.

1.   Introduction

The Grid vision introduced in the end of the nineties has now become a reality with the availability of quite a few Grid infrastructures, most of them experimental but some others will come soon in production. Although most of the research and development efforts have been spent in the design of Grid middleware systems, the question of how to program such large scale computing infrastructures remains open. Programming such computing infrastructures will be quite complex considering its parallel and distributed nature. The programmer vision of a Grid infrastructure is often determined by its programming model. The level of abstraction that is proposed today is rather low, giving the vision either of a parallel machine, with a message-passing layer such as MPI, or a distributed system with a set of services, such as Web Services, to be orchestrated. Both approaches offer a very low level programming abstraction and are not really adequate, limiting the spectrum of applications that could take benefit from Grid infrastructures. Of course such approaches may be sufficient for simple applications but a Grid infrastructure has to be generic enough to also handle complex applications with ease. To overcome this situation, it is required to propose high level abstractions to facilitate the programming of Grid infrastructures and in a longer term to be able to develop more secure and robust next generation Grid middleware systems by using these high level abstractions for their design as well. The current situation is very similar to what happened with computers in the sixties: minimalist operating systems were developed first with assembly languages before being developed, in the seventies, by languages that offer higher levels of abstraction.

Several research groups are already investigating how to design or adapt programming models that provide this required level of abstraction. Among these models, component-oriented programming models are good candidates to deal with the complexity of programming Grid infrastructures. A Grid application can be seen as a collection of components interconnected in a certain way that must be deployed on available computing resources managed by the Grid infrastructure. Components can be reused for new Grid applications, reducing the time to build new applications. However, from our experience such models have to be combined with other programming models that are required within a Grid infrastructure. It is imaginable that a parallel program can be encapsulated within a component. Such a parallel program is based on a parallel programming model which might be for instance message-based or skeleton-based. Moreover, a component oriented programming model can be coupled with a service oriented approach exposing some component ports as services through the use of Web Services.

The results of this is that this combination of several models to design Grid applications leads to a major challenge: the deployment of applications within a Grid infrastructure. Such programming models are always implemented through various runtime or middleware systems that have their own dependencies vis-à-vis of operating systems, making it extremely challenging to deploy applications within a heterogeneous environment, which is an intrinsic property of a Grid infrastructure.

The objective of this paper is to propose a common deployment process based on the experience gained from the ASSIST and GridCCM projects. This paper is organized as follows. Section 2 gives an overview of the ASSIST and GridCCM projects. Section 3 presents our common analysis of what should be the different steps to deploy grid applications. Section 4 shortly describes GEA and Adage, the two deployment systems designed respectively for ASSIST and GridCCM, and how they already conform to the common model. Finally, Section 5 concludes the paper and presents some perspectives.

2. ASSIST and GridCCM Software Component Models

Both University of Pisa and INRIA-Rennes have investigated the problem of deploying component-based Grid applications in the context of the ASSIST and GridCCM programming environments and came out with two approaches with some similarities and differences. In the framework of the CoreGRID Network of Excellence, the two research groups decided to join their efforts to develop a common deployment process suitable for both projects taking benefits of the experience of both groups. In the remaining part of this section, the ASSIST and GridCCM programming and component models are presented, so as to illustrate the common requirements on the deployment system.

2.1 Assist

ASSIST (A Software development System based upon Integrated Skeleton Technology [13]) is a complete programming environment aimed at efficient development of high-performance multi-disciplinary applications. Efficiency is pursued both w.r.t. the development effort and to overall performance, as the ASSIST approach aims at managing the complexity of applications, easing prototyping and decreasing time-to-market.

ASSIST provides a basic modularization of parallel applications by means of sequential and parallel modules (*parmods*), with well-defined interfaces exploiting stream-based communications. The ASSISTcl coordination language describes modules and composition of them.

Sequential modules wrap code written in several languages (e.g. C, C++, FORTRAN). Parmods describe parallel execution of a number of sequential functions within *Virtual Processes* (VPs), mainly activated by stream communications, and possibly exploiting shared state and/or explicit synchronization at the parmod level. The abilities to (1) describe both task and data-parallel

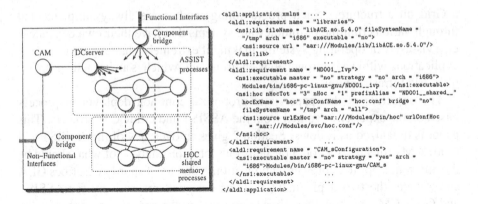

```
<aldl:application xmlns = ... >
  <aldl:requirement name = "libraries">
    <ns1:lib fileName = "libACE.so.5.4.0" fileSystemName =
      "/tmp" arch = "i686" executable = "no">
    <ns1:source url = "aar:///Modules/lib/libACE.so.5.4.0"/>
    </ns1:lib>                        ...
  </aldl:requirement>
  <aldl:requirement name = "NDOO1__Ivp">
    <ns1:executable master = "no" strategy = "no" arch = "i686">
      Modules/bin/i686-pc-linux-gnu/NDOO1__ivp   </ns1:executable>
    <ns1:hoc nHocTot = "3" nHoc = "1" prefixAlias = "NDOO1__shared__"
      hocExName = "hoc" hocConfName = "hoc.conf" bridge = "no"
      fileSystemName = "/tmp" arch = "all">
      <ns1:source urlExHoc = "aar:///Modules/bin/hoc" urlConfHoc
        = "aar:///Modules/svc/hoc.conf"/>
    </ns1:hoc>
  </aldl:requirement>                 ...
  <aldl:requirement name = "CAM_sConfiguration">
    <ns1:executable master = "no" strategy = "yes" arch =
      "i686">Modules/bin/i686-pc-linux-gnu/CAM_s
    </ns1:executable>              ...
  </aldl:requirement>               ...
</aldl:application>
```

Figure 1. The process schema of a simple Grid.it component.

Figure 2. Excerpt from the ALDL describing a Grid.it component (ellipsis shown as . . .).

behavior within a parmod, (2) to fine-control nondeterminism when dealing with multiple communication channels and (3) to compose sequential and parallel modules into arbitrary graphs, they allow expressing parallel semantics and structure in a high-level, structured way. ASSIST implements program adaptivity to changing resource allocation exploiting the VP granularity as a user-provided definition of elementary computation.

ASSIST supports component-based development of software by allowing modules and graph of modules to be compiled into Grid.it components [2], and separately deployed on parallel and Grid computing platforms. The Grid.it framework supports integration with different frameworks (e.g. CCM, Web Services), and implementation of automatic component adaptation to varying resource/program behavior. Component-based applications can exploit both ASSIST native adaptivity and Grid.it higher-level "super-components", which arrange other components into basic parallel patterns and provide dynamic management of graphs of of components within an application.

ASSIST applications and Grid.it components have a platform-independent description encoded in ALDL [4], an XML dialect expressing the structure, the detailed requirements and the execution constraints of all the elementary composing blocks. Support processes shown in Fig. 1 are all described in the ALDL syntax of Fig. 2, e.g. besides those actually performing computation and implementing virtual shared memory support, we include those providing inter-component communications and interfacing to other component frameworks. ALDL is interpreted by the GEA tool (see Section 4.1), which translates requirements into specific actions whenever a new instance of a component has to be executed, or an existing instance dynamically requires new computing resources.

Summing up, the support of the ASSIST/Grid.it environment must deal with (1) heterogeneous resources, (2) dynamically changing availability and allocation of resources, (3) several sets of processes implementing application and components, which need (4) different execution protocols and information (e.g. setting up a shared memory space support versus instantiating a CORBA name service).

Deploying an application is therefore a complex process which takes into account program structure and resource characteristics, involves selecting resources and configuring several sets of processes to cooperate and obtain high-performance. Finally, the deployment task continues during program execution, processing resource requests from components, which utilize run-time reconfiguration to adapt and fulfill specified performance requirements [4].

The GEA tools has to provide these functionalities, shielding the actual application run-time support from the details of the different middleware used to manage the available resources.

2.2 GridCCM: a Parallel Component Model

The model GridCCM [12] is a research prototype that targets scientific code coupling applications. Its programming model extends the CORBA Component Model (CCM) with the concept of parallel components. CCM specifies several models for the definition, the implementation, the packaging and the deployment of distributed components [11]. However, the embedding of a parallel code, such as an MPI-based code, into a CCM component results in a serialization of the communications with another component also embedding a parallel code. Such a bottleneck is removed with GridCCM which enables MxN communications between parallel components.

A parallel component is a component whose implementation is parallel. Typically, it is a SPMD code which can be based on any kind of parallel technology (MPI, PVM, OpenMP, ...). The only requirements of GridCCM that the distributions of input and output data need to be specified. Such distributed data can be the parameters of interface operations or can be the type of event streams. Interactions between parallel components are handled by GridCCM which supports optimized scheduled MxN communications. It is a two phase process. First, data redistribution libraries compute the communication matrices for all the distributed data of an operation invocation. These data redistributions are a priori distinct. Second, a scheduling library takes care of globally optimizing the transfer of all the data associated to the operation invocation with respect to the properties of the network like the latency, the networking card bandwidth and the backbone bandwidth for wide area networks. Data redistributions and communication scheduling libraries may be extended at user-level.

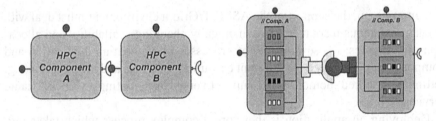

Figure 3.   On the left, a parallel component appears as a standard component. On the right, communications between two parallel components are of type MxN.

```
<softpkg ...>
...
</implementation>
 <GridCCM type="MPI" id="pi1">
  <functional_prgrm>
   <location>
    http://g5k.org/Flow.mpi
   </location>
  </functional_prgrm>
   ...
 </GridCCM>
</softpkg>
```

```
<MPI_application>
 <programs>
  <program id="master_program">
   <binary vendor="MPICH">
    <location>URL...</location>
   </binary>
  </program>
  <application>
   <world_size>32</world_size>
    ...
  </application>
</MPI_application>
```

Figure 4.   Example of a GridCCM description of a MPI-based parallel component.

Figure 5.   Partial view of the description of the MPI-based parallel component implementation.

As illustrated in Figure 3, a parallel component looks like any CCM component and can be connected with any other CCM components. Hence, an application may be incrementally parallelized, one component after the other.

The deployment   The deployment of a GridCCM application turns out to be a complex task because several middleware systems may be involved. There are the component middleware, which implies to deploy CCM applications, and the technology used by the parallel component which may be MPI, PVM or OpenMP for example. Moreover, to deal with network issues, an environment like PadicoTM [5] should be also deployed with the application.

The description of an GridCCM application is achieved thanks to an extension of the XML CCM Component Software Description (CSD) language. As shown in Figure 4, this extension enables the CSD to refer to another file to actually describe the structure of the parallel component implementation as displayed in Figure 5. This solution has been selected because GridCCM does not enforce any parallel technology. More information is provided in [9]. Then, Adage, a deployment tool described in Section 4.2 is used to deploy it.

As GridCCM is an extension of CCM, it implicitly provides the same heterogeneity support than CORBA for operating system, processor, compiler, libraries dependencies, etc.

2.3 Discussion

Both ASSIST and GridCCM expose programming models that required advanced deployment tools to efficiently handle the different elements of an application to be deployed. Moreover, they provide distinct features like the dynamic behavior and the different Grid middleware support of ASSIST and the multi-middleware application support of GridCCM. Hence, a common deployment process will help in integrating features needed for their deployment.

3. General Overview of the Deployment Process

Starting from a description of an application and a user objective function, the deployment process is responsible for automatically performing all the steps needed to start the execution of the application on a set of selected resources. This is done in order to avoid the user from directly dealing with heterogeneous resource management mechanisms.

From the point of view of the execution, a component contains a structured set of binary executables and requirements for their instantiation. Our objectives include generating deployment plans

- to deploy components in a multi-middleware environment,

- to dynamically alter a previous configuration, adding new computational resources to a running application,

- for re-deployment, when a complete restart from a previous checkpoint is needed (severe performance degradation or failure of several resources).

A framework for the automatic execution of applications can be composed of several interacting entities in charge of distinct activities, as depicted in Figure 6. The logical order of the activities is fixed (Submission, Discovery, Selection, Planning, Enactment, Execution). Some steps have to be re-executed when the application configuration is changed at run-time. Moreover, the steps in the grey box, that interact closely, can be iterated until a suitable set of resources is found.

In the following we describe the activities involved in the deployment of an application on a Grid. We also detail the inputs that must be provided by the user or the deployment framework to perform such activities.

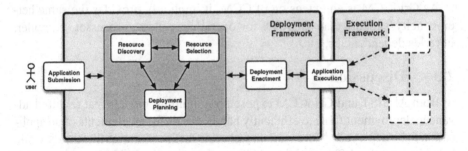

Figure 6.   Activities involved in the deployment process of an application.

3.1   Application Submission

This is the only activity which the user must be involved in, to provide the information necessary to drive the following phases. This information is provided through a file containing a description of the components of the application, of their interactions, and of the required resource characteristics.

3.1.1   Application Description.   The description of (the components of) the submitted application, written in an user-understandable specification language, is composed of various kinds of data. First, the **module description** deals with the executable files, I/O data and configuration files which make up each module (e.g. each process). Second, there is information to guide the stages related to mapping the application onto resources, like the **resource constraints** – characteristics that Grid resources (computational, storage, network) must possess to execute the application, the **execution platform constraints** – software (libraries, middleware systems) that must be installed to satisfy application dependencies, the **placement policies** – restrictions or hints for the placement of subsets of application processes (e.g. co-location, location within a specific network domain, or network performance requirements), and the **resource ranking** – an objective function provided by the user, stating the optimization goal of application mapping. Resource ranking is exploited to select the best resource, or set of them, among those satisfying the given requirements for a single application process. Resource constraints can be expressed as *unitary requirements*, that is requirements that must be respected by a single module or resource (e.g. CPU rating), and as *aggregate requirements*, i.e., requirements that a set of resources or a module group must respect at the same time (e.g. all the resources on the same LAN, access to a shared file system); some placement policies are implicitly aggregate requirements. Third, the **Deployment directives** determine the tasks that must be performed to set up the application runtime environment, and to start the actual execution.

As discussed in the following sections, the provided information is used throughout the deployment process.

3.2 Resource Discovery

This activity is aimed at finding the resources compatible with the execution of the application. In the application description several requirements can be specified that available resources must respect to be eligible for execution. The requirements can specify hardware characteristics (e.g. CPU rating, available memory, disk space), software ones (e.g. OS, libraries, compilers, runtime environments), services needed to deploy components (e.g. accessible TCP ports, specific file transfer protocols), and particular execution services (e.g. to configure the application execution environment).

Resources satisfying unitary requirements can be discovered, interacting with Grid Information Services. Then, the information needed to perform resource selection (that considers also aggregate requirements), must be collected, for each suitable resource found.

The GIS[1] can be composed of various software systems, implementing information providers that communicate with different protocols (MDS-2, MDS-3, MDS-4, NWS, iGrid, custom). Some of these systems provide only static information, while others can report dynamic information about resource state and performance, including network topology and characteristics. In order to interact with such different entities, an intermediate translation layer between the requirements needed by the user and the information provided is necessary. Information retrieved from different sources is mapped to a standard schema for resource description that can be exploited in the following activities independently from the information source.

3.3 Resource Selection

When information about available resources is collected, the proper resources that will host the execution of the application must be selected, and the different parts of each component have to be mapped on some of the selected resources. This activity also implies satisfying all the aggregate requirements within the application. Thus, repeated interaction with the resource discovery mechanisms may be needed to find the best set of resources, also exploiting dynamic information.

At this point, the user objective function must be evaluated against the characteristics and available services of the resources (expressed in the normalized resource description schema), establishing a resource ranking where appropriate in order to find a suitable solution.

---

[1]Grid Information Service

3.4   Deployment Planning

A component-based application can require different services installed on the selected resources to host its execution. Moreover, additional services can be transferred/activated on the resources or configured to set up the hosting environment.

Each of these ancillary applications has a well-defined deployment schema, that describes the workflow of actions needed to set up the hosting environment before the actual execution can start.

After resource selection, an abstract deployment plan is computed by gathering the deployment schemata of all application modules. The abstract plan is then mapped on the resources, and turned into a concrete plan, identifying all the services and protocols that will be exploited in the next phase on each resource, in order to set up and start the runtime environment of the application.

For example, to transfer files we must select a protocol (e.g. HTTP, GridFTP), start or configure the related services and resources, and finally start the transfer. At the end of this phase, the concrete deployment plan must be generated, specifying every single task to perform to deploy the application.

This activity can require repeated interactions with the resource discovery and selection phases because some problems about the transformation from the deployment schema to the deployment plan can arise, thus the elimination of one or more eligible resources can force to find new resources, and restart the whole planning process.

3.5   Deployment Enactment

The concrete deployment plan developed in the previous phase is submitted to the execution framework, which is in charge of the execution of the tasks needed to deploy the application. This service must ensure a correct execution of the deployment tasks while respecting the precedences described in the deployment plan. At the end of this phase, the execution environment of the application must be ready to start the actual execution.

This activity must deal with different kinds of software and middleware systems; the selection of the right ones depends on the concrete deployment plan. The implementation of the services that will perform this activity must be flexible enough to implement the functionalities to interact with different services, as well as to add mechanisms to deal with new services.

Changes in the state of the resources can force a new deployment plan for some tasks. Hence, this phase can require interactions with the previous one.

3.6 Application Execution

The deployment process for adaptive Grid applications does not finish when the application is started. Several activities have to be performed while the application is active, and actually the deployment system must rely on at least one permanent process or daemon. The whole application life-cycle must be managed, in order to support new resource requests for application adaptation, to schedule a restart if an application failure is detected, and to release resources when the normal termination is reached. These monitoring and controlling activities have to be mediated by the deployment support (actual mechanisms depend on the middleware), and it does seem possible to reliably perform them over noisy, low-bandwidth or mobile networks.

4. Current Prototypes

4.1 GEA

In the ASSIST/Grid.it architecture the Grid Abstract Machine (GAM, [2]) is a software level providing the abstractions of security mechanisms, resource discovery, resource selection, (secure) data and code staging and execution. The Grid Execution Agent (GEA, [4]) is the tool to run complex component-based Grid applications, and actually implements part of the GAM. GEA provides virtualization of all the basic functions of deployment w.r.t. the underlying middleware systems (see Tab. 1), translating the abstract specification of deployment actions into executable actions. We outlined GEA's requirements in Sect. 2.1. In order to implement them, GEA has been designed as an open framework with several interfaces. To simplify and make fully portable its implementation, GEA has been written in Java.

As mentioned, GEA takes in charge the ALDL description of each component (Fig. 2) and performs the general deployment process outlined in Sect. 3, interacting with Grid middleware systems as needed. GEA accepts commands through a general purpose interface which can have multiple protocol adaptors (e.g. command-line, HTTP, SSL, Web Service). The first command transfers to the execution agent a compact archival form of the component code, also containing its ALDL description. The ALDL specification is parsed and associated to a specific session code for subsequent commands (GEA supports deploying multiple components concurrently, participating in a same as well as in different applications). Component information is retained within GEA, as the full set of GEA commands accepted by the front-end provides control over the life cycle of a component, including the ability to change its resource allocation (an API is provided to the application runtime to dynamically request new resources) and to create multiple instances of it (this also allows higher-level components to dynamically replicate hosted ones).

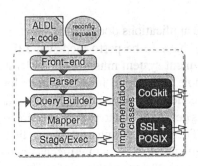
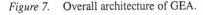

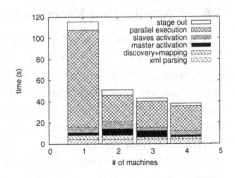

Figure 7.   Overall architecture of GEA.

Figure 8.   GEA launch time of a program over 1–4 nodes in a Globus network.

Each deployment phase described in Sect. 3 corresponds to an implementation class performing that step (see Fig. 7). GEA selects resources, maps application processes onto them, possibly loops back to the research, and finally deploys the processes, handling code and data staging in and out. This tasks are carried on according to the specific design of the class implementing each step, so that we can choose among several mapping and resource selection strategies when needed. In particular, different subclasses are available in the GEA source that handle the different middleware systems and protocols available to perform the deployment.

Current GEA architecture contains classes from the CoGKit to exploit resource location (answering resource queries through Globus MDS), monitoring (through NWS), and resource access on Globus grids. Test results deploying over 1 to 4 nodes in a local network are shown in Fig. 8. GEA also provides classes to gather resource description on clusters and local networks (statically described in XML) and to access them (assuming centralized authentication in this case). Experiments have also been performed with additional modules interfacing to a bandwidth allocation system over an optical network [14].

Different kinds of handshake among the executed processes happen in the general case (e.g. servers or naming services may need to be deployed before other application processes), thus creating a graph of dependencies among the deployment actions. This is especially important whenever a Grid.it component needs to wrap, or interact with, a CCM component or a Web Service. Currently, GEA manages processes belonging to different middleware systems within a component according to the Grid.it component deployment workflow. Work is ongoing to redesign those classes managing execution order and configuration dependencies for the "server" and "slave" processes. This will allow to parameterize the deployment workflow and to fully support different component models and middlewares.

4.2 Adage

Adage [7] (*Automatic Deployment of Applications in a Grid Environment*) is a research project that aims at studying the deployment issues related to multi-middleware applications. One of its originality is to use a generic application description model (GADe) [10] to handle several middleware systems. Adage follows the deployment process described in this paper.

With respect to application submission, Adage requires an application description, which is specific to a programming model, a reference to a resource information service (MDS2, or an XML file), and a control parameter file. The application description is internally translated into a generic description so as to support multi-middleware applications. The control parameter file allows a user to express constraints on the placement policies which are specific to an execution. For example, a constraint may affect the latency and bandwidth between a computational component and a visualization component. However, the implemented schedulers, random and round-robin, do not take into account any control parameters but the constraints of the submission method. Processor architecture and operating system constraints are taking into account.

The generic application description model (GADe) provides a model close to the machines. It contains only four concepts: process, code-do-load, group of processes and interconnection [10]. Hence, this description format is independent of the nature of the application (i.e., distributed or parallel), but complete enough to be exploited by a deployment planning algorithm.

Adage supports multi-middleware applications through GADe and a plug-in mechanism. The plug-in is involved in the conversion from the specific to the generic application description but also during the execution phase so as to deal with specific middleware configuration actions. Translating a specific application description into the generic description turns out to be a straightforward task. Adage supports standard programming models like MPI (MPICH1-P4 and MPICH-G2), CCM and JXTA, as well as more advanced programming models like GridCCM.

Adage currently deploys only static applications. After the generic description is used by the planer to produce a deployment plan. Then, an enactment engine executes it and produces a deployment report which is used to produce two scripts: a script to get the status of deployed processes and a script to clean them up. There is not yet any dynamic support in Adage.

Adage supports resource constraints like operating system, processor architectures, etc. The resource description model of Adage takes into account (grid) networks with a functional view of the network topology. The simplicity of the model does not hinder the description of *complex* network topologies (asymmetric links, firewalls, non-IP networks, non-hierarchical topologies) [8]. A planer integrating such piece of information is being developed.

Table 1. Features of the common deployment process supported by GEA and Adage.

Feature	GEA	Adage
Component description in input	ALDL (generic)	Many, via GADe (MPI, (CCM, GridCCM, JXTA, etc.)
Multi-middleware application	Yes (in progress)	Yes
Dynamic application	Yes	No (in progress)
Resource constraints	Yes	Yes
Execution constraints	Yes	Yes
Grid Middleware	Many, via GAM (GT 2-4, and SSH)	SSH and GT2

4.3   Comparison of GEA and Adage

Table 1 sums up the similarities and difference between GEA and Adage with respect to the features of our common deployment process. The two prototypes are different approximations of the general model: GEA supports dynamic ASSIST applications. Dynamicity, instead, is not currently supported by Adage. On the other hand, multi-middleware applications are fully supported in Adage, as it is a fundamental requirement of GridCCM. Its support in GEA is in progress, following the incorporation of those middleware systems in the ASSIST component framework.

5.   Conclusion

ASSIST and GridCCM programming models requires advanced deployment tools to handle both application and grid complexity. This paper has presented a common deployment process for components within a Grid infrastructure. This model is the result of several visits and meetings that were held during the last past months. It suits well the needs of the two projects, with respect to the support of heterogeneous hardware and middleware, and of dynamic reconfiguration. The current implementations of the two deployment systems – GEA and Adage– share a common subset of features represented in the deployment process. Each prototype implements some of the more advanced features. This motivates the prosecution of the collaboration.

Next steps in the collaboration will focus on the extension of each existing prototype by integrating the useful features present in the other: dynamicity in Adage and extending multi-middleware support in GEA. Another topic of collaboration is the definition of a common API for resource discovery, and a common schema for resource description.

References

[1] M. Aldinucci, S. Campa, M. Coppola, M. Danelutto, D. Laforenza, D. Puppin, L. Scarponi, M. Vanneschi, and C. Zoccolo. Components for high performance Grid programming in the Grid.it project. In V. Getov and T. Kielmann, editors, *Proc. of the Workshop on Component Models and Systems for Grid Applications (June 2004, Saint Malo, France)*. Springer, January 2005.

[2] M. Aldinucci, M. Coppola, M. Danelutto, M. Vanneschi, and C. Zoccolo. ASSIST as a research framework for high-performance Grid programming environments. In J. C. Cunha and O. F. Rana, editors, *Grid Computing: Software environments and Tools*. Springer, Jan. 2006.

[3] M. Aldinucci, A. Petrocelli, E. Pistoletti, M. Torquati, M. Vanneschi, L. Veraldi, and C. Zoccolo. Dynamic reconfiguration of grid-aware applications in ASSIST. In *11th Intl Euro-Par 2005: Parallel and Distributed Computing*, LNCS, pages 771–781, Lisboa, Portugal, August 2005. Springer.

[4] M. Danelutto, M. Vanneschi, C. Zoccolo, N. Tonellotto, R. Baraglia, T. Fagni, D. Laforenza, and A. Paccosi. HPC Application Execution on Grids. In V. Getov, D. Laforenza, and A. Reinefeld, editors, *Future Generation Grids*, CoreGrid series. Springer, 2006. Dagstuhl Seminar 04451 – November 2004.

[5] A. Denis, C. Pérez, and T. Priol. PadicoTM: An open integration framework for communication middleware and runtimes. *Future Generation Computer Systems*, 19(4):575–585, May 2003.

[6] F. Cappello, F. Desprez, M. Dayde, E. Jeannot, Y. Jegou, S. Lanteri, N. Melab, R. Namyst, P. Primet, O. Richard, E. Caron, J. Leduc, and G. Mornet. Grid'5000: A large scale, reconfigurable, controlable and monitorable grid platform. In *Grid2005 6th IEEE/ACM International Workshop on Grid Computing*, November 2005.

[7] S. Lacour, C. Pérez, and T. Priol. A software architecture for automatic deployment of CORBA components using grid technologies. In *Proceedings of the 1st Francophone Conference On Software Deployment and (Re)Configuration (DECOR'2004)*, pages 187–192, Grenoble, France, October 2004.

[8] S. Lacour, C. Pérez, and T. Priol. A Network Topology Description Model for Grid Application Deployment. In *the Proceedings of the 5th IEEE/ACM International Workshop on Grid Computing (GRID 2004)*. Springer, November 2004.

[9] S. Lacour, C. Pérez, and T. Priol. Description and packaging of MPI applications for automatic deployment on computational grids. Research Report RR-5582, INRIA, IRISA, Rennes, France, May 2005.

[10] S. Lacour, C. Pérez, and T. Priol. Generic application description model: Toward automatic deployment of applications on computational grids. In *the Proceedinfs of the 6th IEEE/ACM Int. Workshop on Grid Computing (Grid2005)*. Springer, November 2005.

[11] Open Management Group (OMG). CORBA components, version 3. Document formal/02-06-65, June 2002.

[12] C. Pérez, T. Priol, and A. Ribes. A parallel CORBA component model for numerical code coupling. *The Int. Journal of High Performance Computing Applications*, 17(4):417–429, 2003.

[13] M. Vanneschi. The programming model of ASSIST, an environment for parallel and distributed portable applications. *Parallel Computing*, 28(12):1709–1732, Dec. 2002.

[14] D. Adami, M.Coppola, S. Giordano, D. Laforenza, M. Repeti, N. Tonellotto, Design and
       Implementation of a Grid Network-aware Resource Broker. In *Proc. of the Parallel and
       Distributed Computing and Networks Conf. (PDCN 2006)*. Acta Press, February 2006.

TOWARDS AUTOMATIC CREATION OF WEB SERVICES FOR GRID COMPONENT COMPOSITION

Jan Dünnweber and Sergei Gorlatch
University of Münster, Department of Mathematics and Computer Science
Einsteinstrasse 62, 48149 Münster, Germany
duennweb@uni-muenster.de
gorlatch@uni-muenster.de

Nikos Parlavantzas
Harrow School of Computer Science, University of Westminster, HA1 3TP, U.K.
N.Parlavantzas@westminster.ac.uk

Francoise Baude and Virginie Legrand
INRIA, CNRS-I3S, University of Nice Sophia-Antipolis, France
Francoise.Baude@sophia.inria.fr
Virginie.Legrand@sophia.inria.fr

Abstract   While high-level software components simplify the programming of grid applications and Web services increase their interoperability, developing such components and configuring the interconnecting services is a demanding task.

In this paper, we consider the combination of *Higher-Order Components* (HOCs)
with the *Fractal* component model and the *ProActive* library.

HOCs are parallel programming components, made accessible on the grid via
Web services that use a special class loader enabling code mobility: executable
code can be uploaded to a HOC, allowing one to customize the HOC. Fractal
simplifies the composition of components and the ProActive library offers a generator for automatically creating Web services from components composed with
Fractal, as long as all the parameters of these services have primitive types.

Taking all the advantages of HOCs, ProActive and Fractal together, the obvious
conclusion is that composing HOCs using Fractal and automatically exposing
them as Web services on the grid via ProActive minimizes the required efforts
for building complex grid systems. In this context, we solved the problem of
exchanging code-carrying parameters in automatically generated Web services
by integrating the HOC class loading mechanism into the ProActive library.

Keywords: CoreGRID Component Model (GCM) & Fractal, Higher-Order Components

1.   Introduction

The complexity of developing applications for distributed, heterogeneous systems (grids) is a challenging research topic. A promising idea for simplifying the development process and enhancing the quality of resulting applications is skeleton-based development [9]. This approach is based on the observation that many parallel applications share a common set of recurring patterns such as divide-and-conquer, farm, and pipeline. The idea is to capture such patterns as generic software constructs (skeletons) that can be customized by developers to produce particular applications.

When parallelism is achieved by distributing the data processing across several machines, the software developers must take communication issues into account. Therefore, grid software is typically packaged in the form of components, including, besides the operational code, also the appropriate middleware support. With this support, any data transmission is handled using a portable, usually XML-based format, allowing distributed components to communicate over the network, regardless of its heterogeneity. A recently proposed approach to grid application development is based on *Higher Order Components* (HOCs) [12], which are skeletons implemented as components and exposed via Web services. The technique of implementing skeletons as components consists in the combination of the operational code with an appropriate middleware support, which enables the exchange of data over the network using portable formats. Any Internet-connected client can access HOCs via their Web service ports and request from the HOCs, the execution of standard parallelism patterns on the grid. In order to customize a HOC for running a particular computation, the application-specific pieces of code are sent to the HOC as parameters.

Since HOCs and the customizing code may reside at different locations, the HOC approach includes support for code mobility. HOCs simplify application development because they isolate application programmers from the details of building individual HOCs and configuring the hosting middleware. The HOC approach can meet the requirements of providing a component architecture for grid programming with respect to abstraction and interoperability for two reasons: (1) the skeletal programming model offered by HOCs imposes a clear separation of concerns: the user works with high-level services requesting from him to provide an application-level code only, and (2) any HOC offers a publicly available interface in form of a Web service, thus making it accessible for remote systems without introducing any specific requirements on them, e. g., regarding the use of a particular middleware technology or programming language.

Building new grid applications using HOCs is simple as long as they require only HOCs that are readily available: In this case only some new parameter code must be specified. However, once an application adheres to a parallelism pattern that is not covered by the available HOCs, a new HOC has to be built. Building new HOCs currently requires starting from scratch and working directly with low-level grid middleware, which is tedious and error prone.

We believe that combining the HOC mechanism with another high-level grid programming environment, such as GAT [7] or ProActive [4] can greatly reduce the complexity of developing and deploying new HOCs. This complexity can be reduced further by providing support for composing HOCs out of other HOCs (e. g., in a nested manner) or other reusable functionality. For this reason, we are investigating the uniform use of the ProActive/Fractal [8] component model for implementing HOCs as assemblies of smaller-grained components, and for integrating HOCs with other HOCs and client software. The Fractal component model was recently selected as the starting point for defining a common Grid component model (GCM) used by all partners of the European research community CoreGRID [3]. Our experiments with Fractal-based HOCs can therefore be viewed as a proposal for using HOCs in the context of the forthcoming CoreGRID GCM.

Since HOCs are parameterized with code, the implementation of a HOC as a ProActive/Fractal component poses the following technical problem: how can one pass code-carrying arguments to a component that is accessed via a Web service? This paper describes how this problem is addressed by combining HOC's code mobility mechanism with ProActive/Fractal's mechanism for automatic Web service exposition. The presented techniques can also be applied to other component technologies that use Web services for handling the network communication.

The rest of this paper is structured as follows. Section 2 describes the HOC approach, focusing on the code mobility mechanism. Section 3 discusses how HOCs can be implemented in terms of ProActive/Fractal components. Section 4 presents the solution to the problem of supporting code-carrying parameters, and Section 5 concludes the paper in the context of related work.

2. Higher-Order Components (HOCs)

Higher-Order Components [12] (HOCs) have been introduced with the aim to provide efficient, grid-enabled patterns of parallelism (skeletons). There exist HOC implementations based on different programming languages [11] [10], but our focus in this paper is on Java, which is also the basic technology of the ProActive library [4].

Java-based HOCs are customized by plugging in application-specific Java code at appropriate places in a skeleton implementation. To cope with the data portability requirement of grids, our HOCs are accessed via Web services, and thus, any data that is transmitted over the network is implicitly converted into XML. These conversions are handled by the hosting middleware, e. g., the Globus toolkit, which must be appropriately configured. The middleware configuration depends on the types of input data accepted by a HOC, which are independent from specific applications. Therefore, the required middleware configuration files are pre-packaged with the HOCs during the deployment process, and hidden from the HOC users.

A HOC client application first uses a Web service to specify the customization parameters of a HOC. The goal is to set the behaviors that are left open in the skeletal code inside the HOC, e. g., the particular behavior of the Master and the Workers in the Farm-HOC which describes "embarrassingly parallel" applications without dependencies between tasks. Next, the client invokes operations on the customized HOC to initiate computations and retrieve the results. Any parameter in these invocations, whether it is a data item to be processed or a customizing piece of code, is uploaded to the HOC via Web service operation.

Code is transmitted to a Web service as plain data, since code has no valid representation in the WSDL file defining the service interface, which leads to the difficulty of assigning compatible interfaces to code-carrying parameters for executing them on the receiver side. HOCs make use of the fact that skeletons do not require a possibility to plug in arbitrary codes, but only the codes that match the set of behaviors, which are missing in the server-sided implementation. There is a given set of such code parameter types comprising, e. g, pipeline stages and farm tasks. A non-ambiguous mapping between each HOC and the code parameters it accepts is therefore possible. We use identifiers in the xsd:string-format to map code that is sent to a HOC as a parameter to a compatible interface. Let us demonstrate this feature using the example of the Farm-HOC implementing the farm skeleton, with a Master and an arbitrary number of Workers.

The Farm-HOC implements the dispatching of data emitted from the Master via scattering, i. e., each Worker is sent an equally sized subset of the input. The Farm-HOC implementation is partial since it does neither include the code to split input data into subsets, nor the code to process one single subset. While these application-specific behaviors must be specified by the client, Java interfaces for executing any code expressing these behaviors are independent from an application and fixed by the HOC. The client must provide (in a registry) one code unit that implements the following interface for the Workers:

```
1: public interface<E> Worker {
2:     public E[] compute(E[] input);
3: }
```

and another interface for the Master:

```
1: public interface<E> Master {
2:     public E[][] split (E[] input, int numWorkers);
3:     public E[] join(E[][] input);
4: }
```

The client triggers the execution of the Farm-HOC as follows:

```
1: farmHOC = farmFactory.createHOC();  // create client proxy
2: farmHOC.setMaster("masterID");          // customization of the HOC
3: farmHOC.setWorker("workerID");          // via Web service
4: String[] targetHosts = {"masterH", "workerH1", ...};
5: farmHOC.configureGrid(targetHosts); // choosing of target machines
6: farmHOC.compute(input);
```

Lines 2–3 are the most notable lines of code: here, the HOC is customized by passing the parameter identifiers masterID and workerID. It is an example use of the HOCs' code mobility mechanism, which supports the shipping of codes which implement interfaces like the above Master and Worker from a registry where clients have put them previously. In our Farm-HOC example, the masterID could, e. g, refer to a code in the registry, which splits a rectangular image into multiple tiles. The provision of the registry for mobile codes, also called *code service* [11], is dual-purpose: it stores code units in a byte-array format, enabling their transfer via Web services which treat them as raw data, and it fosters the reuse of code parameters units in different combinations.

The variable data type E in the code parameter interfaces is typically assigned double as the most general type possible. If int is sufficient, it may be used for a more efficient data encoding. However, only primitive types can be assigned to E. The input of a HOC is transferred to a Web service and therefore the input data type must have a representation as an element in the corresponding WSDL-types structure, which is an XML Schema. Choosing Java Object and the general XML Schema type xsd:any as a substitute would not help at all, since no middleware can serialize/deserialize arbitraty data. Any more specific types, derived from the plain Object type, are forbidden, when the defining classes are not present on both, the sender and the receiver side and a plain Object is not suitable to transmit any significant information. Alternatives like Java Beans (i. e., classes composed of attributes and corresponding accessors only) result in fixed types for the data parameters and also require an unnecessary time-consuming marshaling process.

To make the code mobility mechanism transparent to Java programmers, we developed a remote class loader for HOCs that replaces the Java default class loader. The introduced remote loader connects to the *code service* whenever new classes are loaded, that are not available on the local file system. After the bytecode for a particular class is retrieved from the code service, the class is instantiated by the remote class loader using the Java reflection mechanism.

Overall, the code mobility mechanism provides a sort of mapping code parameters implementing the Java interfaces for a given type of HOC, to XML-schema definitions used in WSDL descriptions. This mapping is indirect as it relies on the usage of xsd:string-type identifiers for code parameters (which can obviously be expressed in WSDL). The current implementation of the HOC service architecture [11] does not enable the automatic generation of any middleware configuration, including the basic WSDL and WSDD files required for deploying the Web services used to access a HOC. It is the duty of the programmer of a (new type of) HOC to provide these files.

3. Higher-Order Components (HOCs) built upon ProActive/Fractal

In the following, we will show that HOCs, Fractal and the ProActive library are complementary. ProActive provides various, generally useful utilities for programming grid systems, e. g., the active object construct allowing RMI-based programs to communicate asychronously. ProActive is not only a library, but it also includes the ProActive *runtime*, a middleware for hosting active objects and Fractal components, which are compositions of multiple active objects. In the context of HOCs, we are interested in the following feature of Fractal/ProActive: Web services for accessing Fractal components can be automatically deployed onto a compatible middleware (e. g., Apache Axis [2]), while HOCs that only use Globus as their middleware demand the coding of WSDL and WSDD from the HOC developers.

Let us take a look at a few further features of Fractal/ProActive that are useful for HOC developers. ProActive/Fractal components interconnect active objects and compositions of them via so-called *bindings*. An important feature of Fractal is the support for hierarchical composition of components, i. e., components can be connected and nested into each other up to arbitrary levels of abstraction. By applying Fractal's component composition features to HOCs, we can build, e. g., a farm of multiple pipelines as a new type of HOC, simply by binding the Farm-HOC and the Pipeline-HOC together. Once all the required code parameters for every HOC in such a composition have been installed, the composite component exhibits the same behavior as the outermost HOC it is built of. In a hierarchical composition, the interfaces of the inner components are accessible via the outer ones. The Web service interface for accessing composite HOCs over remote connections offers the same operations as the outermost HOC. Thus, there is exactly one customization operation for altering each single HOC parameter (see Fig. 1).

Component configurations can be specified flexibly using an architecture description language (ADL) and mapped declaratively to arbitrary network topologies using deployment descriptors. In the example in Section 2 which did not use Fractal, we have seen the `configureGrid` method, which required the client to fix the target nodes to be used in the applications code. With Fractal's ADL, the HOC method `configureGrid` becomes obsolete, leading to more flexibility. Moreover, Fractal-based components can be associated with an extensible set of controllers, which enable inspecting and reconfiguring their internal features. The component model is expected to simplify developing and modifying HOCs because it presents a high abstraction level to developers and supports changing configurations and deployment properties without code modifications.

Using ProActive/Fractal, a HOC will be formed as a composite that contains components customizable with externally-provided behavior. Let us consider, again, the Farm-HOC from the previous section, and see how it could be understood as a Fractal component. This would be a *composite* component containing a *primitive* component called `Master`, connected to an arbitrary number of other primitives called `Workers` (Fig. 1). The `Master` and the `Workers` can reside either on a single machine or they can be distributed over multiple nodes of the grid, depending on the ADL configuration. For better performance, the `Master` could dispatch data to `Workers` using the built-in scattering (group communication) mechanism provided by the ProActive library, or the forthcoming multicast GCM interfaces [3].

The `Master` and `Worker` elements of the Farm-HOC are themselves independent components in the Fractal model. Both are customizable with external behavior (depicted with the black cycles) through the following interface exposed on the composite:

```
public interface Customisation {
    public void setMaster(Master m);
    public void setWorker(Worker w);
}
```

To make the Fractal-based farm component accessible as a HOC in the grid, the `Customisation` interface must be exposed via a Web service. However, this requires that one can pass a code-carrying, behavioral argument (e.g., a `Master` implementation) to this Web service. Moreover, the service must be associated with state data, such that the behavior customizations triggered by the `setMaster`/`setWorker`-operations have a persistent effect on the HOC.

A popular solution to this problem are *resource properties* [13], giving the service operations durable access to data records defined in the service configuration. The middleware maintains this data in a way that each record is uniquely identifiable, avoiding conflicts among different, potentially concurrent service operations. However, this solution requires special support by the middleware, which is not present in standard Web service hosting environments (e. g., Axis) but only in Grid toolkits, such as Globus.

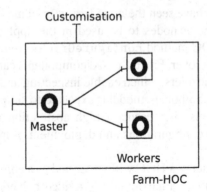

Figure 1.   The Farm-HOC shown using the Fractal symbols

The Web service creation mechanism in ProActive/Fractal cannot automatically build service configurations including resource properties for a grid middleware like Globus. However, the code service and the remote class loader in the HOC service architecture are preconfigured to work with this type of middleware. In the following, we will show, how the HOC service architecture and Fractal/ProActive can be combined to automatically create Web services that allow the interconnection of distributed grid components, which exchange data and code over the network.

4.   Accessing HOC components via ProActive Web services

This section first describes the existing ProActive mechanism for automatically exposing Fractal components as Web services, and then it explains how this mechanism has been extended to solve the technical problem identified in Section 3.

ProActive uses the Axis [2] library to generate WSDL descriptions and the Apache SOAP [1] engine to deploy Web services automatically. Service invocations are routed through a custom ProActive *provider*. When a Fractal component should be exposed as a Web service, the ProActive user simply calls the static library method `exposeComponentAsWebService`, which generates the required service configuration and makes a new Web service available. The URL of this new service is specified as a parameter.

This mechanism supports all parameter types defined in the SOAP specification; Java primitive types are supported, but not complex types. When consumers need to perform a call on a service, they get the description and just perform the call according to the WSDL contract (Fig. 2, step 1).

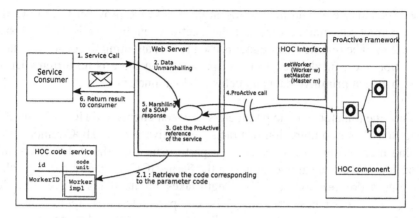

Figure 2. ProActive web services mechanism with HOC remote class loading

ProActive programmers are freed from processing SOAP messages in the code they write: when a call reaches the ProActive provider, the Apache SOAP engine has already unmarshaled the message and knows which method to call on which object (Fig. 2, step 2). Only the logic required to serve the requested operation must be implemented, when a new service should be provided. Specifically, the provider gets a remote reference on the targeted interface (Fig. 2, step 3), it performs a standard ProActive call from the Web server side to the remote ProActive runtime side using the reference (Fig. 2, step 4), and it returns the result to the SOAP engine. The engine then marshals a new SOAP message and sends it back to the service consumer (Fig. 2, steps 5 and 6).

Whenever the `exposeComponentAsWebService` method is called for a HOC, parameters of complex types are transfered indirectly, by passing a primitive identifier, as explained in Section 2. For this purpose, we derived a special HOC-class from the base class for defining a component in Fractal (`Component`), used to represent HOCs built upon Fractal. Java's `instanceof` operator is used to detect the HOC type. When a Web service is created for accessing a HOC, all non-primitive parameters are simply replaced by the `xsd:string` type for carrying parameter identifiers. In the server-sided HOC code, the remote class loader is used to obtain an `Object`-type instances of the classes corresponding to these identifiers. Any such `Object` is then to be cast approriately, for making it available, e. g., as the `Master` in the Farm-HOC. Our extension of the ProActive/Fractal Web service creation mechanism involves two steps:

- First, we generate a WSDL description that maps behavioral parameters to identifiers used to denote code units in the HOC code service as explained above.

- Second, we extend the routing in the ProActive provider to retrieve the correct code unit according to the identifier sent by the client (Fig. 2, step 2.1). The remote class loader is used for instantiating the code via reflection, i. e., inside the service implementation there is no differentiation between primitive data and behavioral parameters.

Since the transfer of code parameters between clients and HOCs is handled using SOAP, our combination of Fractal/ProActive and the HOC remote class loading mechanism introduces a slight performance overhead during the initialization phase of an application. For the Farm-HOC, we measured, e. g., that installing a Worker code of 5KB length takes about 100ms at average. So, if, e. g., 10 Worker hosts run this 5KB code parameter, then approximately 1 additional second installation time will be needed. Marginal performance reductions like this can of course be disregarded w.r.t. the typical runtimes of grid applications. It should also be noted that this time is spent only once during a non-recurring setup step.

5. Conclusion and Perspectives

This paper describes a solution to supporting code-carrying parameters in component interfaces, offering transparency to developers at the code receiving side. A natural direction for future work is to provide tools for interpreting WSDL descriptions containing such parameters, in order to provide transparency also at the code sending side. Further work would also be to devise a general solution for supporting arbitrary types, even a complex Java type, when publishing ProActive/Fractal components as Web services. This paper presents a first step in this direction: it suggests a solution that only applies to some specific parameter types, i.e. those representing behaviors. The general case would call for a solution where the generation of the extended ProActive provider would be totally automated. The solution presented here is specific in the sense that the extended provider has been generated specifically for the case of HOC.

For addressing the general case, we should take into account related work: (1) the *valuetype* construct in CORBA, which supports passing objects by value (both state and behavior) to remote applications [5], (2) possible – not yet standard – extensions of WSDL for passing arguments as complex types using specific SOAP attachments, and (3) standard facilities for XML data binding, such as the Java Architecture for XML Binding 2.0 JAXB [6]. Whatever the solution we would use for passing parameters of arbitrary types, it calls for a generic and automatic mechanism based on reflection techniques and dynamic code generation. Note that legacy software is another example for programs, where the number of code-carrying parameters and their types, i.e. the requirements for executing them, are known. Thus, it is easily possible to extend our parameter matching mechanism, such that a code parameter can be represented, e. g., by an MPI program: therefore, we only need an additional parameter identifier (see Section 2) that causes the HOC to run this parameter on top of the appropriate supporting environment (mpirun in the example case) instead of retrieving a Java interface.

This paper has also discussed how HOCs can be implemented as composite components in the context of the CoreGRID GCM, which is based on the Fractal component model. Our work can thus be considered as a joint effort to devise grid-enabled skeletons based on a fully-fledged component-oriented model, effectively using the dynamic (re)configuration capabilities, and the ability to master complex codes through hierarchical composition. We foresee that a skeleton could be configured by passing it software components as its internal entities. The configuration options could be made broader than in the current HOC model, by adding specific controllers on the composite component representing a whole skeleton, that could recursively affect the included components.

Acknowledgments

This research was conducted within the FP6 Network of Excellence CoreGRID funded by the European Commission (Contract IST-2002-004265).

References

[1] The Apache SOAP web site. http://ws.apache.org/soap.

[2] The AXIS web site. http://ws.apache.org/axis.

[3] The CoreGRID web site. http://coregrid.net.

[4] The ProActive web site. http://www-sop.inria.fr/oasis/ProActive.

[5] *CORBA/IIOP v3.0.3.* Object Management Group, 2004. OMG Document formal/2004-03-01.

[6] *The Java Architecture for XML Binding 2.0, early draft v0.4.* Sun Microsystems, 2004.

[7] G. Allen, K. Davis, T. Goodale, A. Hutanu, H. Kaiser, T. Kielmann, A. Merzky, R. v. Nieuwpoort, A. Reinefeld, F. Schintke, T. Schtt, E. Seidel, and B. Ullmer. The Grid Application Toolkit: Towards generic and easy application programming interfaces for the grid. In *Proceedings of the IEEE, vol. 93, no. 3*, pages 534 – 550, 2005.

[8] F. Baude, D. Caromel, and M. Morel. From distributed objects to hierarchical grid components. In *International Symposium on Distributed Objects and Applications (DOA), Catania, Sicily, Italy, 3-7 November*, 2003.

[9] M. I. Cole. *Algorithmic skeletons: a structured approach to the management of parallel computation.* MIT Press & Pitman, 1989.

[10] J. Dünnweber, A. Benoit, M. Cole, and S. Gorlatch. Integrating MPI-skeletons with Web services. In *Proceedings of the PARCO, Malaga, Spain, 2005*

[11] J. Dünnweber and S. Gorlatch. HOC-SA: A grid Service Architecture for Higher-Order Components. In *International Conference on Services Computing (SCC04), Shanghai, China*, pages 288–294, Washington, USA, 2004. IEEE computer.org.

[12] S. Gorlatch and J. Dünnweber. From grid middleware to grid applications: Bridging the gap with HOCs. In *Future Generation Grids*. Springer Verlag, 2005.

[13] OASIS Technical Committee.   WSRF: The Web Service Resource Framework, http://www.oasis-open.org/committees/wsrf.

ADAPTABLE PARALLEL COMPONENTS FOR GRID PROGRAMMING

Jan Dünnweber and Sergei Gorlatch
University of Münster, Department of Mathematics and Computer Science
Einsteinstrasse 62, 48149 Münster, Germany
duennweb@uni-muenster.de
gorlatch@uni-muenster.de

Marco Aldinucci, Sonia Campa and Marco Danelutto
Università di Pisa, Department of Computer Science
Largo B. Pontecorvo 3, 56127 Pisa, Italy
aldinuc@di.unipi.it
campa@di.unipi.it
marcod@di.unipi.it

Abstract   We suggest that parallel software components used for grid computing should be adaptable to application-specific requirements, instead of developing new components from scratch for each particular application. As an example, we take a parallel farm component which is "embarrassingly parallel", i. e., free of dependencies, and adapt it to the wavefront processing pattern with dependencies that impact its behavior. We describe our approach in the context of Higher-Order Components (HOCs), with the Java-based system Lithium as our implementation framework. The adaptation process relies on HOCs' mobile code parameters that are shipped over the network of the grid. We describe our implementation of the proposed component adaptation method and report first experimental results for a particular grid application – the alignment of DNA sequence pairs, a popular, time-critical problem in computational molecular biology.

Keywords: Grid Components, Adaptable Code, Wavefront Parallelism, Java, Web Services

1.   Introduction

Grids are a promising platform for distributed computing with high demand on data throughput and computing power, but they are still difficult to program due to their highly heterogeneous and dynamic nature. Popular technologies for programming grids are Java, since it enables portabilty for executable code, and Web services, which facilitate the exchange of application data in a portable a format. Thus, multiple Java-based components, distributed across the Internet, can work together using Web services.

Besides interoperability, grid applications require from their runtime environments support for the sharing of data among multiple services and a possibility for issuing non-blocking service requests. The contemporary grid middleware systems, e. g., the Globus Toolkit [6] and Unicore [15] address such recurring issues, thus freeing users from dealing with the same problems again and again. Middleware abstracts over the complex infrastructure of a grid: application code developed by middleware users (which still consists in Java-based Web services in most cases) is not so heavily concerned with the low-level details of network communication and the maintenance of distributed data.

While providing an infrastructure-level abstraction, middleware introduces numerous non-trivial configuration requirements on the system-level, which complicates the development of applications. Therefore, recent approaches to simplifying the programming of grid applications often introduce an additional layer of software components abstracting over the middleware used in the grid.

Software components for the grid aim to be easier to handle than raw middleware. In [14], components are defined as software building-blocks with no implicit dependencies regarding the runtime environment; i. e., components for grid programming are readily integrated with the underlying middleware, hiding it from the grid users. An example for grid programming components is given by the CoreGRID *Grid Component Model* (GCM), a specification which emerged from the component models Fractal [2], HOCs [7], ASSIST [12] and other experimental studies, conducted within the CoreGRID community. While the GCM predecessors are accompanied by framework implementations, providing the users with an API, there is yet no GCM framework. Anyway, there are multiple implementations of Fractal, the HOC-SA [5] for programming with HOCs, the ASSIST framework for data-flow programming and its Java-based variant Lithium [4]. These frameworks allow to experiment with many GCM features and to preliminarily analyse limitations of the model.

This paper addresses grid application programming using a component framework, where applications are built by *selecting*, *customizing* and *combining* components. Selecting means choosing appropriate components from the framework, which may contain several ready-made implementations of commonly used parallel computing schemata (farm, divide-and-conquer, etc. [3]).

By customization, we mean specifying application-specific operations to be executed within the processing schema of a component, e. g., parallel farming of application-specific tasks. Combining various parallel components together for accomplishing one task, can be done, e. g., via Web services.

As our main contribution, we introduce *adaptations* of software components, which extends the traditional notion of *customization*: while customization applies a component's computing schema in a particular context, adaptation modifies the very schema of a component, with the purpose of incorporating new capabilities. Our thrust to use adaptable components is motivated by the fact that a fixed framework is hardly able to cover every potentially useful type of component. The behavior of adaptable components can be altered, thus allowing to apply them in use cases for which they have not been originally designed. We demonstrate that both, traditional customization and adaptation of components can be realized in a grid-aware manner (i. e., also in the context of an upcoming GCM-framework). We use two kinds of components' parameters that are shipped over the network with the purpose of adaptation: these parameters may be either data or executable codes.

As a case study, we take a component that was originally designed for dependency-free *task farming*. By means of an additional code parameter, we adapt this component for the parallel processing of tasks exhibiting data dependencies with a *wavefront* structure.

In Section 2, we explain our *Higher-Order Components* (HOCs) and how they can be made adaptable. Section 3 describes our application case study used throughout the paper: the alignment of sequence pairs, which is a wavefront-type, time-critical problem in computational molecular biology. In Section 4, we show how the HOC-framework enables the use of mobile code, as it is required to apply a component adaptation in the grid context. Section 5 shows our first experimental results for applying the adapted farm component to the alignment problem in different, grid-like infrastructures. Section 6 summarizes the contributions of this paper in the context of related work.

2. Components and Adaptation

When an application requires a component, which is not provided by the employed framework, there are two possibilities: either to code the required component anew or to try and derive it from another available component. The former possibility is more direct, but it has to be done repeatedly for each new application. The latter possibility, which we call adaptation, provides more flexibility and potential for reuse of components. However, it requires from the employed framework to have a special adaptation mechanism.

2.1   Higher-Order Components (HOCs)

Higher-Order Components (HOCs) [7] are called so because they can be parameterized not only with data but also with code, in analogy to higher-order functions that may use other functions as arguments. We illustrate the HOC concept using a particular component, the Farm-HOC, which will be our example throughout the paper. We first present how the Farm-HOC is used in the context of Java and then explain the particular features of HOCs which make them well-suited for adaptation. While many different options (e. g., C + MPI or Pthreads) are available for implementing HOCs, in this paper, our focus is on Java, where multithreading and the concurrency API are standardized parts of the language.

2.2   Example: The Farm-HOC

The farm pattern is only one of many possible patterns of parallelism, arguably one of the simplest, as all its parallel tasks are supposed to be independent from each other. There may be different implementations of the farm, depending on the target computer platform; all these implementations have, however, in common that the input data are partitioned using a code unit called the Master and the tasks on the data parts are processed in parallel using a code unit called the Worker. Our Farm-HOC, has therefore two so-called *customization code parameters*, the Master-parameter and the Worker-parameter, defining the corresponding code units in the farm implementation.

The code parameters specify how the Farm-HOC should be applied in a particular situation. The Master parameter must contain a split method for partitioning data and a corresponding join method for recombining it, while the Worker parameter must contain a compute method for task processing. Farm-HOC users declare these parameters by implementing the following two interfaces:

```
1: public interface Master<E>  {
2:   public E[][] split(E[] input, int grain);
3:   public E[] join(E[][] results);   }
4: public interface Worker<E>  {
5:   public E[] compute(E[] input);   }
```

The Master (line 1–3) determines how an input array of some type E is split into independent subsets, and the Worker (line 4–5) describes how a single subset is processed as a task in the farm. While the Worker-parameter differs in most applications, programmers typically pick the default implementation of the Master from our framework. This Master splits the input regularly, i. e., into equally sized partations. A specific Master-implementation must only be provided, if a regular splitting is undesireable, e. g., for preserving certain data correlations.

Unless an adaptation is applied to it, the processing schema of the Farm-HOC is very general, which is a common property of all HOCs. In the case of the Farm-HOC, after the splitting phase, the schema consists in the parallel execution of the tasks described by the implementation of the above Worker-interface. To allow the execution on multiple servers, the internal implementation of the Farm-HOC adheres to the widely used scheduler/worker-pattern of distributed computing: A single scheduler machine runs the Master-code (the first server given in the call to the configureGrid method, shown below) and the other servers each run a pool of threads, wherein each thread waits for tasks from the scheduler and then processes them using the Worker code parameter, passed during the farm initialization.

The following code shows how the Farm-HOC is invoked on the grid as a Web service via its remote interface farmHOC:

```
1: farmHOC.configureGrid( "masterHost",
2:                        "workerHost1",... ,
3:                        "workerHostN" );
4: farmHOC.process(input, LITHIUM, JAVA5);
```

The programmer can pick the servers to be employed for running the Worker-code via the configureGrid-method (line 1–3), which accepts either host names or IP addresses as parameters. Moreover, the programmer can select, among various implementations, the most adequate version for a particular network topology and for particular server architectures (in the above code, the version based on the grid programming library Lithium [4] is chosen). The JAVA5-constant, passed in the invocation (line 4), specifies that the format of the code parameters to be employed in the execution is Java bytecode compliant to Java virtual machine versions 1.5 or higher.

2.3 The Implementation of Adaptable HOCs

The need for adaptation arises if an application requires a processing schema which is not provided by the available components. Adaptation is used to derive a new component with a different behavior from the original HOC. Our approach is that a particular adaptation is also specified via a code parameter, similar to the customization shown in the preceding section. In contrast to a customizing code parameter, which is applied within the execution of the HOC's schema, a code parameter specifying an adaptation runs in parallel to the execution of the HOC. There is no fixed position for the adaptation code in the HOC implementation; rather the HOC exchanges messages with it in a publish/subscribe-manner. This way, a code parameter can, e. g., block the execution of the HOC's standard processing schema at any time, until some condition is fulfilled.

Our implementation design can be viewed as a general method for making components adaptable. The two most notable, advantageous properties of our implementation are as follows: 1) Using HOCs, adaptation code is placed within one or multiple threads of its own, while the original framework code remains unchanged, and 2) An adaptation code parameter is connected to the HOC using only message exchange, leading to high flexibilty.

This design has the following advantageous properties:

- we clearly separate the adaptation code not only from the component implementation code, but also from the obligatory, customizing code parameters. When a new algorithm with new dependencies is implemented, the customization parameters can still be written as if this algorithm introduced no new data dependencies. This feature is especially obvious in case of the Farm-HOC, as there are no dependencies at all in a farm. Accordingly, the Master and Worker parameters of a component derived from the Farm-HOC are written dependency-free.

- we decouple the adaptation thread from the remaining component structure. There can be an arbitrary number of adaptations. Due to our messaging model, adaptation parameters can easily be changed. Our model promotes better code reusability as compared to passing information between the component implementations and the adaptation code directly via the parameters and return values of the adaptation codes' methods. Any thread can publish messages for delivery to other that provides the publisher with an appropriate interface for receiving messages. Thus, adaptations can also adapt other adaptations and so on.

- Our implementation offers a high degree of location independence: In the Farm-HOC, the data to be processed can be placed locally on the machine running the scheduler or they can be distributed among several remote servers. In contrast to coupling the adaptation code to the Worker code, which would be a consequence of placing it inside the same class, our adaptations are not restricted to affecting only the remote hosts, but can also have an impact on the scheduler host. In our case study, we use this feature to efficiently optimize the scheduling behavior with respect to exploiting data locality: processing a certain amount of data locally in the scheduler significantly increases the efficiency of the computations.

3.   Case Study: Sequence Alignment

Our case study in this paper is one of the fundamental algorithms in bioinformatics – the computation of *distances* between DNA sequences, i. e. , finding the minimum number of operations needed to transform one sequence into another. Sequences are encoded using the nucleotide alphabet $\{A, C, G, T\}$.

The distance, which is the total number of the required transformations, quantifies the similarity of sequences [11] and is often called *global alignment*. Mathematically, global alignment can be expressed using a so-called *similarity matrix S*, whose elements $s_{i,j}$ are defined as follows:

$$s_{i,j} := max \left(s_{i,j-1}+plt, s_{i-1,j-1}+\delta(i,j), s_{i-1,j}+plt \right) \qquad (1)$$

wherein

$$\delta(i,j) := \begin{cases} +1 & \text{, if } \epsilon_1(i) = \epsilon_2(j) \\ -1 & \text{, otherwise} \end{cases} \qquad (2)$$

Here, $\epsilon_k(b)$ denotes the b-th element of sequence k, and plt is a constant that weighs the costs for inserting a space into one of the sequences (typically, $plt = -2$, the "double price" of a mismatch).

The data dependencies imposed by definition (1) imply a particular order of computation of the matrix: elements which can be computed independently of each other, i. e., in parallel, are located on a so-called *wavefront* which "moves" across the matrix as computations proceed. The wavefront is degenerated into a straight line when it is drawn along the single independent elements, but its "wavy" structure becomes apparent when it spans multi-element blocks. In higher-dimensional cases (3 or more input sequences), the wavefront becomes a hyperplane [9].

The wavefront pattern of parallel computation is not specific only to the sequence alignment problem, but is used also in other popular applications: searching in graphs represented via their adjacency matrices, system solvers, character stream conversion problems, motion planning algorithms in robotics etc. Therefore, programmers would benefit if a standard component would capture the wavefront pattern. Our approach is to take the Farm-HOC, as introduced in Section 2, adapt it to the wavefront structure of parallelism and then customize it to the sequence alignment application. Fig. 2 schematically shows this two-step procedure. First, the workspace, holding the partitioned tasks for farming, is sorted according to the wavefront pattern, whereby a new processing order is fixed, which is optimal with respect to the degree of parallelism. Then, the alignment definitions (1) and (2) are employed for processing the sequence alignment application.

4. Adaptations with Globus & WSRF

The Globus middleware and the enclosed implementation of the *Web Services Resource Framework* (WSRF) form the middleware platform used for running HOCs (http://www.oasis-open.org/committees/wsrf).

The WSRF allows to set up stateful resources and connect them to Web services. Such resources can represent application state data and thereby make Web services and their XML-based communication protocol (SOAP) more suitable for grid computing: while usual Web services offer only self-contained operations, which are decoupled from each other and from the caller, Web services hosted with Globus include the notion of context: multiple operations can affect the same data, and changes within this data can trigger callbacks to the service consumer, thus avoiding blocking invocations.

Globus requires from the programmer to manually write a configuration consisting in multiple XML files which must be placed properly within the grid servers' installation directories. These files must explicitly declare all resources, the services used to connect to them, their interfaces and bindings to the employed protocol, in order to make Globus applications accessible in a platform- and programming language-independent manner.

4.1   Enabling Mobile Code

Users of the HOC-framework are freed from the complicated WSRF-setup described above, as all the required files, which are specific for each HOC but independent from applications, are provided for all HOCs in advance.

We provide a special class-loading mechanism allowing class definitions to be exchanged among distributed servers. The code pieces being exchanged among the grid nodes hosting our HOCs are stored as properties of resources that have been configured according to the HOC-requirements; e. g., the Farm-HOC is connected with a resource for holding an implementation of one `Master` and one `Worker` code parameter.

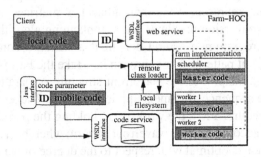

Figure 1.   Transfer of code parameters

Fig. 1 illustrates the transfer of mobile code in the HOC-framework. The bold lines around the Farm-HOC, the *remote class loader* and the *code-service* indicate that these entities are parts of our framework implementation. The Farm-HOC, shown in the right part of the figure, contains an implementation of the farm schema with a scheduler that dispatches tasks to workers (two in the figure). The HOC implementation includes one Web service providing the publicly available interface to this HOC. Application programmers only

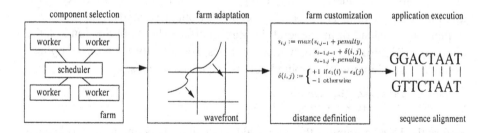

Figure 2. Two-step process: adaptation and customization

provide the code parameters. System programmers, who build HOCs, must assure that these parameters can be interpreted on the target nodes, which may be particularly difficult for heterogeneous grid nodes.

HOCs transfer each code unit as a record holding an identifier (ID) plus the a combination of the code itself and declaration of requirements for running the code. A requirement may, e. g., be the availability of a certain Java virtual machine version. As the format for declaring such requirements, we use string literals, which must coincide with those used in the invocation of the HOC (e. g., JAVA5, as shown in Section 2.2). This requirement-matching mechanism is necessary to bypass the problem that executable code is usually platform-specific, and therefore not mobile: not any code can be executed by an arbitrary host. Before we ship a code parameter, we guide it through the code-service – a Web service connected to a database, where the code parameters are filed as Java bytecode or in a scripting-language format. This design facilitates the reuse of code parameters and their mobility, at least across all nodes that run a compatible Java virtual machine or a portable scripting-language interpreter (e. g., Apache BSF: http://jakarta.apache.org/bsf). The remote class loader in Fig. 1 loads class definitions from the code-service, if they are not available on the local filesystem.

In the following, we illustrate the two-step process of adaptation and customization shown in Fig. 2. For the sake of explanation, we start with the second step (HOC customization), and then consider the farm adaptation.

4.2 Customizing the Farm-HOC for Sequence Alignment

Our HOC framework includes several helper classes that simplify the processing of matrices. It is therefore, e. g., not necessary to write any Master code, which splits matrices into equally sized submatrices, but we can fetch a standard framework procedure from the code service. The only code parameter we must write anew for computing the similarity matrix in our sequence alignment application is the Worker code. In our case study this parameter implements, instead of the general Worker-interface shown in Section 2.2, the alternative Binder-interface, which describes, specifically for matrix applications, how an element is computed depending on its indices:

```
1: public interface Binder<E>   {
2:   public E bind(int i, int j);   }
```

Before the HOC computes the matrix elements, it assigns an empty workspace matrix to the code parameter; i. e., a matrix reference is passed to the parameter object and, thus, made available to the customizing parameter code for accessing the matrix elements.

Our code parameter implementation for calculating matrix elements, accordingly to definition (1) from section 3, reads as follows:

```
1: new Binder<Integer>( ) {
2:   public Integer bind(int i, int j)   {
3:   return max( matrix.get(i, j - 1) + penalty,
4:    matrix.get(i - 1, j - 1) + delta(i, j),
5:    matrix.get(i - 1, j) + penalty );   }   }
```

The helper method delta, used in line 4 of the above code, implements definition (2).

The special Matrix-type used by the above code for representing the distributed matrix is also provided by our framework and it facilitates full location transparency, i.e., it allows to use the same interface for accessing remote elements and local elements. Actually, Matrix is an abstract class, and our framework includes two concrete implementations: LocalMatrix and RemoteMatrix. These classes allow to access elements in adjacent submatrices (using negative indices), which further simplifies the programming of distributed matrix algorithms. Obviously, these framework-specific utilities are quite helpful in the presented case study, but they are not necessary for adaptable components and therefore beyond the scope of this paper.

Farming the tasks described by the above Binder, i. e., the matrix element computations, does not allow data dependencies between the elements. Therefore any farm implementation, including the one in the Lithium library used in our case, would compute the alignment result as a single task, without parallelization, which is unsatisfactory and will be addressed by means of adaptation.

4.3   Adapting the Farm-HOC to the Wavefront Pattern

For the parallel processing of submatrices, the adapted component must, initially, fix the "wavefront order" for processing individual tasks, which is done by sorting the partitions of the workspace matrix arranged by the Master from the HOC-framework, such that independent submatrices are grouped in one wavefront. We compute this sorted partitioning, while iterating over the matrix-antidiagonals as a preliminary step of the adapted farm, similar to the loop-skewing algorithm described in [16]. The central role in our adaptation approach is played by the special *steering thread* that is installed by the user and runs the wavefront-sorting procedure in its initialization method.

After the initialization is finished, the steering thread keeps running concurrently to the original farm scheduler and periodically creates new tasks by executing the following loop:

```
 1: for (List<Task> waveFront : data)  {
 2:  if (waveFront.size( ) < localLimit)
 3:   scheduler.dispatch(wave, true);
 4:  else  {
 5:   remoteTasks = waveFront.size( ) / 2;
 6:   if ((surplus = remoteTasks % machines) != 0)
 7:    remoteTasks -= surplus;
 8:   localTasks = waveFront.size( ) - remoteTasks;
 9:   scheduler.dispatch(
10:    waveFront.subList(0, remoteTasks), false);
11:   scheduler.dispatch(
12:    waveFront.subList(remoteTasks,
13:    remoteTasks + localTasks), true);  }
14:  scheduler.assignAll( );  }
```

Here, the steering thread iterates over all wavefronts, i.e., the submatrices positioned along the anti-diagonals of the similarity matrix being computed.

The assignAll and the dispatch are not part of the standard Java API, but we implemented them ourselves to improve the efficiency of the scheduling as follows: The assignAll-method waits until the tasks to be processed have been assigned to workers. Method dispatch, in its first parameter, expects a list of new tasks to be processed. Via the second boolean parameter, the method allows the caller to decide whether these tasks should be processed locally by the scheduler (see lines 2–3 of the code above): the steering thread checks if the number of tasks is less than a limit set by the client. If so, then all tasks of such a "small" wavefront are marked for local processing, thus avoiding that communication costs exceed the time savings gained by employing remote servers. For wavefront sizes above the given limit, the balance of tasks for local and remote processing is computed in lines 5–8: half of the submatrices are processed locally and the remaining submatrices are evenly distributed among the remote servers. If there is no even distribution, the surplus matrices are assigned for local processing. Then, all submatrices are dispatched, either for local or remote processing (lines 9—13) and the assignAll-method is called

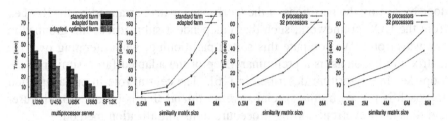

Figure 3. Experiments, from left to right: single multiprocessor servers; employing two servers; multiple multiprocessor servers; same input, zipped transmission

(line 14). The submatrices are processed asynchronously, as `assignAll` only waits until all tasks have been *assigned*, not until they are finished.

Without the `assignAll` and `dispatch`-method, the adaptation parameter can implement the same behavior using a `Condition` from the standard concurrency API for thread coordination, which is a more low-level solution.

5. Experimental Results

We investigated the run time of the application for processing the genome data of various fungi, as archived at `http://www.ncbi.nlm.nih.gov`. The scalability was measured in two dimensions: (1) with increasing number of processors in a single server, and (2) with increasing number of servers.

Table 1. The servers in our grid testbed

Server	Architecture	Processors	Clock Speed
SMP U280	Sparc II	2	750 Mhz
SMP U450	Sparc II	4	900 Mhz
SMP U880	Sparc II	8	900 Mhz
SMP U68K	UltraSparc III+	2	900 Mhz
SMP SF12K	UltraSparc III+	8	1200 Mhz

The first plot in Fig. 3 shows the results for computing a similarity matrix of 1 MB size using the SunFire machines listed above. We have deliberately chosen heterogeneous multiprocessor servers, in order to study a realistic, grid-like scenario.

A standard, non-adapted farm can carry out computations on a single pair of DNA sequences only sequentially, due to the wavefront-structured data dependencies. Using our Farm-HOC, we imitated this behavior by omitting the adaptation parameter and by specifying a partitioning grain equal to the size of an overall similarity matrix. This version was the slowest in our tests. Runtime measurements with the `localLimit` in the `steeringThread` set to a value $>= 0$ are labeled as *adapted, optimized farm*. The locality optimization, explained in Section 4.3, has an extra impact on the first plot in Fig. 3, since it avoids the use of sockets for local communication. To make the comparison with the standard farm version fairer, the localLimit was set to zero in a second series of measurements, which are labeled as *adapted farm* in Fig. 3. Both plots in Fig. 3 show the average results of three measurements. To obtain a measure for the spread, we always computed the variation coefficient; this turned to be less than 5% for all test series.

To investigate the scalability we ran the same application using two Pentium III servers under Linux. While the standard farm can only use one of the servers at a time, the adapted farm sends a part of the load to the second server, which improves the overall performance when the input sequence length increases (see the second plot). For more than two servers the performance was leveled off. We assume that this is due to the increase of communication, for distributing the Binder-tasks (shown in Section 4.2) over the network. The right plots in Fig. 3 support this assumption. We investigated the scalability using the U880 plus a second SunFire 6800 with 24 1350 MHz UltraSPARC-IV processors. As can be seen, the performance of our applications is significantly increased for the 32 processor configuration, since the SMP-machine-interconnection does not require the transmission of all tasks over the network. Curves for the standard farm are not shown in these diagrams, since they lie far above the shown curves and coincide for 8 and 32 processors, which only proves again that this version does not allow for parallelism within the processing of a single sequence pair. The outer right plot shows the effect of another interesting modification: When we compress the submatrices using the Java util.zip Deflater-class before we transmit them over the network, the curves do not grow so fast for small-sized input, but the absolute times for larger matrices are improved.

To estimate the overhead introduced by the adaptation and remote communication in our system, we compared our implementation to the *JAligner*-system, available from the *sourceforge.net* Web-site. Locally *JAligner* was about twice as fast as our system. On the distributed multiprocessor servers, the time for processing 9 MB using *JAligner* was about 1 min., while we measured execution times below 40 seconds for processing the same input using our system. This time advantage is explained by the fact that JAligner only benefits from the big caches of the grid servers, but it cannot make use of more than a single processor at a time. Thus, our adapted farm component outperforms the hand-tuned JAligner implementation, once the size of the processed genome data exceeds 10 MB.

6. Conclusion and Related Work

We adapted a farm component to wavefront computations. Although wavefront exhibits a different parallel behavior than farm, the remote interface, the resource configuration and most parts of a farm component's implementation could be reused due to the presented adaptation technique. Adaptations require that scheduling actions, crucial to the application progress, such as the loading of task data, can be extended by parameter code, which is provided to the component at runtime, as it is possible, e. g., in the upcoming GCM, which includes the HOC code mobility mechanisms. A helpful analytical basis, which allows to derive new component adaptations from any application dependency graph, is given by the *Polytope*-model [10]. Polytope is also a possible starting point for future work on adaptable components, as it allows to automate the creation of adaptation code parameters.

Farm is a popular higher-order construct (i. e., a component parameterized with code) that is available in several parallel programming systems. However, there is typically no wavefront component available. One of the reasons is that there are simply too many different parallel structures encountered in applications, so that it is practically impossible to every particular structure in a single, general component framework like, e. g., CCA (http://www.cca-forum.org).

Of course, component adaptation is not restricted neither to farm components nor to wavefront algorithms. In an adaptation of other HOCs like the Divide-and-Conquer-HOC, our technique can take effect analogously: If, e. g., an application of a divide-and-conquer algorithm allowed to conduct the join-phase in advance to the final data partitioning under certain circumstances, we could apply this optimization using an adaptation without any impact on the standard division-predicate of the algorithm.

Our case study shows that adaptable components allow for run-time rearrangements of software running on a distributed computer infrastructure, in the same flexible way as aspect-oriented programming simplifies code modifications at compile-time.

The use of the wavefront schema for parallel sequence alignment has been analyzed before in [1], where it is classified as a design pattern. While in the CO_2P_3S system the wavefront behavior is a fixed part of the pattern implementation, in our approach, it is only one of many possible adaptations that can be applied to a HOC. We used our adapted Farm-HOC for solving the DNA sequence pair alignment problem. In comparison with the extensive previous work on this challenging application [8, 13], we developed a high-level solution with competitive performance.

Acknowledgments

This research was conducted within the FP6 Network of Excellence Core-GRID funded by the European Commission (Contract IST-2002-004265).

References

[1] J. Anvik, S. MacDonald, D. Szafron, J. Schaeffer, S. Bromling, and K. Tan. Generating parallel programs from the wavefront design pattern. In *7th Workshop on High-Level Parallel Programming Models*. IEEE Computer Society Press, 2002.

[2] F. Baude, D. Caromel, and M. Morel. From distributed objects to hierarchical grid components. In *International Symposium on Distributed Objects and Applications (DOA)*. Springer LNCS, Catania, Sicily, 2003.

[3] M. I. Cole. *Algorithmic Skeletons: A Structured Approach to the Management of Parallel Computation*. Pitman, 1989.

[4] M. Danelutto and P. Teti. Lithium: A structured parallel programming enviroment in Java. In *Proceedings of Computational Science - ICCS*, number 2330 in Lecture Notes in Computer Science, pages 844–853. Springer-Verlag, Apr. 2002.

[5] J. Dünnweber and S. Gorlatch. HOC-SA: A grid service architecture for higher-order components. In *IEEE International Conference on Services Computing, Shanghai, China*, pages 288–294. IEEE Computer Society Press, Sept. 2004.

[6] Globus Alliance. http://www.globus.org, 1996.

[7] S. Gorlatch and J. Dünnweber. From Grid Middleware to Grid Applications: Bridging the Gap with HOCs. In *Future Generation Grids*. Springer Verlag, 2005.

[8] J. Kleinjung, N. Douglas, and J. Heringa. Parallelized multiple alignment. In *Bioinformatics 18*. Oxford University Press, 2002.

[9] L. Lamport. The parallel execution of do loops. In *Commun. ACM*, volume 17, 2, pages 83–93. ACM Press, 1974.

[10] C. Lengauer. Loop parallelization in the polytope model. In *International Conference on Concurrency Theory*, pages 398–416, 1993.

[11] V. I. Levenshtein. Binary codes capable of correcting insertions and reversals. In *Soviet Physics Dokl. Volume 10*, pages 707–710, 1966.

[12] M. Aldinucci, S. Campa et al. The implementation of ASSIST, an environment for parallel and distributed programming. In H. Kosch, L. Böszörményi, and H. Hellwagner, editors, *Proc. of the Euro-Par 2003*, number 2790 in lncs, pages 712–721. Springer, Aug. 2003.

[13] M. Schmollinger, K. Nieselt, M. Kaufmann, and B. Morgenstern. Dialign p: Fast pairwise and multiple sequence alignment using parallel processors. In *BMC Bioinformatics 5*. BioMed Central, 2004.

[14] C. Szyperski. *Component software: Beyond object-oriented programming*. Addison Wesley, 1998.

[15] Unicore Forum e.V. UNICORE-Grid, http://www.unicore.org, 1997.

[16] M. Wolfe. Loop skewing: the wavefront method revisited. In *Journal of Parallel Programming, Volume 15*, pages 279–293, 1986.

SKELETON PARALLEL PROGRAMMING AND PARALLEL OBJECTS

Marcelo Pasin
CoreGRID fellow
on leave from Universidade Federal de Santa Maria
Santa Maria RS, Brasil
pasin@inf.ufsm.br

Pierre Kuonen
Haute Ecole Specialisï¿½ de Suisse Occidentale
ï¿½ole d'ingï¿½ieurs et d'architects de Fribourg
Fribourg, Suisse
pierre.kuonen@eif.ch

Marco Danelutto and Marco Aldinucci
Universitï¿½di Pisa
Dipartimento d'Informatica
Pisa, Italia
marcod@di.unipi.it
aldinuc@di.unipi.it

Abstract   This paper describes the ongoing work aimed at integrating the POP-C++ parallel object programming environment with the ASSIST component based parallel programming environment. Both these programming environments are shortly outlined, then several possibilities of integration are considered. For each one of these integration opportunities, the advantages and synergies that can be possibly achieved are outlined and discussed.

      The text explains how GEA, the ASSIST deployer can be considered as the basis for the integration of such different systems. An architecture is proposed, extending the existing tools to work together. The current status of integration of the two environments is discussed, along with the expected results and fallouts on the two programming environments.

Keywords: Parallel, programming, grid, skeletons, object-oriented, deployment, execution.

1.   Introduction

This is a prospective article on the integration of ASSIST and POP-C++ tools for parallel programming. POP-C++ is a C++ extension for parallel programming, offering parallel objects with asynchronous method calls. Section 2 describes POP-C++. ASSIST is a skeleton parallel programming system that ofers a structured framework for developing parallel applications starting from sequential components. ASSIST is described in Section 3 as well as some of its components, namely ADHOC and GEA.

This paper also describes some initial ideas of cooperative work on integrating parts of ASSIST and POP-C++, in order to obtain a broader and better range of parallel programming tools. It has been clearly identified that the distributed resource discovery and matching, as well as the distributed object deployment found in ASSIST could be used also by POP-C++. An architecture is devised in order to support the integration. An open question, and an interesting research problem, is whether POP-C++ could be used inside skeleton components for ASSIST. Section 4 is consacrated to these discussions.

2.   Parallel Object-Oriented Programming

It is a very common sense in software engineering today that object-oriented programming and its abstractions improve software development. Besides that, the own nature of objects incorporate many possibilities of program parallelism. Several objects can act concurrently and independently from each other, and several operations in the same object can be concurrently carried out. For these reasons, a parallel object seems to be a very general and straightforward model to express concurrency, and thus to parallel programming.

POP stands for Parallel Object Programming, a programming model in which parallel objects are generalizations of traditional sequential objects. POP-C++ is an extension of C++ that implements the POP model, integrating distributed objects, several remote method invocations semantics, and resource requirements. The extension is kept as close as possible to C++ so that programmers can easily learn POP-C++ and existing C++ libraries can be parallelized with little effort. It results in an object-oriented system for developing high-performance computing applications for the Grid [13].

POP-C++ incorporates a runtime system in order to execute applications on different distributed computing tools (as Globus [10] or SSH [17]). This runtime system has a modular object-oriented service structure. Services are instantiated inside each application and can be combined to perform specific tasks using different lower level services (middleware, operating system). This design can be used to glue current and future distributed programming toolkits together to create a broader environment for executing high performance computing applications.

Parallel objects have all the properties of traditional objects, added to distributed resource-driven creation and asynchronous invocation. Each object creation has the ability to specify its requirements, making possible transparent optimized resource allocation. Each object is allocated in a separate address space, but references to an object are shareable, allowing for remote invocation. Shared objects with encapsulated data allow programmers to implement global data sharing in distributed environments. In order to share parallel objects, POP-C++ programs can arbitrarily pass their references from one place to another as arguments of method invocations. The runtime system is responsible for managing parallel object references.

Parallel objects support any mixture of synchronous, asynchronous, exclusive or concurrent method invocations. Without an invocation, a parallel object lies in an inactive state, only being activated a method invocation request. Syntactically, method invocations on POP objects are identical to those on traditional sequential objects. However, each method has its own invocation semantics, specified by the programmer. These semantics define different behaviours at both sides (caller and object) of a method call. Even though these semantics are important to define the POP model, they are irrelevant for the scope of this paper and will not be detailed here.

Prior to allocate a new POP object it is necessary to select an adequate placeholder. Similarly, when an object is no longer in use, it must be destroyed to release the resources it is occupying. POP-C++ provides (in its runtime system) automatic placeholder selection, object allocation, and object destruction. This automatic features result in a dynamic usage of computational resources and gives to the applications the ability to adapt to changes in both the environment and application behaviour.

Resource requirements can be expressed by the quality of service that components require from the environment. POP-C++ integrates the requirements into the code under the form of resource descriptions. Each parallel object constructor is associated with an **object description** that depicts the characteristics of the resources needed to create the object. Currently, resource requirements are expressed in terms of resource name, computing power, amount of memory, expected communication bandwidth and latency. Work is being done in order do broaden the expressiveness of the resource requirements.

The runtime system incorporates a server process called **job manager**, implementing services for object creation and for resource discovery. A simple distributed peer-to-peer resource discovery model is integrated, yet it does not scale well. Object creation is seen as a new process, which can be started with different management systems such as LSF [9], PBS [12] or even Globus [10].

3.   Structured parallel programming with ASSIST

The development of efficient parallel programs is especially difficult with large-scale heterogeneous and distributed computing platforms as the Grid. Previous research on that subject exploited **skeletons** as a parallel coordination layer of functional modules, made of conventional sequential code [3]. This model allows to relieve the programmer from many concerns of classical, non structured parallel programming frameworks. With skeletons, mapping, scheduling, load balancing and data sharing, and maybe more, can be managed by either the compiler or the runtime system. In addition to that, using skeletons several optimizations can be efficently implemented, because the source code contains a description of the structure for the parallelism. That is much harder to do automatically when the parallelism pattern is unknown.

ASSIST is a parallel programming environment providing a skeleton based coordination language. It includes a skeleton compiler and runtime libraries. Parallel application are structured as generic graphs. The nodes are either parallel modules or sequential code. The edges are data streams. Sequential code can be written in C, C++ and Fortran, allowing to reuse existing code. The programmer can experiment different parallelisation strategies just changing a few lines of code and recompiling.

A **parallel module** is used to model the parallel activities of an ASSIST program. It can be specialized to behave as the most common parallelism patterns as farms, pipelines, or geometric and data parallel computations. Skeletons and coordination technology are exploited in such a way that parallel applications with complex parallelism patterns can be implemented without handling error prone details as process and communication setup, scheduling, mapping, etc.

The language allows to define, inside a parallel module, a set of virtual processors and to assign them tasks. The same task can be assigned to all virtual processors or to a certain group of them, or even to a single one. A parallel module can concurrently access state variables, and can interact with the external world using standard object access methods (like CORBA, for instance). A parallel module can handle as many input and output streams as needed. Non deterministic control is provided to accept inputs from different streams and explicit commands are provided to output items on the output streams.

Several optimizations are performed to efficiently execute ASSIST programs [15, 1]. The environment was recently extended to support a component model (GRID.it) [2], that can interact with foreign component models, as CORBA CCM and Web Services. ASSIST components are supplied with autonomic managers [4] that adapt the execution to dynamic changes in the grid features (node or link faults, different load levels, etc.).

Along with binary executable files, the compiler generates an XML configuration file that represent the descriptor of the parallel application. GEA (see Section 3.1) is a deployer built to run the program based on the XML file. It takes care of all the activities needed to stage the code at remote nodes, to start auxiliary runtime processes, to run the application code and to gather the results back to the node where the program has been launched.

Grid applications often need access to fast, scalable and reliable data storage. ADHOC (Adaptive Distributed Herd of Object Caches) is a distributed persistent object repository toolkit [5], conceived in the context of the ASSIST project. ADHOC creates a single distributed data repository by the cooperation between multiple local memories. It separates management of computation and storage, supporting a broad class of parallel applications while achieving good performance. Clients access objects through proxies, that can implement protocols as complex as needed (e.g. distributed agreement). The toolkit enables object creation, set, get, removal and method call. The following section presents GEA in more detail.

3.1   Grid Application Deployment

ASSIST applications are deployed using GEA, the Grid Execution Agent. It is a parallel process launcher targeting distinct architectures, as clusters and the Grid. It has a modular design, intended for aggressive adaptation to different system architectures and to different application structures. GEA deploys applications and its infrastructure based on XML description files. It makes possible to configure and lauch processes in virtually any combination and order needed, adapting to different types of applications.

GEA has already been adapted for deployment on Globus grids and Unix computers supporting SSH access as well. Other different environments can be added without any modification in GEA's structure, because it is implemented using the Commodity Grid toolkit [16]. It currently supports the deployment of three different flavors of ASSIST applications, each one with a different process startup scheme. In the deployment of ASSIST applications, the compiler generates the necessary XML files, creating an automatic process to describe and launch applications. Besides the work described in this paper, the deployment of GridCCM components [8] is as well under way.

At the deployment of an application, after parsing the XML file that describe the resources needed, a suitable number of computing resources (nodes) are recruited to host the application processes. The application code is deployed to the selected remote nodes, by transferring the needed files to the appropriated places in the local filesystems. Data files and result files are transfered as well, respectively prior and after the execution of the application processes.

The necessary support processes to run the applications are also started at the necessary nodes.

The procedure for launching and connecting these processes with the application processes is automatized inside customized deployment modules. For example, ASSIST applications need processes to implement the data flow streams interconnecting their processes. ASSIST components need also supplementary processes for adaptation and dynamic connection. Other different launching patterns can be added with new modules, without any modification in GEA's structure.

4. Objects and skeletons getting along

Work is under progress within the CoreGRID network of excellence in order to establish a common programming model for the Grid. This model must implement a component system that keeps interoperability with the systems currently in use. ASSIST and POP-C++ have been designed and developed with different programming models in mind, but with a common goal: provide grid programmers with advanced tools suitable to develop efficient grid applications. They together represent two major and different parallel programming models (skeletons and distributed objects). Even if they may conduct the construction of the CoreGRID programming model to different directions, the set of issues addressed in both contexts has a large intersection. Compile or runtime enhancements made for any of them may be easily adapted to be used by other programming systems (possibly not only skeletal or object-oriented). Many infrastructural tools can be shared, as presented later in this text.

The possible relations between POP-C++ and ASSIST, one object-oriented and another based on skeletons are being studied inside CoreGRID. Work has been done to identify the possibilities to integrate both tools in such a way that effectively improve each one of them exploiting the original results already achieved in the other. Three possibilities that seem to provide suitable solutions have been studied:

1 Deploy POP-C++ objects using ASSIST deployment;

2 Adapt both to use the same type of shared memory;

3 Build ASSIST components of POP-C++ objects.

The first two cases actually improve the possibilities offered by POP-C++ by exploiting ASSIST technology. The third case improves the possibilities offered by ASSIST to assemble complex programs out of components written accordingly to different models. Currently such components can only be written using the ASSIST coordination language or inherited from CCM or Web Services. The following sections detail these three possibilities and discuss their relative advantages.

4.1   Same memory for ASSIST and POP-C++

POP-C++ implements asynchronous remote method invocations, using very basic system features, as TCP/IP sockets and POSIX threads. Instead of using those natively implemented parallel objects, POP-C++ could be adapted to use ADHOC objects. Calls to POP objects would be converted into calls to ADHOC objects. This would have the added advantage of being possible to somehow mix ADHOC applications and POP-C++ as they would share the same type of distributed object. This would as well add persistence to POP-C++ objects.

ADHOC objects are shared in a distributed system, as POP objects are. But they do not incorporate any concurrent semantics on the object side, neither their calls are asynchronous. In order to offer the same semantics, ADHOC objects (at both caller and callee sides) would have to be wrapped in jackets, which would implement the concurrent semantics using something like POSIX threads. This does not appear to be a good solution, neither about performance nor about elegance.

ADHOC has been implemented in C++. It should be relatively simple to extend its classes to be used inside a POP-C++ program, as it would with any other C++ class libraries. It means that it is already possible to use the current version of ADHOC to share data between POP-C++ and ASSIST applications. For all these reasons the idea of adopting ADHOC to implement regular POP-C++ objects has been precluded.

4.2   ASSIST components written in POP-C++

Currently, the ASSIST framework allows component programs to be developed with two type of components: **native** components and **wrapped** legacy components. Native components can either be sequential or parallel. They provide both a functional interface, exposing the computing capabilities of the component, and a non functional interface, exposing methods that can be used to control the component (e.g. to monitor its behaviour). They provide as well a **performance contract** that the component itself ensures by exploiting its internal autonomic control features implemented in the non functional code. Wrapped legacy components, on the other hand, are either CCM components or plain Web Services that can be automatically wrapped by the ASSIST framework tools to look like a native component.

The ASSIST framework can be extended in such a way that POP-C++ programs can also be wrapped to look like native components and therefore be used in plain native component programs. As the parallelism patterns allowed in native components are restricted to the ones provided by the ASSIST coordination language, POP-C++ components introduce in the ASSIST framework the possibility of having completely general parallel components. Of course, the efficiency of POP-C++ components would be completely in charge of POP-C++ compiler and its runtime environment.

Some interesting possibilities appear when exploring object oriented programming techniques to implement the non functional parts of the native component. In other words, one could try to fully exploit POP-C++ features to implement a customizable autonomic application manager providing the same non functional interface of native ASSIST components. These extensions, either in ASSIST or in POP-C++ can be subject to further research, especially in the context of CoreGRID, when its component model would be more clearly defined.

If eventually an ASSIST component should be written in POP-C++, it will be necessary to deploy and launch it. To launch an application, different types of components will have to be deployed. ASSIST has a deployer that is not capable of dealing with POP-C++ objects. One first step to enable their integration should be the construction of a common deployment tool, capable of executing both types of components.

4.3   Deploying ASSIST and POP-C++ alike

ASSIST provides a large set of tools, including infrastructure for launching processes, integrated with functions for matching needs to resouces capabilities. The POP-C++ runtime library could hook up with GEA, the ASSIST deployer, in different levels. The most straightforward is to replace the parts of the POP-C++ job manager related to object creation and resource discovery with calls to GEA.

As seen in Section 3.1, GEA was build to be extended. It is currently able to deploy ASSIST applications, each type of it being handled by a different deployer module. Adding support for POP-C++ processes, or objects, can be done by writing another such module. POP-C++ objects are executed by independent processes that depend on very little. Basically, the newly created process has to allocate the new object, use the network to connect with the creator, and wait for messages on the connection. The connection to establish is defined by arguments in the command line, which are passed by the caller (the creator of the new object). The POP-C++ deployer module is actually a simplified version of those used for ASSIST applications.

Process execution and resource selection in both ASSIST and POP-C++ happen in very different patterns. ASSIST relies on the structure of the application and is performance contract to specify the type of the resources needed to execute it. This allows for a resource allocation strategy based on graphs, specified ahead of the whole execution. Chosen a given set of resources, all processes are started. The adaptation follow certain rules and cannot happen without boundaries. POP-C++ on the other hand does not impose any program structure. A new resource must be located on-the-fly for every new object created. The characteristics of the resources are completely variable, and cannot be determined previous to the object creation.

It seems clear that a good starting point for integration of POP-C++ and ASSIST is the deployer, and some work has been done in that direction. The next section of this paper discusses the architecture of the extensions designed to support the deployment of POP objects with with GEA, the ASSIST deployer.

5.   Architecture for a common deployer

The modular design of GEA allows for extensions. Nevertheless, it is written in Java. The runtime of POP-C++ was written in C++ and it must be able to reach code running in Java. Anticipating such uses, GEA was built to run as a server, exporting a TCP/IP interface. Client libraries to connect and send requests to it were written in both Java and C++. The runtime library of POP-C++ has then to be extended to include calls to GEA's client library.

In order to assess the implications of the integration proposed here, the object creation procedure inside the POP-C++ runtime library has to be seen more into detail. The steps are as following:

1 A proxy object is created inside the address space of the creator process, called **interface**.

2 The interface evaluates the object description (written in C++) and calls a resource discovery service to find a suitable resource.

3 The interface launches a remote process to host the new object in the given resource and waits.

4 The new process running remotely connects with the interface, receives the constructor arguments, creates the object in the local address space and tells the interface that the creation ended.

5 The interface returns the proxy object to the caller.

GEA can currently only be instructed to, at once, choose an adequate resource, then load and launch a process. An independant discovery service, as required by the POP-C++ interface, is not yet implemented in GEA. On the other hand, in can be used as it is just rewriting the calls in the POP-C++ object interface. The modifications are:

- The resource discovery service call has to be rewritten to just build an XML description of the resource based on the object description.

- The remote process launch should be rewritten to call the GEA C++ client library, passing the XML description formrly built.

Requests to launch processes have some restrictions on GEA. Its currently structured model matches the structured model of ASSIST. Nodes are divided into administrative domains, and each domain is managed by a single GEA server. The ASSIST model dictates a fixed structure, with parallel modules connected in a predefined way. All processes of parallel modules are assigned to resources when the execution starts. It is eventually possible to adjust on the number of processes inside of a running parallel module, but the new processes must be started in the same domain.

POP-C++ needs a completely dynamic model to run parallel objects. An object running in a domain must be able to start new objects in different domains. Even a sigle server for all domains is not a good idea, as it may become a bottleneck. In order to support multiple domains, GEA has to be extended to a more flexible model. GEA servers must forward execution calls between each other. Resource discovery for new processes must also take into account the resources in all domains (not only the local one). That is a second reason why the resource discovery and the process launch were left to be done together.

GEA is build to forward a call to create a process to the corresponding process type module, called **gear**. With POP-C++, the POP gear will be called by GEA for every process creation. The POP gear inspects all resources available and associates the process creation request with a suitable resource. The CoG kit will eventually be called to launch the process in the associated resource. This scenario is illustrated in Figure 1. A problem arises when no suitable resource is available in the local domain, as GEA does not share resource information with other servers.

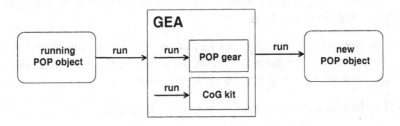

Figure 1.   GEA with a cetralized POP-C++ gear

By keeping together the descriptions of the program and the resource, the mapping decision can be postponed to the last minute. The Figure 2 shows a scenario, where a POP gear does not find a suitable resource locally. A peer-to-peer network, established with GEA servers and their POP gears would forward the request until it is eventually satisfied, or a timeout is reached. A similar model was proposed as a Grid Information Service, using routing indexes to improve performance [14].

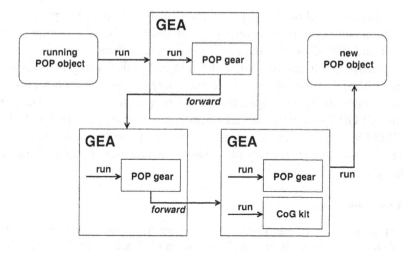

Figure 2. GEA with a peer-to-peer POP-C++ gear

In the context of POP-C++ (and in other similar systems, as ProActive [7], for instance), the allocation is dynamic, with every new process created idependently of the others. Structured systems as ASSIST need to express application needs as a whole prior to the execution. Finding good mappings in a distributed algorithm is clearly an optimisation problem, that could eventually be solved with heuristics expoiting a certain degree of locality. Requirements and resource sets must be split into parts and mixed and matched in a distributed and incremental (partial) fashion [11].

In either contexts (static or dynamic), resources would better be described without a predefined structure. Descriptions could be of any type, not just amounts of memory, CPU or network capacity. Requirements sould be expressed as predicates that evaluate to a certain degree of satisfaction [6]. The languages needed to express requirements and resources, as well as efficient distributed resource matching algorithms are still interesting research problems.

6. Conclusion

The questions discussed in this paper entail a CoreGRID fellowship. All the possibilities described in the previous sections were considered, and the focus of interest was directed to the integration of GEA as the POP-C++ launcher and resource manager. This will impose modifications on POP-C++ runtime library and new funcionalities for GEA. Both systems are expected to improve thanks to this interaction, as POP-C++ will profit from better resource discovery and GEA will implement a less restricted model.

Further research on the matching model will lead to new approaches on expressing and matching application requirements and resource capabilities.

This model should allow a distributed implementation that dynamically adapt the requirements as well as the resource availability, being able to express both ASSIST and POP-C++ requirements, and probably others.

A subsequent step can be a higher level of integration, using POP-C++ programs as ASSIST components. This could allow to exploit full object oriented parallel programming techniques in ASSIST programs on the Grid. The implications of POP-C++ parallel object oriented modules on the structured model of ASSIST are not fully identified, especially due to the dynamic aspects of the objects created. Supplementary study has to be done in order to devise its real advantages and consequences.

References

[1] M. Aldinucci, S. Campa, P. Ciullo, M. Coppola, S. Magini, P. Pesciullesi, L. Potiti, R. Ravazzoloand M. Torquati, M. Vanneschi, and C. Zoccolo. The Implementation of ASSIST, an Environment for Parallel and Distributed Programming. In *Proc. of EuroPar2003*, number 2790 in "Lecture Notes in Computer Science". Springer, 2003.

[2] M. Aldinucci, S. Campa, M. Coppola, M. Danelutto, D. Laforenza, D. Puppin, L. Scarponi, M. Vanneschi, and C. Zoccolo. Components for High-Performance Grid Programming in GRID.it. In *Component modes and systems for Grid applications*, CoreGRID. Springer, 2005.

[3] M. Aldinucci, M. Danelutto, and P. Teti. An advanced environment supporting structured parallel programming in Java. *Future Generation Computer Systems*, 19(5):611–626, 2003. Elsevier Science.

[4] M. Aldinucci, A. Petrocelli, E. Pistoletti, M. Torquati, M. Vanneschi, L. Veraldi, and C. Zoccolo. Dynamic reconfiguration of grid-aware applications in ASSIST. In *11th Intl Euro-Par 2005: Parallel and Distributed Computing*, number 3149 in "Lecture Notes in Computer Science". Springer Verlag, 2004.

[5] M. Aldinucci and M. Torquati. Accelerating apache farms through ad-HOC distributed scalable object repository. In M. Danelutto, M. Vanneschi, and D. Laforenza, editors, *10th Intl Euro-Par 2004: Parallel and Distributed Computing*, volume 3149 of *"Lecture Notes in Computer Science"*, pages 596–605, Pisa, Italy, August 2004. "Springer".

[6] S. Andreozzi, P. Ciancarini, D. Montesi, and R. Moretti. Towards a metamodeling based method for representing and selecting grid services. In Mario Jeckle, Ryszard Kowalczyk, and Peter Braun II, editors, *GSEM*, volume 3270 of *Lecture Notes in Computer Science*, pages 78–93. Springer, 2004.

[7] F. Baude, D. Caromel, L. Mestre, F. Huet, and J. Vayssiï¿½e. Interactive and descriptor-based deployment of object-oriented grid applications. In *Proceedings of the 11th IEEE Intl Symposium on High Performance Distributed Computing*, pages 93–102, Edinburgh, Scotland, July 2002. IEEE Computer Society.

[8] Massimo Coppola, Marco Danelutto, Sï¿½astien Lacour, Christian Pï¿½ez, Thierry Priol, Nicola Tonellotto, and Corrado Zoccolo. Towards a common deployment model for grid systems. In Sergei Gorlatch and Marco Danelutto, editors, *CoreGRID Workshop on Integrated research in Grid Computing*, pages 31–40, Pisa, Italy, November 2005. CoreGRID.

[9] Platform Computing Corporation. *Running Jobs with Platform LSF*, 2003.

[10] I. Foster and C. Kesselman. Globus: A metacomputing infrastructure toolkit. *Intl Journal of Supercomputer Applications and High Performance Computing*, 11(2):115–128, 1997.

[11] Felix Heine, Matthias Hovestadt, and Odej Kao. Towards ontology-driven p2p grid resource discovery. In Rajkumar Buyya, editor, *GRID*, pages 76–83. IEEE Computer Society, 2004.

[12] R. Henderson and D. Tweten. Portable batch system: External reference specification. Technical report, NASA, Ames Research Center, 1996.

[13] T.-A. Nguyen and P. Kuonen. ParoC++: A requirement-driven parallel object-oriented programming language. In *Eighth Intl Workshop on High-Level Parallel Programming Models and Supportive Environments (HIPS'03), April 22-22, 2003, Nice, France*, pages 25–33. IEEE Computer Society, 2003.

[14] Diego Puppin, Stefano Moncelli, Ranieri Baraglia, Nicola Tonellotto, and Fabrizio Silvestri. A grid information service based on peer-to-peer. In *Lecture Notes in Computer Science 2648, Proceeeding of Euro-Par*, pages 454–464, 2005.

[15] M. Vanneschi. The Programming Model of ASSIST, an Environment for Parallel and Distributed Portable Applications . *Parallel Computing*, 12, December 2002.

[16] Gregor von Laszewski, Ian Foster, and Jarek Gawor. CoG kits: a bridge between commodity distributed computing and high-performance grids. In *Proceedings of the ACM Java Grande Conference*, pages 97–106, June 2000.

[17] T. Ylonen. SSH - secure login connections over the internet. In *Proceedings of the 6th Security Symposium*, page 37, Berkeley, 1996. USENIX Association.

TOWARDS THE AUTOMATIC MAPPING OF ASSIST APPLICATIONS FOR THE GRID

Marco Aldinucci
Computer Science Departement, University of Pisa
Largo Bruno Pontecorvo 3, I-56127 Pisa, Italy
aldinuc@di.unipi.it

Anne Benoit
LIP, Ecole Normale Supérieure de Lyon
46 Allée d'Italie, 69364 Lyon Cedex 07, France
Anne.Benoit@ens-lyon.fr

Abstract   One of the most promising technical innovations in present-day computing is the invention of grid technologies which harness the computational power of widely distributed collections of computers. However, the programming and optimisation burden of a low level approach to grid computing is clearly unacceptable for large scale, complex applications. The development of grid applications can be simplified by using high-level programming environments. In the present work, we address the problem of the mapping of a high-level grid application onto the computational resources. In order to optimise the mapping of the application, we propose to automatically generate performance models from the application using the process algebra PEPA. We target in this work applications written with the high-level environment ASSIST, since the use of such a structured environment allows us to automate the study of the application more effectively.

Keywords: high-level parallel programming, grid, ASSIST, PEPA, automatic model generation, skeletons.

1.   Introduction

A grid system is a geographically distributed collection of possibly parallel, interconnected processing elements, which all run some form of common grid middleware (e.g. Globus services) [16]. The key idea behind grid-aware applications is to make use of the aggregate power of distributed resources, thus benefiting from a computing power that falls far beyond the current availability threshold in a single site. However, developing programs able to exploit this potential is highly programming intensive. Programmers must design concurrent programs that can execute on large-scale platforms that cannot be assumed to be homogeneous, secure, reliable or centrally managed. They must then implement these programs correctly and efficiently. As a result, in order to build efficient grid-aware applications, programmers have to address the classical problems of parallel computing as well as grid-specific ones:

1. Programming: code all the program details, take care about concurrency exploitation, among the others: concurrent activities set up, mapping/scheduling, communication/synchronisation handling and data allocation.

2. Mapping & Deploying: deploy application processes according to a suitable mapping onto grid platforms. These may be highly heterogeneous in architecture and performance. Moreover, they are organised in a cluster-of-clusters fashion, thus exhibiting different connectivity properties among all pairs of platforms.

3. Dynamic environment: manage resource unreliability and dynamic availability, network topology, latency and bandwidth unsteadiness.

Hence, the number and quality of problems to be resolved in order to draw a given QoS (in term of performance, robustness, etc.) from grid-aware applications is quite large. The lesson learnt from parallel computing suggests that any low-level approach to grid programming is likely to raise the programmer's burden to an unacceptable level for any real world application.

Therefore, we envision a layered, high-level programming model for the grid, which is currently pursued by several research initiatives and programming environments, such as ASSIST [22], eSkel [10], GrADS [20], ProActive [7], Ibis [21], Higher Order Components [13–14]. In such an environment, most of the grid specific efforts are moved from programmers to grid tools and run-time systems. Thus, the programmers have only the responsibility of organising the application specific code, while the programming tools (i.e. the compiling tools and/or the run-time systems) deal with the interaction with the grid, through collective protocols and services [15].

In such a scenario, the QoS and performance constraints of the application can either be specified at compile time or varying at run-time. In both cases, the run-time system should actively operate in order to fulfil QoS requirements of the application, since any static resource assignment may violate QoS constraints due to the very uneven performance of grid resources over time. As an example, ASSIST applications exploit an autonomic (self-optimisation) behavior. They may be equipped with a QoS contract describing the degree of performance the application is required to provide. The ASSIST run-time environment tries to keep the QoS contract valid for the duration of the application run despite possible variations of platforms' performance at the level of grid fabric [6, 5]. The autonomic features of an ASSIST application rely heavily on run-time application monitoring, and thus they are not fully effective for application deployment since the application is not yet running. In order to deploy an application onto the grid, a suitable mapping of application processes onto grid platforms should be established, and this process is quite critical for application performance.

This problem can be addressed by defining a performance model of an AS-SIST application in order to statically optimise the mapping of the application onto a heterogeneous environment, as shown in [1]. The model is generated from the source code of the application, before the initial mapping. It is expressed with the process algebra PEPA [18], designed for performance evaluation. The use of a stochastic model allows us to take into account aspects of uncertainty which are inherent to grid computing, and to use classical techniques of resolution based on Markov chains to obtain performance results. This static analysis of the application is complementary with the autonomic reconfiguration of ASSIST applications, which works on a dynamic basis. In this work we concentrated on the static part to optimise the mapping, while the dynamic management is done at run-time. It is thus an orthogonal but complementary approach.

Structure of the paper. The next section introduces the ASSIST high-level programming environment and its run-time support. Section 4.2 introduces the Performance Evaluation Process Algebra PEPA, which can be used to model ASSIST applications. These performance models help to optimise the mapping of the application. We present our approach in Section 4, and give an overview of future working directions. Finally, concluding remarks are given in Section 5.

2. The ASSIST environment and its run-time support

ASSIST (A Software System based on Integrated Skeleton Technology) is a programming environment aimed at the development of distributed high-performance applications [22, 3]. ASSIST applications should be compiled in binary packages that can be deployed and run on grids, including those exhibiting heterogeneous platforms. Deployment and run is provided through standard middleware services (e.g. Globus) enriched with the ASSIST run-time support.

2.1   The ASSIST coordination language

ASSIST applications are described by means of a coordination language, which can express arbitrary graphs of modules, interconnected by typed streams of data. Each stream realises a one-way asynchronous channel between two sets of endpoint modules: sources and sinks. Data items injected from sources are broadcast to all sinks. All data items injected into a stream should match the stream type.

Modules can be either sequential or parallel. A sequential module wraps a sequential function. A parallel module *(parmod)* can be used to describe the parallel execution of a number of sequential functions that are activated and run as *Virtual Processes* (VPs) on items arriving from input streams. The VPs may synchronise with the others through barriers. The sequential functions can be programmed by using a standard sequential language (C, C++, Fortran). A *parmod* may behave in a data-parallel (e.g. SPMD/for-all/apply-to-all) or task-parallel (e.g. farm) way and it may exploit a distributed shared state that survives the VPs lifespan. A module can nondeterministically accept from one or more input streams a number of input items according to a CSP specification included in the module [19]. Once accepted, each stream item may be decomposed in parts and used as function parameters to instantiate VPs according to the input and distribution rules specified in the parmod. The VPs may send items or parts of items onto the output streams, and these are gathered according to the output rules. Details on the ASSIST coordination language can be found in [22, 3].

2.2   The ASSIST run-time support

The ASSIST compiler translates a graph of modules into a network of processes. As sketched in Fig. 1, sequential modules are translated into sequential processes, while parallel modules are translated into a parametric (w.r.t. the parallelism degree) network of processes: one *Input Section Manager* (ISM), one *Output Section Manager* (OSM), and a set of *Virtual Processes Managers* (VPMs, each of them running a set of Virtual Processes). The ISM implements a CSP interpreter that can send data items to VPMs via collective communications. The number of VMPs gives the actual parallelism degree of a parmod instance. Also, a number of processes are devoted to application dynamic QoS control, e.g. a *Module Adaptation Manager* (MAM), and an *Application Manager* (AM) [6, 5].

The processes that compose an ASSIST application communicate via ASSIST support channels. These can be implemented on top of a number of grid middleware communication mechanisms (e.g. shared memory, TCP/IP, Globus, CORBA-IIOP, SOAP-WS). The suitable communication mechanism between each pair of processes is selected at launch time depending on the mapping of the processes.

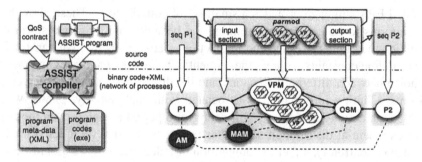

Figure 1. An ASSIST application and a QoS contract are compiled in a set of executable codes and its meta-data [3]. This information is used to set up a processes network at launch time.

2.3 Towards fully grid-aware applications

ASSIST applications can already cope with platform heterogeneity [2], either in space (various architectures) or in time (varying load) [6]. These are definite features of a grid, however they are not the only ones. Grids are usually organised in sites on which processing elements are organised in networks with private addresses allowing only outbound connections. Also, they are often fed through job schedulers. In these cases, setting up a multi-site parallel application onto the grid is a challenge in its own right (irrespectively of its performance). Advance reservation, co-allocation, multi-site launching are currently hot topics of research for a large part of the grid community. Nevertheless, many of these problems should be targeted at the middleware layer level and they are largely independent of the logical mapping of application processes on a suitable set of resources, given that the mapping is consistent with deployment constraints.

In our work, we assume that the middleware level supplies (or will supply) suitable services for co-allocation, staging and execution. These are actually the minimal requirements in order to imagine the bare existence of any non-trivial, multi-site parallel application. Thus we can analyse how to map an ASSIST application, assuming that we can exploit middleware tools to deploy and launch applications [12].

3. Introduction to performance evaluation and PEPA

In this section, we briefly introduce the Performance Evaluation Process Algebra PEPA [18], with which we can model an ASSIST application. The use of a process algebra allows us to include the aspects of uncertainty relative to both the grid and the application, and to use standard methods to easily and quickly obtain performance results.

The PEPA language provides a small set of combinators. These allow language terms to be constructed defining the behavior of components, via the activities they undertake and the interactions between them. We can for instance define constants, express the sequential behavior of a given component, a choice between different behaviors, and the direct interaction between components. Timing information is associated with each activity. Thus, when enabled, an activity $a = (\alpha, r)$ will delay for a period sampled from the negative exponential distribution which has parameter r. If several activities are enabled concurrently, either in competition or independently, we assume that a *race condition* exists between them.

The dynamic behavior of a PEPA model is represented by the evolution of its components, as governed by the operational semantics of PEPA terms [18]. Thus, as in classical process algebra, the semantics of each term is given via a labelled *multi-transition* system (the multiplicity of arcs are significant). In the transition system a state corresponds to each syntactic term of the language, or *derivative*, and an arc represents the activity which causes one derivative to evolve into another. The complete set of reachable states is termed the *derivative set* and these form the nodes of the *derivation graph*, which is formed by applying the semantic rules exhaustively. The derivation graph is the basis of the underlying Continuous Time Markov Chain (CTMC) which is used to derive performance measures from a PEPA model. The graph is systematically reduced to a form where it can be treated as the state transition diagram of the underlying CTMC. Each derivative is then a state in the CTMC. The *transition rate* between two derivatives P and Q in the derivation graph is the rate at which the system changes from behaving as component P to behaving as Q. Examples of derivation graphs can be found in [18].

It is important to note that in our models the rates are represented as random variables, not constant values. These random variables are exponentially distributed. Repeated samples from the distribution will follow the distribution and conform to the mean but individual samples may potentially take any positive value. The use of such distribution is quite realistic and it allows us to use standard methods on CTMCs to readily obtain performance results. There are indeed several methods and tools available for analysing PEPA models. Thus, the PEPA Workbench [17] allows us to generate the state space of a PEPA model and the infinitesimal generator matrix of the underlying Markov chain. The state space of the model is represented as a sparse matrix. The PEPA Workbench can then compute the steady-state probability distribution of the system, and performance measures such as throughput and utilisation can be directly computed from this.

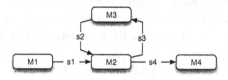

Figure 2.   Graph representation of our example application.

4. Performance models of ASSIST applications

PEPA can easily be used to model an ASSIST application since such applications are based on stream communications, and the graph structure deduced from these streams can be modelled with PEPA. Given the probabilistic information about the performance of each of the ASSIST modules and streams, we then aim to find information about the global behavior of the application, which is expressed by the steady-state of the system. The model thus allows us to predict the run-time behavior of the application in the long time run, taking into account information obtained from a static analysis of the program. This behavior is not known in advance, it is a result of the PEPA model.

4.1 The ASSIST application

As we have seen in Section 2, an ASSIST application consists of a series of modules and streams connecting the modules. The structure of the application is represented by a graph, where the modules are the nodes and the streams the arcs.

We illustrate in this paper our modeling process on an example of a graph, but the process can be easily generalized to any ASSIST applications since the information about the graph can be extracted directly from ASSIST source code, and the model can be generated automatically from the graph.

A model of a data mining classification algorithm has been presented in [1], as well as the corresponding ASSIST source code. For the purpose of our methodology and in order to generalize our approach, we concentrate here only on the graph of an application.

The graph of the application that we consider in this paper is similar to the one of [1], consisting of four modules. Figure 2 represents the graph of this application.

4.2 The PEPA model

Each ASSIST module is represented as a PEPA component, and the different components are synchronised through the streams of data to model the overall application. The performance results obtained are the probabilities to be in either of the states of the system. From this information, we can determine the bottleneck of the system and decide the best way to map the application onto the available resources.

The PEPA model is generated automatically from the ASSIST source code, during a pre-compilation phase. The information required for the generation is provided by the user directly in the source code, and particularly the rates associated to the different activities of the PEPA model. These rates are related to the theoretical complexity of the modules and of the communications. In particular, rates of the communications depend on: a) the speed of the links and b) data size and communications frequencies. A module may include a parallel computation, thus its rate depend on a) computing power of the platforms running the module and b) parallel computation complexity, its size, its parallel degree, and its speedup.

Observe that aspect a) of both modules and communications rates strictly depend on mapping, while aspect b) is much more dependent by application logical structure and algorithms.

The PEPA components of the modules are shown in Fig. 3. The modules are working in a sequential way: the module MX (X = 1..4) is initially in the state MX1, waiting for data on its input streams. Then, in the state MX2, it processes the piece of data and evolves to its third state MX3. Finally, the module sends the output data on its output streams and goes back into its first state.

The system evolves from one state to another when an activity occurs. The activity sX ($X = 1..4$) represents the transfer of data through the stream X, with the associated rate λ_X. The rate reflects the complexity of the communication. The activity pX ($X = 1..4$) represents the processing of a data by module MX, which is done at a rate μ_X. These rates are related to the theoretical complexity of the modules.

The overall PEPA model is then obtained by a collaboration of the different modules in their initial states: $M11 \bowtie_{s1} M21 \bowtie_{s2,s3} M31 \bowtie_{s4} M41$.

The performance results obtained are the probability to be in either of the states of the system. We compute the probability to be waiting for a processing activity pX, or to wait for a transfer activity sX. From this information, we can determine the bottleneck of the system and decide the best way to map the application onto the available resources.

4.3   Automatic generation of the model

To allow an automatic generation of the PEPA model from the ASSIST source code, we ask the user to provide some information directly in the main procedure of the application. This information must specify the rates of the different activities of the PEPA model. We are interested in the relative computational

$$M11 \stackrel{def}{=} M12$$
$$M12 \stackrel{def}{=} (p1, \mu_1).M13$$
$$M13 \stackrel{def}{=} (s1, \lambda_1).M11$$

$$M21 \stackrel{def}{=} (s1, \top).M22 + (s2, \top).M22$$
$$M22 \stackrel{def}{=} (p2, \mu_2).M23$$
$$M23 \stackrel{def}{=} (s3, \lambda_3).M21 + (s4, \lambda_4).M21$$

$$M31 \stackrel{def}{=} (s3, \top).M32$$
$$M32 \stackrel{def}{=} (p3, \mu_3).M33$$
$$M33 \stackrel{def}{=} (s2, \lambda_2).M31$$

$$M41 \stackrel{def}{=} (s4, \top).M42$$
$$M42 \stackrel{def}{=} (p4, \mu_4).M43$$
$$M43 \stackrel{def}{=} M41$$

Figure 3. PEPA model for the example

and communication costs of the different parts of the system, but we define numerical values to allow a numerical resolution of the PEPA model.

The complexity of the modules depends on the number of computations done, and also on the degree of parallelism used for a parallel module. It is directly related to the time needed to compute one input. The rates associated with the streams depends on the amount of the data transiting on each stream. In ASSIST, the object transiting on the stream is often a reference to the real object, since the actual data is available in a shared memory, and this is beyond the scope of our PEPA model.

This information is defined directly in the ASSIST source code of the application, by calling a `rate` function, which takes as a parameter the name of the modules and streams. This function should be called once for each module and each stream to fix the rates of the corresponding PEPA activities.

The PEPA model is generated during a precompilation of the source code of ASSIST. The parser identifies the `main` procedure and extracts the useful information from it: the modules and streams, the connections between them, and the rates of the different activities. The main difficulty consists in identifying the schemes of input and output behavior in the case of several streams. This information can be found in the input and output section of the parmod code. Regarding the input section, the parser looks at the guards. Details on the different types of guards can be found in [22, 3].

As an example, a disjoint guard means that the module takes input from either of the streams when some data arrives. This is translated by a choice in the PEPA model, as illustrated in our example. However, some more complex behavior may also be expressed, for instance the parmod can be instructed to start executing only when it has data from both streams. In this case, the PEPA model is changed with some sequential composition to express this behavior. For example, $M21 \stackrel{def}{=} (s1, \top).(s2, \top).M22 + (s2, \top).(s1, \top).M22$.

Another problem may arise from the variables in guards, since these may change the frequency of accessing data from a stream. Since the variables may depend on the input data, we cannot automatically extract static information from them. They are currently ignored, but we plan to address this problem by asking the programmer to provide the relative frequency of the guard. The considerations for the output section are similar.

4.4   Performance results

Once the PEPA model has been generated, performance results can be obtained easily with the PEPA Workbench [17]. Some additional information is generated in the PEPA source code to specify the performance results that we are interested in. This information is the following:

```
moduleM1 = 100 * {M12 ||  **  ||  **  ||  ** };
moduleM2 = 100 * {**  || M22 ||  **  ||  ** };
moduleM3 = 100 * {**  ||  **  || M32 ||  ** };
moduleM4 = 100 * {**  ||  **  ||  **  || M42};

stream1  = 100 * {M13 || M21 ||  **  ||  ** };
stream2  = 100 * {**  || M21 || M33 ||  ** };
stream3  = 100 * {**  || M23 || M31 ||  ** };
stream4  = 100 * {**  || M23 ||  **  || M41};
```

The expression in brackets describes the states of the PEPA model corresponding to a particular state of the system. For each module MX (X = 1..4), the result moduleMX corresponds to the percentage of time spent waiting to process and processing this module. The steady-state probability is multiplied by 100 for readability and interpretation reasons. A similar result is obtained for each stream.

We expect the complexity of the PEPA model to be quite simple and the resolution straightforward for most of the ASSIST applications. In our example, the PEPA model consists in 36 states and 80 transitions, and it requires less than 0.1 seconds to generate the state space of the model and to compute the steady state solution, using the linear biconjugate gradient method [17].

Experiment 1 For the purpose of our example, we choose the following rates, meaning that the module $M3$ is computationally more intensive than the other modules. In our case, $M3$ has an average duration of 1 sec. compared to 0.01 sec. for the others: $\mu_1 = 100; \mu_2 = 100; \mu_3 = 1; \mu_4 = 100;$

The rates for the streams correspond to an average duration of 0.1 sec: $\lambda_1 = 10; \lambda_2 = 10; \lambda_3 = 10; \lambda_4 = 10;$

The results for this example are shown in Table 1 (row *Case 1*).

These results confirm the fact that most of the time is spent in module M3, which is the most computationally demanding. Moreover, module M1 (respectively M4) spends most of its time waiting to send data on s1 (respectively waiting to receive data from s4). M2 is computing quickly, and this module is often receiving/sending from stream s2/s3 (little time spent waiting on these streams in comparison with streams s1/s4).

If we study the computational rate, we can thus decide to map M3 alone on a powerful processor because it has the highest value between the different steady states probabilities of the modules. One should be careful to map the streams s1 and s4 onto sufficiently fast network links to increase the overall throughput of the network. A mapping that performs well can thus be deduced from this information, by adjusting the reasoning to the architecture of the available system.

Experiment 2 We can reproduce the same experiment but for a different application: one in which there are a lot of data to be transfered inside the loop. Here, for one input on $s1$, the module M2 makes several calls to the server M3 for computations. In this case, the rates of the streams are different, for instance $\lambda_1 = \lambda_4 = 1000$ and $\lambda_2 = \lambda_3 = 1$.

The results for this experiment are shown in Table 1 (row *Case 2*). In this table, we can see that M3 is quite idle, waiting to receive data 89.4% of the time (i.e. this is the time it is not processing). Moreover, we can see in the stream results that s2 and s3 are busier than the other streams. In this case a good solution might be to map M2 and M3 on to the same cluster, since M3 is no longer the computational bottleneck. We could thus have fast communication links for s2 and s3, which are demanding a lot of network resources.

Table 1. Performance results for the example.

	Modules				Streams			
	M1	M2	M3	M4	s1	s2	s3	s4
Case 1	4.2	5.1	67.0	4.2	47.0	6.7	6.7	47.0
Case 2	52.1	52.2	10.6	52.1	5.2	10.6	10.6	5.2

4.5   Analysis summary

As mentioned in Section 4.2, PEPA rates model both aspects strictly related to the mapping and to the application's logical structure (such as algorithms implemented in the modules, communication patterns and size). The predictive analysis conducted in this work provides performance results which are related only to the application's logical behavior. On the PEPA model this translates on the assumption that all sites includes platforms with the same computing power, and all links have an uniform speed. In other words, we assume to deal with a homogeneous grid to obtain the relative requirements of power among links and platforms. This information is used as a hint for the mapping in a heterogeneous grid.

It is of value to have a general idea of a good mapping solution for the application, and this reasoning can be easily refined with new models including the mapping peculiarities, as demonstrated in our previous work [1]. However, the modeling technique exposed in the present paper allows us to highlight individual resources (links and processors) requirements, that are used to label the application graph.

These labels represent the expected relative requirements of each module (stream) with respect to other modules (streams) during the application run. In the case of a module the described requirement can be interpreted as the aggregate power of the site on which it will be mapped. On the other hand, a stream requirement can be interpreted as the bandwidth of the network link on which it will be mapped. The relative requirements of parmods and streams may be used to implement mapping heuristics which assign more demanding parmods to more powerful sites, and more demanding streams to links exhibiting higher bandwidths. When a fully automatic application mapping is not required, modules and streams requirements can be used to drive a user-assisted mapping process.

Moreover, each parmod exhibits a structured parallelism pattern (a.k.a. skeleton). In many cases, it is thus possible to draw a reliable relationship between the site fabric level information (number and kind of processors, processors and network benchmarks) and the expected aggregate power of the site running a given parmod exhibiting a parallelism pattern [5, 4, 9]. This may enable the development of a mapping heuristic, which needs only information about sites fabric level information, and can automatically derive the performance of a given parmod on a given site.

The use of models taking into account both of the system architecture characteristics can then eventually validate this heuristic, and give expected results about the performance of the application for a specified mapping.

4.6   Future work

The approach described here considers the ASSIST modules as blocks and does not model the internal behavior of each module. A more sophisticated approach might be to consider using known models of individual modules and to integrate these with the global ASSIST model, thus providing a more accurate indication of the performance of the application. At this level of detail, distributed shared memory and external services (e.g. DB, storage services, etc) interactions can be taken into account and integrated to enrich the network of processes with dummy nodes representing external services. PEPA models have already been developed for pipeline or deal skeletons [8–9], and we could integrate such models when the parmod module has been adapted to follow such a pattern.

Analysis precision can be improved by taking into account historical (past runs) or synthetic (benchmark) performance data of individual modules and their communications. This kind of information should be scaled with respect to the expected performances of fabric resources (platform and network performances), which can be retrieved via the middleware information system (e.g. Globus GIS).

We believe that this approach is particularly suitable for modeling applications that can be described by a graph, not just ASSIST applications (such as applications described in the forthcoming CoreGrid Grid Component Model [11]). In particular the technique described here helps to derive some information about the pressure (on modules and links) within a loop of the graph. Loops are quite common patterns; they can be used to describe simple interactions between modules (e.g. client-server RPC behavior) or mutual recursive dependency between modules. These two cases lead to very different behaviors in term of pressure or resources within the loop; in the former case this pressure is variable over time.

The mapping decision is inherently a static process, and especially for loops in the graph, it is important to make decisions on the expected common case. This is modeled by the PEPA steady state probabilities, that indeed try to give some static information on dynamic processes. Observe that PEPA is known to give much more precise information compared to other known methods, such as networks of queues, which cannot model finite buffering in queues, but it is possible with PEPA. Clearly this is important, particularly for loops within the graph.

5.   Conclusions

In this paper we have presented a method to automatically generate PEPA models from an ASSIST application with the aim of improving the mapping of the application. This is an important problem in grid application optimisation.

It is our belief that having an automated procedure to generate PEPA models and obtain performance information may significantly assist in taking mapping decisions. However, the impact of this mapping on the performance of the application with real code requires further experimental verification. This work is ongoing, and is coupled with further studies on more complex applications.

This ongoing research is a collaboration between two CoreGRID partners: the University of Pisa, Italy (WP3 - Programming Model), and the ENS (CNRS) in Lyon, France (WP6 - Institute on Resource Management and Scheduling).

Acknowledgments

This work has been partially supported by Italian national FIRB project no. RBNE01KNFP *GRID.it*, by Italian national strategic projects *legge 449/97* No. 02.00470.ST97 and 02.00640.ST97, and by the FP6 Network of Excellence CoreGRID funded by the European Commission (Contract IST-2002-004265).

References

[1] M. Aldinucci and A. Benoit. Automatic mapping of ASSIST applications using process algebra. Technical report TR-0016, CoreGRID, Oct. 2005.

[2] M. Aldinucci, S. Campa, M. Coppola, S. Magini, P. Pesciullesi, L. Potiti, R. Ravazzolo, M. Torquati, and C. Zoccolo. Targeting heterogeneous architectures in ASSIST: Experimental results. In M. Danelutto, M. Vanneschi, and D. Laforenza, editors, *Proc. of 10th Intl. Euro-Par 2004 Parallel Processing*, volume 3149 of *LNCS*, pages 638–643. Springer Verlag, Aug. 2004.

[3] M. Aldinucci, M. Coppola, M. Danelutto, M. Vanneschi, and C. Zoccolo. ASSIST as a research framework for high-performance grid programming environments. In J. C. Cunha and O. F. Rana, editors, *Grid Computing: Software environments and Tools*, chapter 10, pages 230–256. Springer Verlag, Jan. 2006.

[4] M. Aldinucci, M. Danelutto, J. Dünnweber, and S. Gorlatch. Optimization techniques for skeletons on grid. In L. Grandinetti, editor, *Grid Computing and New Frontiers of High Performance Processing*, volume 14 of *Advances in Parallel Computing*, chapter 2, pages 255–273. Elsevier, Oct. 2005.

[5] M. Aldinucci, M. Danelutto, and M. Vanneschi. Autonomic QoS in ASSIST grid-aware components. In *Proc. of Intl. Euromicro PDP 2006: Parallel Distributed and network-based Processing*, pages 221–230, Montbéliard, France, Feb. 2006. IEEE.

[6] M. Aldinucci, A. Petrocelli, E. Pistoletti, M. Torquati, M. Vanneschi, L. Veraldi, and C. Zoccolo. Dynamic reconfiguration of grid-aware applications in ASSIST. In J. C. Cunha and P. D. Medeiros, editors, *Proc. of 11th Intl. Euro-Par 2005 Parallel Processing*, volume 3648 of *LNCS*, pages 771–781. Springer Verlag, Aug. 2005.

[7] F. Baude, D. Caromel, and M. Morel. On hierarchical, parallel and distributed components for grid programming. In V. Getov and T. Kielmann, editors, *Proc. of the Intl. Workshop on Component Models and Systems for Grid Applications*, CoreGRID series, pages 97–108, Saint-Malo, France, Jan. 2005. Springer Verlag.

[8] A. Benoit, M. Cole, S. Gilmore, and J. Hillston. Evaluating the performance of skeleton-based high level parallel programs. In M. Bubak, D. van Albada, P. Sloot, and J. Dongarra,

editors, *The Intl. Conference on Computational Science (ICCS 2004), Part III*, LNCS, pages 299–306. Springer Verlag, 2004.

 [9] A. Benoit, M. Cole, S. Gilmore, and J. Hillston. Scheduling skeleton-based grid applications using PEPA and NWS. *The Computer Journal*, 48(3):369–378, 2005.

[10] M. Cole. Bringing Skeletons out of the Closet: A Pragmatic Manifesto for Skeletal Parallel Programming. *Parallel Computing*, 30(3):389–406, 2004.

[11] CoreGRID NoE deliverable series, Institute on Programming Model. *Deliverable D.PM.02 – Proposals for a Grid Component Model*, Nov. 2005.

[12] M. Danelutto, M. Vanneschi, C. Zoccolo, N. Tonellotto, S. Orlando, R. Baraglia, T. Fagni, D. Laforenza, and A. Paccosi. HPC application execution on grids. In V. Getov, D. Laforenza, and A. Reinefeld, editors, *Future Generation Grids*, CoreGRID series, pages 263–282. Springer Verlag, Nov. 2005.

[13] J. Dünnweber and S. Gorlatch. HOC-SA: A grid service architecture for higher-order components. In *IEEE Intl. Conference on Services Computing, Shanghai, China*, pages 288–294. IEEE Computer Society Press, Sept. 2004.

[14] J. Dünnweber, S. Gorlatch, S. Campa, M. Aldinucci, and M. Danelutto. Behavior customization of parallel components application programming. Technical Report TR-0002, Institute on Programming Model, CoreGRID - Network of Excellence, Apr. 2005.

[15] I. Foster, C. Kesselman, and S. Tuecke. The anatomy of the Grid: Enabling scalable virtual organization. *The Intl. Journal of High Performance Computing Applications*, 15(3):200–222, Fall 2001.

[16] I. Foster and C. Kesselmann, editors. *The Grid 2: Blueprint for a New Computing Infrastructure*. Morgan Kaufmann, Dec. 2003.

[17] S. Gilmore and J. Hillston. The PEPA Workbench: A Tool to Support a Process Algebra-based Approach to Performance Modelling. In *Proc. of the 7th Int. Conf. on Modelling Techniques and Tools for Computer Performance Evaluation*, number 794 in LNCS, pages 353–368, Vienna, May 1994. Springer-Verlag.

[18] J. Hillston. *A Compositional Approach to Performance Modelling*. Cambridge University Press, 1996.

[19] C. A. R. Hoare. Communicating Sequential Processes. *Communications of ACM*, 21(8):666–677, Aug. 1978.

[20] S. Vadhiyar and J. Dongarra. Self adaptability in grid computing. *Concurrency & Computation: Practice & Experience*, 17(2–4):235–257, 2005.

[21] R. V. van Nieuwpoort, J. Maassen, G. Wrzesinska, R. Hofman, C. Jacobs, T. Kielmann, and H. E. Bal. Ibis: a flexible and efficient Java-based grid programming environment. *Concurrency & Computation: Practice & Experience*, 17(7-8):1079–1107, 2005.

[22] M. Vanneschi. The programming model of ASSIST, an environment for parallel and distributed portable applications. *Parallel Computing*, 28(12):1709–1732, Dec. 2002.

AN ABSTRACT SCHEMA MODELING ADAPTIVITY MANAGEMENT

Marco Aldinucci and Sonia Campa and Massimo Coppola and Marco Danelutto and Corrado Zoccolo
University of Pisa
Department of Computer Science
Largo B. Pontecorvo 3, 56127 Pisa, Italy
aldinuc@di.unipi.it
campa@di.unipi.it
coppola@di.unipi.it
marcod@di.unipi.it
zoccolo@di.unipi.it

Francoise André and Jérémy Buisson
IRISA / University of Rennes 1
avenue du Général Leclerc, 35042 Rennes, France
fandre@irisa.fr
jbuisson@irisa.fr

Abstract   Nowadays, component application adaptivity in Grid environments has been afforded in different ways, such those provided by the Dynaco/AFPAC framework and by the ASSIST environment. We propose an abstract schema that catches all the designing aspects a model for parallel component applications on Grid should define in order to uniformly handle the dynamic behavior of computing resources within complex parallel applications. The abstraction is validated by demonstrating how two different approaches to adaptivity, ASSIST and Dynaco/AFPAC, easily map to such schema.

Keywords: Abstract schema, component adaptivity, Grid parallel component application.

1.   An Abstract Schema for Adaptation

Adaptivity is a concept that recent framework proposals for Computational Grid take into great account. In fact, due to the unstable nature of the Grid (nodes that disappear because of network problems, changes in user requirements/computing power, variations in network bandwidth, etc.), even assuming a perfect initial mapping of an application over the computing resources, the performance level could be suddenly compromised and the framework has to be able to take reconfiguring decisions in order to keep the expected QoS.

The need to handle adaptivity has been already addressed in several projects (AppLeS [6], GrADS [12], PCL [9], ProActive [5]). These works focus on several aspects of reconfiguration, e.g. adaptation techniques (GrADS, PCL, ProActive), strategies to decide reconfigurations (GrADS), and how to modify the application configuration to optimize the running application (AppLes, GrADS, PCL). In these projects concrete problems posed by adaptivity have been faced, but little investigation has been done on common abstractions and methodology [10].

In this work we discuss, at a very high level of abstraction, a general model of the activities we need to perform to handle adaptivity in parallel and distributed programs.

Our intention is to start drawing a methodology for designing adaptive component environments, leaving in the meanwhile a high degree of freedom in the implementation and optimization choices. In fact, our model is abstract with respect to the implemented adaptation techniques, monitoring infrastructure and reconfiguration strategy; in this way we can uncover the common aspects that have to be addressed when developing a programming framework for reconfigurable applications.

Moreover, we will validate our abstract schema by demonstrating how two completely different approaches to adaptivity fit its structure. We will discuss the Dynaco/AFPAC [7] approach and the ASSIST [4] approach and we will show how, despite several differences in the implementation technologies used, they can be firmly abstracted by the schema we propose.

Before demonstrating its suitability to the two implemented frameworks, we exemplify its application in a significant case study: component-based, high-level parallel programs. The adaptive behavior is derived by specializing the abstract model introduced here. We get significant results on the performance side, thus showing that the model maps to worthwhile and effective implementations [4].

This work is structured as follows. Sec. 2 introduces the abstract model. The various phases required by the general schema are detailed with an example in Sec. 3. Sec. 4 explains how the schema is mapped in the Dynaco/AFPAC framework, where self-adapting code is obtained by semi automated restruc-

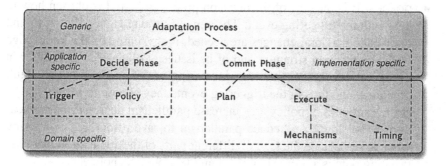

Figure 1. Abstract schema of an adaptation manager.

turing of existing code. Sec. 5 describes how the same schema is employed in the ASSIST programming environment, exploiting explicit program structure to automatically generate autonomic dynamicity-handling code. Sec. 6 summarizes those two mappings of the abstract schema.

2. Adaptivity

The abstract model of dynamicity management we propose is shown in Fig. 1, where high-level actions rely on lower-level actions and mechanisms. The model is based on the separation of application-oriented abstractions and implementation mechanisms, and is also deliberately specified in minimal way, in order not to introduce details that may constrain possible implementations. As an example, the schema does not impose a strict time ordering among its leaves. The process of adapting the behavior of a parallel/distributed application to the dynamic features of the target architecture is built of two distinct phases: a decision phase, and a commit phase, as outlined in Fig. 1. The outcome of the decide phase is an abstract adaptation strategy that the commit phase has to implement. We separate the decisions on the strategy to be used to adapt the application behavior from the way this strategy is actually performed. The decide phase thus represents an abstraction related to the application structure and behavior, while commit phase concerns the abstraction of the run-time support needed to adapt. Both phases are split into different items. The decide phase is composed of:

- trigger – It is essentially an interface towards the external world, assessing the need to perform corrective actions. Triggering events can result from various monitoring activities of the platform, from the user requesting a dynamic change at run-time, or from the application itself reacting to some kind of algorithm-related load unbalance.

- policy – It is the part of the decision process where it is chosen how to deal with the triggering event. The aim of the adaptation policy is to find out what behavioral changes are needed, if any, based on the knowledge of the application structure and of its issues. Policies can also differ in the objectives they pursue, e.g. increasing performance, accuracy, fault tolerance, and thus in the triggering events they choose to react to.

  Basic examples of policy are "increase parallelism degree if the application is too slow", or "reduce parallelism to save resources". Choosing when to re-balance the load of different parts of the application by redistributing data is a more significant and less obvious policy.

In order to provide the decide phase with a policy, we must identify in the code a pattern of parallel computation, and evaluate possible strategies to improve/adapt the pattern features to the current target architecture. This will result either in specifying a user-defined policy or picking one from a library of policies for common computation patterns. Ideally, the adaptation policy should depend on the chosen pattern and not on its implementation details.

In the commit phase, the decision previously taken is implemented. In order to do that, some assessed plan of execution has to be adopted.

- plan – It states how the decision can be actually implemented, i.e. what list of steps has to be performed to come to the new configuration of the running application, and according to which control flow (total or partial order).
- execute – Once the detailed plan has been devised, the execute phase takes it in charge, relying on two kinds of functionalities of the support code
    - the different mechanisms provided by the underlying target architecture, and
    - a timing functionality to activate the elementary steps in the plan, taking into account their control flow and the needed synchronizations among processes/threads in the application.

The actual adapting action depends on both the way the application has been implemented (e.g. message passing or shared memory) and the mechanisms provided by the target architecture to interact with the running application (e.g. adding and removing processes to the application, moving data between processing nodes and so on). The general schema does not constrain the adaptation handling code to a specific form. It can either consist in library calls, or be template-generated, it can result from instrumenting the application or as a side effect of using explicit code structures/library primitives in writing the application. The approaches clearly differ in the degree of user intervention required to achieve dynamicity.

3. Example of the abstract decomposition

We exemplify the abstract adaptation schema on a task-parallel computation organized around a centralized task scheduler, continuously dispatching works to be performed to the set of available processing elements. For this kind of pattern, both a performance model and a balancing policy are well known, and several different implementations are feasible (e.g. multi-threaded on SMP machines, or processes in a cluster and/or on the Grid). At steady state, maximum efficiency is achieved when the overall service time of the set of processing elements is slightly less than the service time of the dispatcher element.

Triggers are activated, for instance, when (1) the average inter-arrival time of task incoming is much lower/higher than the service time of the system, (2) on explicit user request to satisfy a new performance contract/level of performance, (3) when built-in monitoring reports increased load on some of the processing elements, even before service time increases too much.

Assuming we care first for computation performance and then resource utilization, the adaptation policy could be like the following: *i)* when steady state is reached, no configuration change is needed; *ii)* if the set of processing elements is slower than the dispatcher, new processing elements should be added to support the computation and reach the steady state *iii)* if the processing elements are much faster than the dispatcher, reduce their number to increase efficiency.

Applying this policy, the decide phase will eventually determine the increase/decrease of a certain magnitude in the allocated computing power, independently of the kind of computing resources.

This decision is passed to the commit phase, where we must produce a detailed plan to implement it (finding/choosing resources, devising a mapping of application processes where appropriate).

Assuming we want to increase the parallelism degree, we will often come up with a simple plan like the following: *a)* find a set of available processing elements $\{P_i\}$; *b)* install code to be executed at the chosen $\{P_i\}$ (i.e. application code, code that interacts with the task scheduler and for dinamicity handling) ;*c)* register with the scheduler all the $\{P_i\}$ for task dispatching; *d)* inform the monitoring system that new processing element have joined the execution. It is worthwhile that the given plan is general enough to be customized depending on the implementation, that is it could be rewritten/reordered on the basis of the desired target.

Once the detailed plan has been devised, it has to be executed and its actions have to be orchestrated, choosing proper timing in order that they do not to interfere with each other and with the ongoing computation.

Abstract timing depends on the implementation of the mechanisms, and on the precedence relationship that may be given in the plan. In the given example, steps 1 and 2 can be executed in sequence, but without internal constraint on timing. Step 3 requires a form of synchronization with the scheduler to update its data, or to suspend all the computing elements, depending on actual implementation of the scheduler/worker synchronization. For the same reason, execution of step 4 also may/may not require a restart/update of the monitoring subsystem to take into account the new resources.

We also want to point out that in case of data parallel computation (as a fast Fourier transformation, as instance), we could again use policies like *i)-iii* and plans like *a-d*.

4.   Dynaco/AFPAC: a generic framework for developers to manage adaptation

Dynaco is a framework allowing developers to add dynamic adaptability to software components without constraining the programming paradigms and tools that can be used. While Dynaco aims at addressing general adaptability problems, AFPAC focuses on the specific case of parallel components.

4.1   Dynaco: generic dynamic adaptation framework

Dynaco provides the major functional decomposition of dynamic adaptability. It is the part that is the closest from the abstract schema described in section 2. Its design has benefited from the joint work about the abstract schema. As depicted by Fig. 2, Dynaco defines 3 major functions for dynamic adaptability: decision-making, planning and execution. Coarsely, those decision-making and execution functions match respectively the **decide** and **commit** phases of the abstract schema.

For the decision-making function, the *decider* decides whether the component should adapt itself or not. If it should, a strategy is produced that describes the configuration the component should adopt. The framework states that the

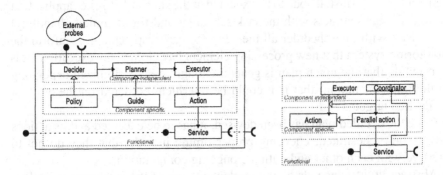

Figure 2.   Overall architecture of a Dynaco component.

Figure 3.   Architecture of AFPAC as a specialization of Dynaco.

decider is independent from the actual component: it is a generic decision-making engine. It is specialized to the actual component by a *policy*, which plays the same role as its homonym in the abstract schema. While the abstract schema reifies in trigger the events triggering the decision-making, Dynaco does not: the *decider* only exports interfaces to the outside of the component. Monitoring engines are considered to be external to the component and to its adaptability, even if the component can bind to itself in order to be one of its monitors.

The planning function is implemented by the *planner*. Given a *strategy* that has been previously decided, it aims at determining a *plan* that indicates how to adopt the *strategy*. The *plan* matches exactly its homonym of the abstract schema. Similarly to the *decider*, the *planner* is a generic engine that is specialized to the actual component by a *guide*.

While not being a phase in the abstract schema, planning has been promoted to a major function within Dynaco, at the same level as decision-making and execution. As a consequence, Dynaco introduces a planning *guide* in order to specialize the planning function in the same way that there is a *policy* that specializes the decision-making function. On the contrary, the abstract schema exhibits a plan which actually links the decide and commit phases. This vision is consistent with the goal of not constraining possible implementations. Dynaco is one interpretation of the abstract schema, while another would have been to have the decide phase directly produce the plan, for example.

The execution function is realized by the *executor* that interprets the instructions of the *plan*. Two kinds of instructions can be used in *plan*s: invocations of elementary *action*s, which match the mechanisms of the abstract schema; and control instructions, which match the timing functionality of the abstract schema. While the former are provided by developers as component-specific entities, the latter are implemented by the *executor* in a component-independent manner.

4.2   AFPAC: dynamic adaptation of parallel components

As seen by AFPAC, parallel components are components that encapsulate a parallel code, such as GridCCM [11] components: they have several processes that execute the *service* they provides. AFPAC is depicted by Fig. 3. It is a specialization of Dynaco's *executor* for parallel components. Through its *coordinator* component, which partly implements the timing functionality of the abstract schema, AFPAC provides an additional control instruction for expressing *plan*s. This instruction makes all of *service* processes execute an *action* in parallel. Such an action is labeled *parallel action* on Fig. 3. This kind of instruction is particularly useful to execute redistribution in the case of data-parallel applications.

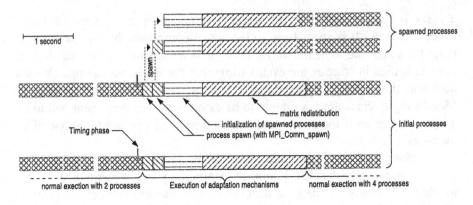

Figure 4.   Scenario of an adaptation with AFPAC

AFPAC addresses the consistency problems of the global states from which the parallel *action*s are executed. Those problems have been discussed in [7]; we have proposed in [8] an algorithm that chooses the next upcoming consistent global state. To do so, it relies on *adaptation point*s: a global state is said consistent if every service process is at such a point. It also requires control structures to be annotated thanks to aspect-oriented programming in order to locate *adaptation point*s as the execution progresses. The algorithm and the consistency criterion it implements suits well to SPMD codes such as the ones using MPI.

Fig. 4 shows the sequence of actions when a data-parallel code working on matrices adapts itself thanks to AFPAC. In this example, the application spawns 2 new processes in order to increase its parallelism degree up to 4. Firstly, the timing phase of the abstract schema is executed by the *coordinator* component concurrently to the normal execution of the parallel code. During this phase, the *coordinator* takes a rendez-vous with every executing *service* process at an *adaptation point*. When *service* processes reach the rendez-vous *adaptation point*, they execute the requested *action*s. Once every action of the *plan* has been executed, the *service* resumes its normal execution. This experiment shows well that most of the overhead lies in incompressible *action*s like matrix redistribution.

5.   ASSIST: Managing dynamicity using language and compilation approaches

ASSIST applications are described by means of a coordination language, which can express arbitrary graphs of (possibly) parallel modules, interconnected by typed streams of data. A parallel module (*parmod*) coordinates a set of concurrent activities called *Virtual Processes* (VPs). Each VP execute a sequential function (that can be programmed using standard sequential languages e.g. C, C++, Fortran) on input data and internal state.

Groups of VPs are grouped together in processes called *Virtual Processes Manager* (VPM). VPs assigned to the same VPM execute sequentially, while different VPMs run in parallel: therefore the actual parallelism exploited in a *parmod* is given by the number of VPMs that are allocated.

Overall, a *parmod* may behave in a data-parallel (e.g. SPMD/for-all/apply-to-all) or task-parallel way (e.g. farm, pipeline), and it can nondeterministically accept from one or more input streams a number of input items, which may be decomposed in parts and used as function parameters to activate VPs. A *parmod* may also exploit a distributed shared state, which survives between VP activations related to different stream items. More details on the ASSIST environment can be found in [13, 2].

An ASSIST module (or a graph of modules) can be declared as a component, which is characterized by *provide* and *use* ports (both one-way and RPC-like), and by *Non-Functional* ports. The latter are responsible of specifying those aspects related to the management/coordination of the computation, as well as the required performance level of the whole application or of the single component. As instance, among the non-functional interfaces there are those related to QoS control (performance, reconfiguration strategy and allocation constraints).

Each ASSIST module in the graph encapsulated by the component is controlled by its own MAM (Module Adaptation Manager), a process that coordinates the configuration and adaptation of the module itself. The MAM dynamically decides the number of allocated VPMs and their mapping onto the processing elements acquired through a retargetable middle-ware, that can be adapted to exploit clusters as well as grid platforms.

Hierarchically, the set of MAMs is coordinated by the Component Adaptation Manager (CAM) that manages the configuration of the whole component. At a higher level, these lower-level entities are coordinated by a (possibly distributed) Application Manager (AM), to pursue a global QoS for the whole application.

The starting configuration is determined at load time by hierarchically splitting the user provided QoS contract between each component and module. In case of a QoS contract violation during the application run, managing processes react by issuing (asynchronous) adaptation requests to controlled entities [4]. According to the locality principle, violations and corrective actions are detected and issued as near as possible to the leaves of the hierarchy (i.e. the modules with their MAM). Higher-level managers are notified of violations when lower-level managers cannot handle them locally. In these cases, CAMs or the AM can coordinate the actions of several MAMs and CAMs (e.g. by re-negotiating contracts with them) in order to implement a non-local adaptation strategy.

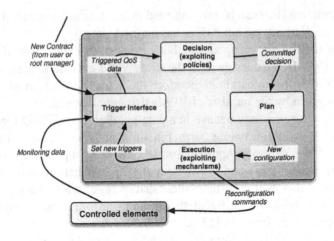

Figure 5.   ASSIST framework.

The corrective actions that can be undertaken in order to fulfill the contracts, eventually lead to the adaptation of component configurations, in terms of parallelism degree, and process mapping [4].

Reconfiguration requests to the adaptation mechanism are triggered by new QoS needs or by monitoring feedbacks. Such requests flow in an autonomic manner through the AM to the lower level managers of the hierarchy (or vice versa). If the contract is broken a new configuration is defined by evaluating the related performance model. It is then applied at each involved party (component or module), in order to reach a state in which the contract is fulfilled.

The adaptation mechanisms adopted in ASSIST completely instantiates the abstract schema provided above by organizing its leafs, left to right in an autonomic control loop (see Fig.5). The trigger functionality is represented by the collection of the stream of monitoring data. Such data come from the running environment and can cause a framework reaction if a contract violation is observed. A component performance model is evaluated (policy phase) on the basis of the collected monitoring data, according to a selected goal (currently, in ASSIST we implemented two predefined policies, pursuing two different goals; for special needs, user-defined policies can be programmed).

If the QoS contract is broken, a decision has to be taken about how to adapt the component: such decision could involve a single component or a compound component. In the latter case, the decision has to flow through the hierarchy of managers in order to harmonize the whole application performance. The decision phase uses the policies in order to reach the contract requirements. Examples of policies are: reaching a *desired service time* (as seen above, it could happen if one VPM becomes overloaded), or realizing the *best effort* in

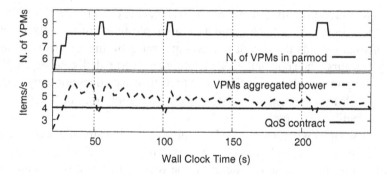

Figure 6. MAM's reaction to a contract violation

the performance/resource trade-off (by releasing unused PE, as instance). The decision phase result is a target for the commit phase (increasing of computing power, as an example). Such target is represented by a plan provided by the homonymous phase that lists the actions (e.g. add or remove resource to/from computation and computation remapping, with associated data migration and global state consolidation) to be taken.

Finally, the execute functionality exploits support code statically generated by the ASSIST compiler, and coordinates it with services provided by the component framework to interface to the middle-ware (e.g. for resource recruiting), according to the schedule provided by timing functionality.

Timing functionality is related to the so-called *reconf-safe* points [4], i.e. points in the application code where the distributed computation and state are known to be consistent and can be efficiently synchronized. Each mechanism that is exploited to reconfigure the application at run time can take advantage (e.g. can be optimized) of reconf-safe points to appropriately orchestrate synchronizations in a transparent manner. Moreover, the generated code is tailored for the given application structure and features, exploiting the set of concrete mechanisms provided by the language run-time support. For instance, no state migration code is inserted for stateless computations, and depending on the parallelism pattern (e.g. stream versus data parallel), VPMs involved in the synchronization can be a subset of those within the component being reconfigured.

Our experiments [4] show that the adaptation mechanisms do not introduce overhead with respect to non-adaptive versions of the same code, when no configuration change is performed, and that issued adaptations are achieved with minimal (of the order of milliseconds) impact on the ongoing computation.

Fig. 6 shows the behavior of an ASSIST parallel application with adaptivity managers enabled, run on a collection of homogeneous Linux workstations interconnected by switched Fast Ethernet. In particular, it shows the reaction of a MAM to a sudden contract violation with respect to the number of VPMs. The application represents a farm computing a simple function with fixed service time on stream items flowing at a fixed input rate. In this scenario, a contract violation occurs when one of the VPMs becomes overloaded, causing the VPMs aggregated power to decrease. The MAM reacts to such decrement by mapping as many VPMs as needed to satisfy the contract (only one in this case) onto fresh computing resources.

In this example, when a new VPM mapping occurs because of the overloading of one (or more) of the allocated ones, removing the overloaded one does not lead to a contract violation. Therefore the MAM, that is also responsible to manage over-dimensioned resource usage, removes the overloaded PE almost immediately. The MAM can reduce resource usage also (not shown in this example) when the incoming data rate decreases or the contract requirements are weakened.

6. A comparative discussion

As it is clear from the previous presentations, Dynaco (and its parallel-component specialization AFPAC) and ASSIST fit the abstract schema proposed in Section 2 in different manner. The frameworks have been developed independently with each other but both aim at offering a platform to handle dynamically adaptable components.

Dynaco can be seen as a pipelined implementation of the abstract schema fed by an external monitoring engine. In particular, the three major functions (decision-making, planning and execution) are specialized by component-specific sub-phases. On the other hand, ASSIST provides a circular implementation of the schema leafs, while decision and commit can be seen as macro-steps of the autonomic loop.

The decision-making functionalities are triggered by the external monitoring engine in Dynaco, while in ASSIST the concept of performance contract is exploited in order to specify the performance level to be guaranteed.

In ASSIST the code related to the execution phase is automatically generated at compile time, while the Dynaco developer is asked to provide the code for policy, guide and action entities. Both the frameworks offer the possibility to configure certain points of the code as "safe-points" from which recovery/re-configuration is possible. In Dynaco such points are defined by aspect-oriented technologies, while in ASSIST they are defined by the language semantics, and determined by the compiler.

From the discussion above, it is clear that each framework affords the adaptivity problem by means of individual solutions. What we want to point out in this work is that, despite their technological diversity, both solutions can be inscribed in the general abstract schema presented in Section 2. Such schema is general enough to abstract from any kind of implementative solution but it is also sufficiently strong to catch the salient aspects a model has to consider while designing adaptive component frameworks. By summing up, it can be seen as a reference guide for modeling adaptable environments independently from the implementations, technologies, languages, constraints or architectures involved.

7. Conclusions

We have described a general model to provide adaptive behavior in Grid-oriented component-based applications. The general schema we have shown is independent of implementation choices, such as the responsibility for inserting the adaptation code (either left to the programmer, as it happens in the Dynaco/AFPAC framework, or performed by exploiting knowledge of the high level program structure, as it happens in the ASSIST context). The model also encompasses user-driven as well as autonomic adaptation.

The abstract model helps in separating application and run-time programming concerns of adaptation, exposing adaptive behavior as an aspect of application programming, formalizing the concerns to be addressed, and encouraging an abstract view of the run-time mechanisms for dynamic reconfiguration.

This formalization gives the basis for defining a methodology. The given case study provide with valuable clues about how to solve different concerns, and how to identify common parts of the adaptation that can be generalized in support frameworks. The model can be thus also usefully applied within other programming frameworks, like GrADS, which do not enforce a strong separation of adaptivity issues into design and implementation.

We expect that such a methodology will lead to more portable and understandable adaptive applications and components, and it will also promote layered software architectures for adaptation, simplifying implementation of both the programming framework and the applications.

Acknowledgments

This research work is carried out under the FP6 Network of Excellence *CoreGRID* funded by the European Commission (Contract IST-2002-004265), and it was partially supported by the Italian MIUR FIRB project *Grid.it* (n. RBNE01KNFP) on High-performance Grid platforms and tools.

References

[1] M. Aldinucci, F. André, J. Buisson, S. Campa, M. Coppola, M. Danelutto, and C. Zoccolo. Parallel program/component adaptivity management. In *Proc. of Intl. PARCO 2005: Parallel Computing*, Sept. 2005.

[2] M. Aldinucci, S. Campa, M. Coppola, M. Danelutto, D. Laforenza, D. Puppin, L. Scarponi, M. Vanneschi, and C. Zoccolo. Components for high performance grid programming in grid.it. In V. Getov and T. Kielmann, editors, *Proc. of the Intl. Workshop on Component Models and Systems for Grid Applications*, CoreGRID series, pages 19–38, Saint-Malo, France, Jan. 2005. Springer.

[3] M. Aldinucci, M. Coppola, M. Danelutto, M. Vanneschi, and C. Zoccolo. ASSIST as a research framework for high-performance grid programming environments. In J. C. Cunha and O. F. Rana, editors, *Grid Computing: Software environments and Tools*, chapter 10, pages 230–256. Springer, Jan. 2006.

[4] M. Aldinucci, A. Petrocelli, A. Pistoletti, M. Torquati, M. Vanneschi, L. Veraldi, and C. Zoccolo. Dynamic reconfiguration of Grid-aware applications in ASSIST. In José. Cunha and Pedro D. Medeiros, editors, *Euro-Par 2005 Parallel Processing: 11th International Euro-Par Conference, Lisbon, Portugal, August 30 - September 2, 2005. Proceedings*, volume 3648 of *LNCS*, pages 711–781. Springer-Verlag, August 2005.

[5] F. Baude, D. Caromel, and M. Morel. On hierarchical, parallel and distributed components for Grid programming. In V. Getov and T. Kielmann, editors, *Workshop on component Models and Systems for Grid Applications*, ICS '04, Saint-Malo, France, June 2004.

[6] F. D. Berman, R. Wolski, S. Figueira, J. Schopf, and G. Shao. Application-level scheduling on distributed heterogeneous networks. In *Supercomputing '96: Proc. of the 1996 ACM/IEEE Conf. on Supercomputing (CDROM)*, page 39, 1996.

[7] J. Buisson, F. André, and J.-L. Pazat. Dynamic adaptation for grid computing. In P.M.A. Sloot, A.G. Hoekstra, T. Priol, A. Reinefeld, and M. Bubak, editors, *Advances in Grid Computing - EGC 2005 (European Grid Conference, Amsterdam, The Netherlands, February 14-16, 2005, Revised Selected Papers)*, volume 3470 of *LNCS*, pages 538–547, Amsterdam, June 2005. Springer-Verlag.

[8] J. Buisson, F. André, and J.-L. Pazat. Enforcing consistency during the adaptation of a parallel component. In *The 4th Int.l Symposium on Parallel and Distributed Computing*, July 2005.

[9] B. Ensink, J. Stanley, and V. Adve. Program control language: a programming language for adaptive distributed applications. *Journal of Parallel and Distributed Computing*, 63(11):1082–1104, November 2003.

[10] M. McIlhagga, A. Light, and I. Wakeman. Towards a design methodology for adaptive applications. In *Mobile Computing and Networking*, pages 133–144, May 1998.

[11] Christian Pérez, Thierry Priol, and André Ribes. A parallel corba component model for numerical code coupling. *The International Journal of High Performance Computing Applications (IJHPCA)*, 17(4):417–429, 2003.

[12] S. Vadhiyar and J. Dongarra. Self adaptability in grid computing. *International Journal Computation and Currency: Practice and Experience*, 2005. To appear.

[13] M. Vanneschi. The programming model of ASSIST, an environment for parallel and distributed portable applications. *Parallel Computing*, 28(12):1709–1732, December 2002.

A FEEDBACK-BASED APPROACH TO REDUCE DUPLICATE MESSAGES IN UNSTRUCTURED PEER-TO-PEER NETWORKS

Charis Papadakis, Paraskevi Fragopoulou, Evangelos P. Markatos, and Elias Athanasopoulos
Institute of Computer Science, Foundation for Research and Technology-Hellas
P.O. Box 1385, 71 110 Heraklion-Crete, Greece
{adanar,fragopou,elathan,markatos}@ics.forth.gr

Marios Dikaiakos
Department of Computer Science, University of Cyprus, P.O. Box 537, CY-1678 Nicosia, Cyprus
mdd@ucy.ac.cy

Alexandros Labrinidis
Department of Computer Science, University of Pittsburgh, Pittsburgh, PA 15260, USA
labrinid@cs.pitt.edu

Abstract   Resource location in unstructured P2P systems is mainly performed by having each node forward each incoming query message to all of its neighbors, a process called *flooding*. Although this algorithm has excellent response time and is very simple to implement, it creates a large volume of unnecessary traffic in today's Internet because each node may receive the same query several times through different paths. We propose an innovative technique, the *feedback-based approach* that aims to improve the scalability of flooding. The main idea behind our algorithm is to monitor the ratio of duplicate messages transmitted over each network connection, and not forward query messages over connections whose ratio exceeds some threshold. Through extensive simulation we show that this algorithm exhibits significant reduction of traffic in random and small-world graphs, the two most common types of graph that have been studied in the context of P2P systems, while conserving network coverage.

Keywords: Peer-to-peer, resource location, flooding, network coverage, query message.

1.   Introduction

In unstructured P2P networks, such as Gnutella and KaZaA, each node is directly connected to a small set of other nodes, called neighbors. Most of today's commercial P2P systems are unstructured and rely on random overlay networks [7, 9]. Unstructured P2P systems have used flooding as their prevailing resource location method [7, 9]. A node looking for a file issues a query which is broadcast in the network. An important parameter in the flooding algorithm is the Time-To-Live (TTL). The TTL indicates the number of hops away from its source a query should propagate. The node that initiates the flooding sets the query's TTL to a small positive integer. Each receiving node decreases by one the query's TTL value before broadcasting it to its neighbors. The query propagation terminates when its TTL reaches zero.

The basic problem with the flooding mechanism is that it creates a large volume of unnecessary traffic in the network mainly because a node may receive the same queries multiple times through different paths. The reason behind the duplicate messages is the existence of cycles in the underlying network topology. Duplicates constitute a large percentage of the total number of messages generated during flooding. In a network of N nodes and average degree d and for TTL value equal to the diameter of the graph, there are $N(d-2)$ duplicate messages for a single query while only $N-1$ messages are needed to reach all network nodes. The TTL was incorporated in the flooding algorithm in order to reduce the number of messages produced thus reducing the overall network traffic. Since the paths traversed by the flooding messages are short, there is a small probability that those paths will form cycles and thus generate duplicates. However, as we will see below, even this observation is not valid for small-world graphs. Furthermore, a small TTL value can reduce the network coverage defined as the percentage of network nodes that receive a query.

In an effort to alleviate the large volumes of unnecessary traffic produced during flooding several variations have been proposed [11]. Most of these rely on randomly or selectively propagating the query messages to a small number of each node's neighbors. The neighbor selection criteria is the number of responses received, the node capacity, or the link latency. Although these methods succeed in reducing excessive network traffic, they usually incur significant loss in network coverage, meaning that only a small part of the network's nodes are queried, thus a much smaller number of query answers are returned to the requesting node. This can be a problem especially when the search targets rare items for which often no response is returned. Other search methods such as random walks or multiple random walks suffer from slow response time.

In this paper, we aim to alleviate the excessive network traffic problem while at the same time maintain high network coverage. Towards this, we devise an innovative technique, the feedback-based algorithm, that attacks the problem by monitoring the number of duplicates on each network connection and trying to forward queries over connections that do not produce an excessive number of duplicates. During an initial and relatively short warm-up phase, a feedback is returned for each duplicate that is encountered on an edge to the upstream node. Following the warm-up phase, each node decides to forward incoming messages on each of its incident edges based on whether the percentage of duplicates on that edge during the warm-up phase does not exceed some pre-defined threshold value. We show through extensive simulation, for different values of the parameters involved, that this algorithm is very efficient in terms of traffic reduction in random and small-world graphs, the two most common types of graph that have been studied in the context of P2P systems, while the algorithm exhibits minor loss in network coverage.

The remainder of this paper is organized as follows: Following the related work section, the feedback-based algorithm is presented in Section 3. The two most common types of graphs that were studied in the context of P2P systems, and on which we conducted our experiments, are presented in Section 4. The simulation details and the experimental results on static graphs are presented in Section 5. Finally, the algorithm's behavior on dynamic graphs, assuming that nodes can leave the network and new nodes can enter at any time, is presented in Section 6. We conclude in Section 7 with a summary of the results.

2. Related work

Many algorithms have been proposed in the literature to alleviate the excessive traffic problem and to deal with the traffic/coverage trade-off [11]. One of the first alternatives proposed was random walk. Each node forwards each query it receives to a single neighboring node chosen at random. In this case the TTL parameter designates the number of hops the walker should propagate. Random walks produce very little traffic, just one query message per visited node, but reduce considerably network coverage and have long response time. As an alternative, multiple random walks have been proposed. The node that originates the query forwards it to k of its neighbors. Each node receiving an incoming query transmits it to a single randomly chosen neighbor. Although compared to the single random walk this method has better behavior, it still suffers from low network coverage and slow response time. Hybrid methods that combine flooding and random walks have been proposed in [5].

In another family of algorithms, query messages are forwarded not randomly but rather selectively to part of a node's neighbors based on some criteria or statistical information. For example, each node selects the first k neighbors that returned the most query responses, or the k highest capacity nodes, or the k connections with the smallest latency to forward new queries [6]. A somewhat different approach named forwarding indices [2] builds a structure that resembles a routing table at each node. This structure stores the number of responses returned through each neighbor on each one of a pre-selected list of topics. Other techniques include query caching, and the incorporation of semantic information in the network [3, 10].

The specific problem we deal with in this paper, namely the problem of duplicate messages, has been identified and some results appear in the literature. In [12] a randomized and a selective approach is adopted and each query message is sent to a portion of a node's neighbors. The algorithm is shown to reduce the number of duplicates and to maintain network coverage. However, the performance of the algorithm is demonstrated on graphs of limited size. In another effort to reduce the excessive traffic in flooding, Gkatsidis and Mihail [5] proposed to direct messages along edges which are parts of shortest paths. They rely on the use of PING and PONG messages to find the edges that lie on shortest paths. However, due to PONG caching this is not a reliable technique. Furthermore, their algorithm degenerates to simple flooding for random graphs, meaning that in this case no duplicate messages are eliminated. Finally, in [8] the authors proposed to construct a shortest paths spanning tree rooted at each network node. However, this algorithm is not very scalable since the state each network node has to keep is in the order of $O(Nd)$, where N is the number of network nodes and d its average degree.

3.   The Feedback-based algorithm

The basic idea of the feedback-based algorithm is to identify edges on which an excessive number of duplicates are produced and to avoid forwarding messages over these edges. In the algorithm's warm-up phase, during which flooding is used, a feedback message is returned to the upstream node for each duplicate message. The objective of the algorithm is to count the number of duplicates produced on each edge, and during the execution phase, using this count, to decide whether to forward a query message over an edge or not.

In a static graph, a message transmitted over an edge is a duplicate if this edge is not on the shortest path from the origin to the downstream node. One of the key points in the feedback-based algorithm is the following: Each network node A forms groups of the other nodes, and a different count is kept on each one of A's incident edges for duplicate messages originating from nodes of each different group. The objective is for each node A to group together the other nodes so that messages originating from nodes of the same group either produce many duplicates or few duplicates on each one of A's incident edges. An incident edge of a node A that produces only a few duplicates for messages originating from nodes of a group must belong to many shortest paths connecting nodes of this group to the downstream node. An incident edge of node A that produces many duplicates for messages originating from nodes of a group must belong

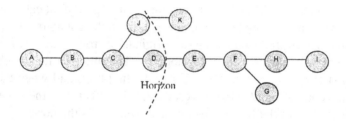

Figure 1. Illustration of the horizon criterion for node A and for horizon value 3.

to few shortest paths connecting nodes of this group to the downstream node. Notice that if all duplicate messages produced on an edge were counted together (independent of their origin), then the algorithm would be inconclusive. In this case the duplicate count on all edges would be the same since each node would receive the same query though all of its incident edges. The criteria used by each node to group together the other nodes are critical for the algorithm's performance and the intuition for their choice is explained below.

A sketch of the feedback-based algorithm is the following:
- Each node A groups together the rest of the nodes according to some criteria.
- During the warm-up phase, each node A keeps a count of the number of duplicates on each of its incident edges, originating from nodes of each different group.
- Subsequently, during the execution phase, messages originating from nodes of a group are forwarded over an incident edge e of node A, if the percentage of duplicates for this group on edge e during the warm-up phase is below a predefined threshold value.

Two different grouping criteria, namely, the *hops criterion* and the *horizon criterion*, as well as a combination of them, *horizon+hops*, are used that lead to three variations of the feedback-based algorithm.
- **Hops criterion:** Each node A keeps a different count on each of its incident edges for duplicates originating k hops away (k ranges from 1 up to the graph's diameter). The intuition for this choice is that in random graphs small hops produce few duplicates and large hops produce mostly duplicates. Thus, messages originating from close by nodes are most probably not duplicates while most messages originating from distant nodes are duplicates. In order for this grouping criterion to work each query message should store the number of hops traversed so far.
- **Horizon criterion:** The horizon is a small integer. A node is in the horizon of some node A if its distance in hops from A is less than the horizon value, while all other nodes are outside A's horizon (Fig. 1). For each node inside A's horizon a different count is kept by A on each of its incident edges. Duplicate messages originating from nodes outside A's horizon are added up to the count

of their entry node in A's horizon. For example, in Fig. 1, duplicates produced by queries originating from node K are added up to the counters kept for node J, while duplicates produced by queries originating from nodes E, F, G, H, I are added up to the counters kept for node D. The intuition for the choice of this criterion is that shortest paths differ in the first hops and when they meet they follow a common route. For this criterion to be effective, a message should store the identities of the last k nodes visited, where k is the horizon value.

• **Horizon+Hops criterion:** This criterion combines the two previous ones. Duplicates are counted separately on each one of A's incident edges for each node in A's horizon. Nodes outside A's horizon are grouped together according (1) to their distance in hops from A and (2) to the entry node of their messages in A's horizon.

In what follows, we present three variations of the feedback-based algorithm that are based on the grouping criteria used. The algorithm using the hops criterion is shown below. The groups formed by node A in the graph of Fig. 1 according to the hops criterion are shown in Table 1.

Feedback-based algorithm using the Hops criterion
1. **Warm-up phase**
   a. Each incoming non-duplicate query message is forwarded to all neighbors except the upstream one.
   b. For each incoming duplicate query message received, a duplicate feedback message is returned to the upstream node.
   c. Each node A, for each incident edge e, counts the percentage of duplicate feedback messages produced on edge e for all queries messages originating k hops away. Let us denote this count by De,k
2. **Execution phase**
   a. Each node A forwards an incoming non-duplicate query message that originates k hops away over its incident edges e if the count De,k does not exceed a predefined threshold.

Table 1.   Groups for the Horizon criterion based on the example of Fig. 1.

Hops	1	2	3	4	5	6	7
Groups formed by node A	B	C	D,J	E,K	F	G,H	I

The algorithm using the horizon criterion is shown below. The groups formed by node A in the graph of Fig. 1 according to the horizon criterion are shown in Table 2.

Feedback-based algorithm using the Horizon criterion
1. Warm-up phase
    a & b. Same as in the Hops criterion algorithm.

    c. Each node A, for each incident edge e, counts the percentage of duplicate messages produced on edge e for all query messages originating from a node B inside the horizon, or entered the horizon at node B. Let us denote this count by $D_{e,B}$.

2. Execution phase
    a. Each node A forwards an incoming non-duplicate query message that originates at a node B inside the horizon, or which entered the horizon at node B over its incident edges e if the count $D_{e,B}$ does not exceed a predefined threshold value.

Table 2. Groups for the Horizon criterion based on the example of Fig. 1.

Node in A's horizon	B	C	D	J
Groups formed by node A	B	C	D,E,F,G,H,I	J,K

The algorithm using the combination of the two criteria described above, namely the horizon+hops, is shown below. The groups formed by node A in Fig. 1 for the horizon+hops criterion are shown in Table 3.

Feedback-based algorithm using the Horizon+Hops criterion
1. Warm-up phase
    a & b. Same as in the Hops criterion algorithm.

    c. Each node A, for each incident edge e, counts the percentage of duplicate messages produced on edge e for all queries messages originating from a node B inside A's horizon, or which entered A's horizon at node B and originated k hops away. Let us denote this count by $D_{e,B,k}$.

2. Execution phase
    a. Each node A forwards an incoming non-duplicate query message originating from some node B inside A's horizon, or which entered A's horizon at node B and originated k hops away, over its incident edges e if the count $D_{e,B,k}$ does not exceed a predefined threshold.

We should emphasize that in order to avoid increasing the network traffic due to feedback messages, a single collective feedback message is returned to each upstream node at the end of the warm-up phase.

Table 3.   Groups for the Horizon+Hops criterion based on the example of Fig. 1.

Node in A's horizon and Hop	B 1	C 2	D 3	D 4	D 5	D 6	D 7	J 3	J 4
Groups formed by node A	B	C	D	E	F	G,H	I	J	K

4.   Random vs. small-world graphs

Two types of graphs have been mainly studied in the context of P2P systems. The first is random graphs which constitute the underlining topology in today's commercial P2P systems [7, 9]. The second type is small-world graphs which emerged in the modelling of social networks [4]. It has been demonstrated that P2P resource location algorithms could benefit from small-world properties. If the benefit proves to be substantial then the node connection protocol in P2P systems could be modified so that small-world properties are intentionally incorporated in their network topologies.

In random graphs each node is randomly connected to a number of other nodes equal to its degree. Random graphs have small diameter and small average diameter. The diameter of a graph is the length (number of hops for unweighted graphs) of the longest among the shortest paths that connect any pair of nodes. The average diameter of a graph is the average of all longest shortest paths from any node to any other node.

A clustered graph is a graph that contains densely connected "neighborhoods" of nodes, while nodes that lie in different neighborhoods are more loosely connected. A metric that captures the degree of clustering that graphs exhibit is the clustering coefficient. Given a graph G, the clustering coefficient of a node A in G is defined as the ratio of the number of edges that exist between the neighbors of A over the maximum number of edges that can exist between its neighbors (which equals to $k(k-1)$ for k neighbors). The clustering coefficient of a graph G is the average of the clustering coefficients of all its nodes. Clustered graphs have, in general, higher diameter and higher average diameter than their random counterparts with about the same number of nodes and degree.

A small-world graph is a graph with high clustering coefficient yet low average diameter. The small-world graphs we use in our experiments are constructed according to the Strogatz-Watts model [4]. Initially, a regular, clustered graph of N nodes is constructed as follows: each node is assigned a unique identifier from 0 to $N-1$. Two nodes are connected if their identity difference is less than or equal to k (in $modN$ arithmetic). Subsequently, each edge of the graph is rewired to a random node according to a given rewiring probability p. If the rewiring probability of edges is relatively small, a small-world graph

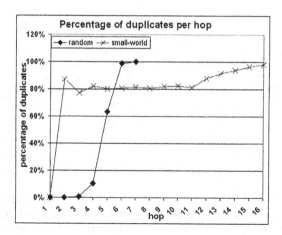

Figure 2. Percentage of duplicate messages per hop in random and small-world graphs.

is produced (high clustering coefficient and small average diameter). As the rewiring probability increases the graph becomes more random (the clustering coefficient decreases). For rewiring probability $p = 1$, all graph edges are rewired to random nodes, and this results in a random graph.

The clustering coefficient of each graph is normalized with respect to the maximum clustering coefficient of a graph with the same number of nodes and average degree. In what follows, when we refer to the clustering coefficient of a graph with N nodes and average degree d, denoted by CC, we refer to the percentage of its clustering coefficient over the maximum clustering coefficient of a graph with the same number of nodes and average degree. The maximum clustering coefficient of a graph with N nodes and average degree d is the clustering coefficient of the clustered graph defined according to the Strogatz-Watts model, before any edge rewiring takes place.

Fig. 2 shows the percentage of duplicates messages generated per hop over the messages generated on that hop on a random and on a small-world graph of 2000 nodes and average degree 6. We can see from this figure that in a random graph there are very few duplicate messages in the first few hops (1-4), while almost all messages in the last hops (6-7) are duplicates. On the contrary, in small-world graphs duplicate messages appear from the first hops and their percentage remains almost constant till the last hops.

5. Experimental results on static graphs

Our evaluation study was performed using sP2Ps (simple P2P simulator) developed at our lab. The experiments were conducted on graphs with 2000 nodes and average degree of 6. The clustering coefficient (CC) ranged from 0.0001 to 0.6, which is the maximum clustering coefficient of a graph with $N =$

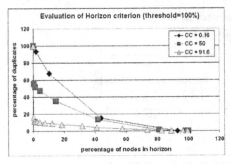
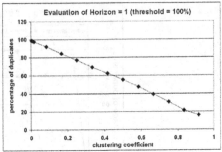

Figure 3. Percentage of duplicates as a function of the percentage of graph nodes in the horizon for three graphs with clustering coefficients 0.16, 50, and 91.6, and threshold value 100%.

Figure 4. Percentage of duplicates as a function of the clustering coefficient for horizon value 1 and threshold value 100%.

2000 and $d = 6$. We shall refer to CC values from now on, as percentages of that max value. We conducted experiments for different values of the algorithm's parameters. The horizon value varied from 0 (were practically the horizon criterion is not used) up to the diameter of the graph. Furthermore, we used two different threshold values, namely 75% and 100%, to select the connections over which messages are forwarded. The TTL value is set to the diameter of the graph.

The efficiency of our algorithm is evaluated based on two metrics: (1) the percentage of duplicates sent by the algorithm, compared to the naive flooding and (2) the network coverage defined as the percentage of network nodes reached by the query. Thus, the lower the duplicates percentage and the higher the coverage percentage is, the better. Notice that a threshold value of 100% indicates that messages originating from the nodes of a group are not forwarded only over edges that produce exclusively (100%) duplicates for all nodes of that group during the warm-up phase. In this case we do not experience any loss in network coverage, but the efficiency of the algorithm in duplicate elimination could be limited. In all experiments on static graphs, the warm-up phase included one flooding from each node. In the execution phase, during which the feedback-based algorithm is applied, again one flooding is performed from each node in order to gather the results of the simulation experiment.

In Figs 3-6 we can see the experimental results for the feedback-based algorithm with the horizon criterion. In Fig. 3 we can see the percentage of duplicates produced as a function of the percentage of graph nodes in the horizon for three graphs (random with $CC = 0.16$, clustered with $CC = 50$, and small-world with $CC = 91.6$) and for threshold value 100%, which means that there is no loss in network coverage. We can deduce from this figure that

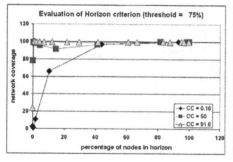

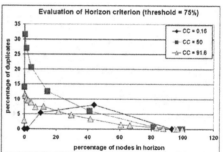

Figure 5. Network coverage as a function of the percentage of graph nodes in the horizon for three graphs with clustering coefficients 0.16, 50, and 91.6 and threshold 75%.

Figure 6. Percentage of duplicates as a function of the percentage of graph nodes in the horizon for three graphs with clustering coefficients 0.16, 50, and 91.6 and threshold 75%.

the efficiency of this algorithm is high for clustered graphs and increases with the percentage of graph nodes in the horizon. Notice that in clustered graphs, with a small horizon value a larger percentage of the graph is in the horizon as compared to random graphs. In Fig. 4 we plot the percentage of duplicates produced by the algorithm as a function of the clustering coefficient for horizon value 1 and threshold 100%. We can see that even for such a small horizon value the efficiency of the algorithm increases linearly with the clustering coefficient of the graph. We can thus conclude that the feedback-based algorithm with the horizon criterion is efficient for clustered and small-world graphs.

Even if the percentage of graph nodes in the horizon decreases, in case the graph size increases and the horizon value remains constant, the efficiency of the algorithm will remain unchanged, because in clustered graphs the clustering coefficient does change significantly with the graph size. Thus, the horizon criterion is scalable for clustered graphs. In contrast, in random graphs, in order to maintain the same efficiency as the graph size increases, one would need to increase the horizon value, in order to maintain the same percentage of graph nodes in the horizon. Thus the horizon criterion is not scalable on random graphs.

Figs 5 and 6 show the efficiency of the algorithm with the horizon criterion in duplicate elimination for threshold 75%. We can see from these figures that the algorithm is very efficient on clustered graphs. From the same figures we can see that with this threshold value in random graphs ($CC = 0.16$) most duplicate messages are eliminated but there is loss in network coverage. Thus, even if we lower the threshold value, the horizon criterion does not work well for random graphs.

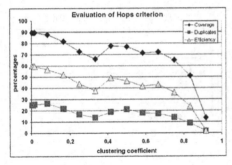

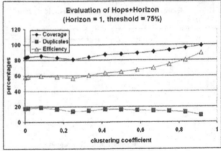

Figure 7.   Network coverage, percentage of duplicates, and efficiency of the algorithm with the hops criterion as a function of the clustering coefficient.

Figure 8.   Network coverage, percentage of duplicates, and efficiency of the algorithm with the horizon+hops criterion as a function of the clustering coefficient.

In Fig. 7 we can see the experimental results for the algorithm with the hops criterion while varying the clustering coefficient. We can see in this figure that the hops criterion is very efficient in duplicate elimination, while maintaining high network coverage, for graphs with small clustering coefficient. This means that this criterion exhibits very good behavior on random graphs. As the clustering coefficient increases, the performance of the algorithm with the hops criterion decreases. This behavior can be easily explained from Fig. 2, where the percentage of duplicates per hop is plotted for random and small-world graphs. We can see from this figure that in random graphs, the small hops produce very few duplicates, while large hops produce too many. Thus, based on the hops criterion only, we were able to eliminate a large percentage of duplicates without greatly sacrificing network coverage.

As mentioned before, the hops criterion works better for random graphs. In case the graph size increases, the number of hops also increases (recall that the diameter of a random graph with N nodes and average degree d is $log(N)/log(d)$). Thus, the hops criterion is scalable on random graphs.

In Fig. 8, we see the efficiency of the algorithm for the horizon+hops criterion. As we can see from this figure this combination of criteria constitutes the feedback based algorithm efficient in graphs with all clustering coefficients, random and small-world. In Fig. 8, three different metrics are plotted, the network coverage, the percentage of duplicates, and the efficiency as a function of the clustering coefficient of the graph. If we denote the duplicate elimination by D and the network coverage by C, the efficiency of the algorithm is defined as $C^2 D$. We can see that for any clustering coefficient the network coverage is always above 80%, while the percentage of duplicate messages not eliminated is always less than 20%. This behavior is achieved for random and small-world graphs for horizon value of only 1. Thus the horizon+hops criterion is scalable on all types of graphs.

6. Experimental results on dynamic graphs

In what follows, we introduce dynamic changes to the graph, meaning that a graph node can leave and some other node can enter the graph, and we monitor how these changes influence the algorithm's efficiency. We introduced a new parameter to our experiments in order to capture the rate of graph change. This parameter measures in query-floods the lifetime of a node in the graph. A graph rate change of r means that each node will initiate, on the average, r query-floods before leaving the network. Insertion of new nodes is performed so as to preserve the clustering coefficient of the graph.

We also introduce a dynamic way to determine when the warm-up phase can terminate, meaning that we have collected enough measurements. The warm-up phase for a group of nodes terminates after the percentage of duplicates seen on an edge for messages originating from nodes of the group stops to oscillate significantly. More specifically, the warm-up phase terminates on an edge for a group of nodes, if in each of the last 20 rounds the change in the count (percentage of the number of duplicates seen on that edge for messages originating from nodes of the that group) was smaller that 2% and the total change over the last 20 rounds was smaller that 1%.

We perform experiments for random graphs and for small-world graphs with clustering coefficient $CC = 33$ and $CC = 84$. For each of these graphs, the value of the change rate equals 0 (static graph), 1, 50, and 200. A change rate of 200 indicates that each node will make 200 query-floods before leaving the network, which is a reasonable assumption for Gnutella 2 [7]. This is because each Ultrapeer contains, on the average, 30 leaves. A leaf node has in general much smaller average lifetime than an Ultrapeer, which means that each Ultrapeer will "see" more than 30 unique leaves in its lifetime. If we assume that each leaf node will send one query through the Ultrapeer, this explains the fact that real-world measures with an Ultrapeer show that each Ultrapeer sends about 100 queries per hour. For each of these graphs and change rates, we run experiments with the following Horizon values: Horizon values 1 and 2 for random graphs and for small-world graphs with $CC = 33$, and Horizon values 1 and 4 for small-world graphs with $CC = 84$.

We performed two experiments with the same horizon value, one using the hops criterion and one without the hops criterion. The threshold value was set to 75%. Each experiment performed 25*2000 floods. The difference between the values "0 wo act. threshold" and "0 with act. threshold" in the x axis in Figs 9 and 10 indicates that in both cases the change rate is 0 (static graph), but in the first case, the numbers are taken from the experiments described in the

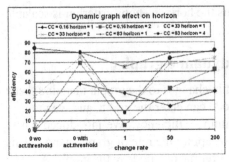

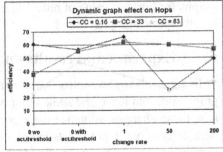

Figure 9. Performance of the algorithm on a dynamic graph for the horizon criterion.

Figure 10. Performance of the algorithm on a dynamic graph for the hops criterion.

previous section, while in the second case the activation threshold was used to terminate the warm-up phase. This enables us to clearly see the benefit of the activation threshold.

Fig. 9 shows how the algorithm performs on dynamic graphs for the horizon criterion. We should note that the use of the activation threshold increases the efficiency of the algorithm significantly. This happens because nodes gradually start eliminating traffic for certain groups of nodes instead of all of them starting eliminating duplicates for all groups simultaneously. We can see that the efficiency of the algorithm decreases when the change rate is 1. The reason for this is not that the measurements for each group quickly become stale, but rather because each node needs some warm-up period to learn the topology of the network. A certain amount of traffic needs to be "seen" by any node, to make the necessary measurements. If that time is a large fraction of the node's lifetime, it means that it will spend most of its time measuring instead of regulating traffic according to the measurements. Finally and most importantly, we can see that the results for a change rate of 200 are the same as those of a change rate of 0 with activation threshold, which shows that, given that the warm-up phase is shorter than the time during which the nodes use the algorithm (execution phase), the changes of the graph do not affect the algorithm's efficiency.

In Fig. 10 we can see that the activation threshold is beneficial to the algorithm with the hops criterion. Furthermore, from the same figure, it becomes clear that the efficiency of the feedback-based algorithm with the hops criterion is not greatly affected by the dynamic changes in the graph. We should however point out that it seems to slightly affect the efficiency of the algorithm in highly clustered graphs.

7. Conclusions

We presented the feedback-based algorithm, an innovative method which reduces significantly the number of duplicates produced by flooding while maintaining high network coverage. The algorithm monitors the percentage of duplicates on each connection during a warm-up phase, and directs traffic to connections that do not produce excessive number of duplicates during the execution phase. In order for this approach to work, each network node groups together the rest of the nodes according to some criteria, so that nodes that produce many duplicates on its incident edges are in different groups than those that produce only few duplicates. The efficiency of the algorithm was demonstrated through extensive simulation on random and small-world graphs. The experiments involved graphs of 2000 nodes. The feedback-based algorithm was shown to reduce to less than 20% the number of duplicates of flooding while conserving network coverage above 80%. The memory requirements in each node are much less compared to the algorithm that constructs shortest paths trees from each network node. The efficiency of our algorithm was demonstrated on static and dynamic graphs.

Acknowledgments

This research work was carried out under the FP6 NoE CoreGRID funded by the EC (IST-2002-004265) and was supported by project SecSPeer (GGET USA-031) funded by the Greek Secreteriat for Research and Technology.

References

[1] Y. Chawathe, S. Ratnasamy, and L. Breslau. Making Gnutella-like P2P Systems Scalable. *ACM SIGCOMM*, 2003.

[2] A. Crespo and H. Garcia-Molina. Routing Indices for Peer-to-Peer Systems. *Int. Conf. Distributed Comp. Systems*, 2002.

[3] A. Crespo and H. Garcia-Molina. Semantic Overlay Networks for P2P Systems. 2002.

[4] Duncan, J. Watts, and S. H. Strongatz. Collective Dynamics of Small-world Networks. *Nature*, **393**:440-442, 1998.

[5] C. Gkantsidis, M. Mihail, and A.Saberi. Hybrid Search Schemes for Unstructured Peer-to-Peer Networks. *IEEE INFOCOM*, 2005.

[6] Q. Lv, P. Cao, E. Cohen, K. Li, and S. Shenker. Search and Replication in Unstructured Peer-to-Peer Networks. *Int. ACM Conf. Supercomputing*, 2002.

[7] R. Manfredi and T. Klingberg. Gnutella 0.6 Specification, http://rfc-gnutella.sourceforge.net/src/rfc-0.6-draft.html

[8] M. Ripenau, I. Foster, A. Iamnitchi, and A. Rogers. UMM: A Dynamically Adaptive, Unstructured, Multicast Overlay. In *Service Management and Self-Organization in IP-based Networks*, Dagstuhl Seminar Proceedings, 2005.

[9] Sharman Industries. Kazaa, http://www.kazaa.com

[10] K. Sripanidkulchai, B. Maggs, and H. Zhang. Efficient Content Location using Interest-Based Locality in Peer-to-Peer Systems. *IEEE INFOCOM*, 2003.

[11] D. Tsoumakos and N. Roussopoulos. A Comparison of Peer-to-Peer Search Methods. *Int. Workshop on the Web and Databases*, 2003.

[12] Z. Zhuang, Y. Liu, L. Xiao, and L.M. Ni. Hybrid Periodical Flooding in Unstructured Peer-to-Peer Networks. *Int.l Conf. Parallel Computing*, 2003.

FAULT-INJECTION AND DEPENDABILITY BENCHMARKING FOR GRID COMPUTING MIDDLEWARE

William Hoarau and Sébastien Tixeuil
LRI-CNRS 8623 & INRIA Grand Large,
Université Paris Sud XI, France
hoarau@lri.fr
tixeuil@lri.fr

Luis Silva
Dep. Engenharia Informï¿½ica, University of Coimbra,
Polo II, 3030-Coimbra, Portugal
luis@dei.uc.pt

Abstract   We present the state-of-the-art about fault-injection and dependability bench-marking and we explain the importance of this kind of tools for dependability assessment of Grid-based applications and Grid middleware. Our emphasis goes to the FAIL-FCI fault-injection software that has been de-veloped in INRIA Grand Large, and a benchmark tool called QUAKE that was developed by the University of Coimbra. We present some experimental results taken with these two tools.

Keywords: Fault-injection, dependability benchmarking, grid middleware.

1.   Introduction

One of the topics of paramount importance in the development of Grid middleware is the impact of faults since their probability of occurrence in a Grid infrastructure and in large-scale distributed system is actually very high. So it is mandatory that Grid middleware should be itself reliable and should provide a comprehensive support for fault-tolerance mechanisms, like failure-detection, checkpointing-recovery, replication, software rejuvenation, component-based reconfiguration, among others. One of the techniques to evaluate the effectiveness of those fault-tolerance mechanisms and the reliability level of the Grid middleware it to make use of some fault-injection tool and robustness tester to conduct some experimental assessment of the dependability metrics of the target system. Dependability benchmarking must provide a uniform, repeatable and cost-effective way of performing experiments in different systems, mechanisms or components [1]. Those three metrics can be achieved with the development of software tools that will be used in the process and in the definition of the dependability benchmark. In this paper we present two tools that have been developed by the two partners of WP4 from CoreGrid (INRIA and Univ. Coimbra) and we explain some of our on-going projects with these tools. The ultimate goal of our common work is to provide some contributions for the definition of a dependability-benchmark for Grid computing and to provide a set of tools and techniques that can be used by the community.

2.   Related Works

2.1   Fault-injection

When considering solutions for software fault injection in distributed systems, there are several important parameters to consider. The main criteria is the usability of the fault injection platform. If it is more difficult to write fault scenarios than to actually write the tested applications, those fault scenarios are likely to be dropped from the set of performed tests. The issues in testing component-based distributed systems have already been described and methodology for testing components and systems has already been proposed [2–3]. However, testing for fault tolerance remains a challeng-ing issue. Indeed, in available systems, the fault-recovery code is rarely executed in the test-bed as faults rarely get triggered. As the ability of a system to perform well in the presence of faults depends on the correctness of the fault-recovery code, it is man-datory to actually test this code. Testing based on fault-injection can be used to test for fault-tolerance by injecting faults into a system under test and observing its behavior. The most obvious point is that simple tests (*e.g.* every few minutes or so, a randomly chosen machine crashes) should be simple to write and deploy. On the other hand, it should be possible to inject faults for very specific cases (*e.g.* in a particular global state of the application), even if it requires a better understanding of the tested application. Also, decoupling the fault injection platform from the tested application is a desirable property, as different groups can concentrate on different aspects of fault-tolerance. Decoupling requires that no source code modification of the tested application should be necessary to inject faults. Finally, to properly evaluate a distributed application in the context of faults, the impact of the fault injection platform should be kept low, even if the number of machines is high. Of course, the impact is doomed to increase with the complexity of the fault scenario, *e.g.* when every action of every processor is likely to trigger a fault action, injecting those faults will induce an over-head that is certainly not negligible. Table 1 captures the main differences between the main solutions for distributed fault injection relatively to those criteria.

Table 1.   Comparison of Faul-injection Tools

Criteria	ORCHESTRA [4]	NFTAPE [5]	LOKI [6]	FAIL-FCI
High Expressiveness	no	yes	no	yes
High-level Language	no	no	no	yes
No Source Code Modification	yes	no	no	yes
Scalability	yes	no	yes	yes
Probabilistic Scenario	yes	yes	no	yes
Global-state-based Injection	no	yes	yes	yes

2.2   Dependability benchmarking

The idea of dependability benchmarking is now a hot-topic of research and there are already several publications in the literature. The components of a dependability benchmark have been defined in [1]. In [10] is proposed a dependability benchmark for transactional systems (DBench-OLTP). Another dependability benchmark for transactional systems is proposed in [11]. Both benchmarks adopted the workload from the TPC-C performance benchmark. While the system presented in [10] used software-based faults the work described on [11] considered a fault-load based on hardware faults. In [12] the authors present a proposal for the classification of dependability in transactional database systems [12]. A dependability benchmark for operating systems was proposed by [13]. That benchmark was targeted for the study of the operating system robustness in the scenario of faulty applications. Another study about the behavior of the operating system in the presence of software faults in OS components was presented in [14]. The research presented in [15] addresses the impact of human errors in system dependability. In [16] is presented a methodology to evaluate human-assisted failure-recovery tools and processes in server systems. Another work was presented in [17] that focus on the availability benchmarking of computer systems. Research work at Sun Microsystems defined a high-level framework that is targeted to availability benchmarking [18]. Within the scope of that framework, they have developed two benchmarks: one that addresses specific aspects of a system's robustness on handling maintenance events such as the replacement of a failed hard-ware component or the installation of software patch [19], and another benchmark that is related to system recovery [20].

At IBM, the Autonomic Computing initiative is also developing benchmarks to quantify the autonomic capability of a system [21]. In that paper they have discussed the requirements of benchmarks to assess the self-* properties of a system and they proposed a set of metrics for evaluation. In [22] is presented a further discussion about benchmarking the autonomic capabilities of a system. The authors present the main challenges and pitfalls. In [23] is presented an interesting approach to conduct bench-marking of the configuration complexity. A benchmark for assessing the self-healing capabilities of a potential autonomic system was presented in [24]. In [25] the authors present a dependability benchmark for Web-Servers (Web-DB). This tool used the experimental setup, the workload and the performance measures specified in the SPECWeb99 performance benchmark.

The dependability benchmark tool that is presented in this paper is targeted to Grid and Web-Services.

3. Our proposal

3.1 FAIL-FCI

FAIL-FCI [9] is a recently developed tool from INRIA. First, FAIL (for FAult In-jection Language) is a language that permits to easily described fault scenarios. Second, FCI (for FAIL Cluster Implementation) is a distributed fault injection platform whose input language for describing fault scenarios is FAIL. Both components are developed as part of the Grid eXplorer project [7] which aims at emulating large-scale networks on smaller clusters or grids. The FAIL language allows defining fault scenarios. A scenario describes, using a high-level abstract language, state machines which model fault occurrences. The FAIL language also describes the association between these state machines and a computer (or a group of computers) in the network. The FCI platform is composed of several building blocks:

1 **The FCI compiler**: The fault scenarios written in FAIL are pre-compiled by the FCI compiler which generates C++ source files and default configuration files.

2 **The FCI library**: The files generated by the FCI compiler are bundled with the FCI library into several archives, and then distributed across the network to the target machines according to the user-defined configuration files. Both the FCI compiler generated files and the FCI library files are provided as source code archives, to enable support for heterogeneous clusters.

3 **The FCI daemon**: The source files that have been distributed to the target machines are then extracted and compiled to generate specific executable files for every computer in the system. Those executables are referred to as the FCI daemons. When the experiment begins, the distributed application to be tested is executed through the FCI daemon installed on every computer, to allow its instrumentation and its handling according to the fault scenario.

The approach is based on the use of a software debugger. Like the Mantis parallel debugger [8], FCI communicates to and from gdb (the Free Software Foundation's portable sequential debugging environment) through Unix pipes. But contrary to Mantis approach, communications with the debugger must be kept to a minimum to guarantee low overhead of the fault injection platform (in our approach, the debugger is only used to trigger and inject software faults). The tested application can be interrupted when it calls a particular function or upon executing a particular line of its source code. Its execution can be resumed depending on the considered fault scenario.

With FCI, every physical machine is associated to a fault injection daemon. The fault scenario is described in a high-level language and compiled to obtain a C++ code which will be distributed on the machines participating to the experiment. This C++ code is compiled on every machine to generate the fault injection daemon. Once this preliminary task has been performed, the experience is then ready to be launched. The daemon associated to a particular computer consists in:

1 a state machine implementing the fault scenario,

2 a module for communicating with the other daemons (e.g. to inject faults based on a global state of the system),

3 a module for time-management (e.g. to allow time-based fault injection),

4 a module to instrument the tested application (by driving the debugger), and

5 a module for managing events (to trigger faults).

FCI is thus a Debugger-based Fault Injector because the injection of faults and the instrumentation of the tested application is made using a debugger. This makes it possible not to have to modify the source code of the tested application, while enabling the possibility of injecting arbitrary faults (modification of the program counter or the local variables to simulate a buffer overflow attack, etc.). From the user point of view, it is sufficient to specify a fault scenario written in FAIL to define an experiment. The source code of the fault injection daemons is automatically generated. These daemons communicate between them explicitly according to the user-defined scenario. This allows the injection of faults based either on a global state of the system or on more complex mechanisms involving several machines (*e.g.* a cascading fault injection). In addition, the fully distributed architecture of the FCI daemons makes it scalable, which is necessary in the context of emulating large-scale distributed systems. FCI daemons have two operating modes: a random mode and a deterministic mode. These two modes allow fault injection based on a probabilistic fault scenario (for the first case) or based on a deterministic and reproducible fault scenario (for the second case). Using a debugger to trigger faults also permits to limit the intrusion of the fault injector during the experiment. Indeed, the debugger places breakpoints which correspond to the user-defined fault scenario and then runs the tested application. As long as no breakpoint is reached the application runs normally and the debugger remains inactive.

3.2   QUAKE: A Dependability Benchmark Tool for Grid Services

QUAKE is a benchmark tool that can be used to study the dependability properties of Grid and Web-Services.

3.2.1   Experimental Setup and Benchmark Procedure.

The QUAKE tool is composed by the following components presented in Figure 3.2.1. The main components are the Benchmark Management System (BMS) and the System Under Test (SUT). The SUT consists of a SOAP server running some Web/Grid service. From the point of view of the benchmark the SUT corresponds to a web-based application server, a SOAP router and a web-service. That web-service will execute under some workload, and optionally will be affected by some fault-load. There are several client machines that invoke requests in the server using SOAP-XML requests. All the machines in the infrastructure are clock-synchronized using NTP. The application under test is not limited to a SOAP-based application: in fact, the benchmark infrastructure can also be used with other examples of client-server applications that use other different middleware technologies.

The Benchmark Management System (BMS) is a collection of software tools that allows the automatic execution of the benchmark. It includes a module for the definition of the benchmark, a set of procedures and rules, definition of the workload that will be produced in the SUT, a module that collects all the benchmark results and produces some results that are expressed as a set of dependability metrics. The BMS system may activate a set of clients (running in separate machines) that inject the defined workload in the SUT by making SOAP requests to the Web Service. The execution of the client machines is timely synchronized and all the partial results collected by each individual client are merged into a global set of results that generated the final assessment of the dependability metrics. The BMS system includes a reporting tool that presents the final results in a readable and graphic format. The results generated by each benchmark run are expressed as throughput-over-time (requests-per-second in a time axis), the total turnaround time of the execution, the average latency, the functionality of the services, the occurrence of failures in the Web-Service, the characterization of those failures (crash, hang, zombie-server), the correctness of the final results and the failure scenarios that are observed at the client machines (explicit SOAP error messages or time-outs).

From the side of the SUT system, there are four modules that also make part of the QUAKE benchmark tool: a fault-load injector, a configuration manager, a collector of logs with the benchmark results and a watchdog of the SUT system. The configuration manager helps in the definition of the configuration parameters of the SUT middleware. It is absolutely that the configuration parameters may have a considerable impact in the robustness of the SUT system. By changing those parameters in different runs of the benchmark it allow us to assess the impact of those parameters in the re-sults expressed as dependability metrics.

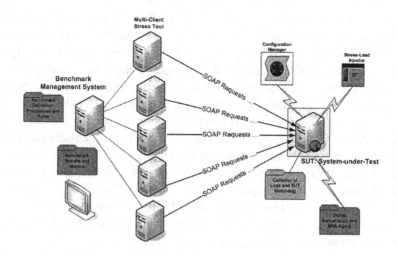

Figure 1. Experimental setup of the QUAKE tool.

The SUT system should also be installed with a module to collect raw data from the benchmark execution. This log data will be then sent to the BMS server that will merge and compare with the data collected from the client machines. The final module is a SUT-Watchdog that detects when a SUT system crashes or hangs when the benchmark is executing. When a crash or hang is detected the watchdog generates a restart of the SUT system and associated applications, thereby allowing an automatic execution of the benchmark runs without user intervention.

There is another external module - the Online Surveillance System - that is respon-sible for the online monitoring of some key parameters that may indicate the occurrence of software aging, namely: throughput (requests-per-second), average response time of requests and the memory usage at the server under test.

4.   Experimental Results

4.1   Fault Injection

We conducted a series of tests to validate our approach by injecting faults on actual distributed applications. We chose the XtremWeb platform [14] to perform our experiments. XtremWeb is a general purpose platform that can be used for high performance distributed calculus. The original XtremWeb application is written in Java, but we used FCI on the C++ version of the software, that is meant to be the most efficient version. XtremWeb participants are usually divided according to the kind of jobs they are doing: the dispatcher distributes jobs that are to be executed by the clients, each client querying and performing the actual work. The XtremWeb application that was run on the platform is POV-Ray, which creates three-dimensional, photo-realistic images using a rendering technique called raytracing. We used the same cluster of computers as in the FCI overhead experiment, but only 35 cluster nodes were participating to the raytracing to the calculus. We considered the task of calculating the same picture twice. Calculating a POV-Ray picture runs as follows: first, the dispatcher divides the image to be calculated into parts, each to be computed by a client, then, after each client has computed its image portion and sent it back to the dispatcher, the dispatcher selects a simple client to collect parts of the image and aggregate them into a single final image, that is finally sent back to the dispatcher. With this application, we designed a fault scenario using FAIL. The dispatcher is run on Computer 1 and is not subject to faults (it simply waits for clients to connect and feeds them jobs). Then, XtremWeb clients are run on the remaining 34 computers and are subject to fault events. The fault scenario that is run on every client is as follows:

1 Every 5 seconds, an XtremWeb client is likely to crash with probability x,

2 After a crash, every 5 seconds, a client may restart with probability 0.3,

3 A client may crash only once.

We carried out this test using various values for x (0.1, 0.3, 0.5, 0.7, and 0.9), and the experiment results are summarized in Figure 4.1. In that Figure, "Added 1" and "Added 2" correspond to the time when the dispatcher collected all image parts from all con-cerned clients for the first and second images, respectively. "Completed 1" and "Completed 2" correspond to the time when the dispatcher received the final first and second images, respectively. Also, the test for failure probability 0 serves as a reference test.

The outcome of these fault injections is consistent with what could be expected. First, for any fault appearance probability, the time needed to complete the second image is less than twice the time to complete the second image. This is due to our scenario where a machine may not fail twice, so that if it failed while calculating the first image and recovered (this happens with probability 0.3), it may not fail again while calculating the second image. When the probability x of fault appearance is low (under 0.5), the execution time of the image parts calculation is kept low, since clients are only responsible for a small percentage of the global result, so that the load of crashed clients can be carried out by someone else quickly. However, the full image completion time is high, because if a node crashes in that part, it is the only one responsible for carrying out the final image, so its failure has high impact. When the probability of fault appearance is high (more than 0.5), the execution time of the image parts calculation is very high since a large number of clients are likely to crash in this process. The final image completion time is high too, but the overhead of this part is not as high as when the fault appearance probability is low, simply because most faults occurred while calculating the images, so most clients will not fail again in the last phase of the calculus.

A more comprehensive study by using FAIL-FCI with 170 machines was presented in [26]. That study shows some insights about the scalability of this fault-injection tool, which allows us to consider its use in large-scale Grid applications.

4.2 Dependability Benchmarking

In this section we present some experimental results taken with the QUAKE benchmark. To easily evaluate the correctness of the application after the execution of several benchmark runs we have developed a SOAP service that make access to a data-base and provide a simulated online e-banking application. This way we can easily check at the end of each run if the database contains

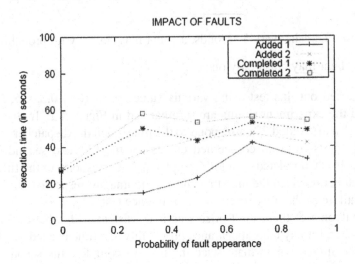

Figure 2.   FCI fault-injection results

corrected data and the at-most-once semantics has been followed in the execution of the SOAP service. This was the synthetic application that has been used in the experiments that will be described herein. Other Web-Services and Grid Services are currently under assessment by the QUAKE tool.

The testing infrastructure was composed by a cluster with 12 machines running Linux and Java 1.4. The SOAP service was running on a central node (dual-processor) of the cluster and we have use a Tomcat-AXIS server running on top of Linux. As far as we know, most of the Java-based Web-Services and Grid-Services are currently using Tomcat-Axis so we were interested to evaluate the robustness of this middleware.

From those 12 machines, one was running the SUT application, other was dedicated to the BMS system, and the remaining 10 machines were running instances of the clients that were in practice the workload generators. For these results herein presented we have chosen the following parameters:

1 Default configuration parameters of the JVM, Tomcat and Axis.

2 The Tomcat JVM was running with the implicit Java garbage-collector.

3 In the overall, the client machines will send 1 million of SOAP requests.

4 The request will follow the "continuous-burst" distribution.

5 There are no retransmission of SOAP requests when a client gets a response error. This way there are no repeated messages and the "at-most-once" semantics is not violated;

6 No fault-load is introduced in the SUT system. We ran the SOAP services in a dedicated server and all the operating system resources were available to the application. This means we are testing a Web-Service in a normal environment with any perturbations at the system-level.

The results of the first experiment are presented in Figure 4.2. The Figure presents the number of requests-per-second that is served by the SOAP service over the time axis. In this benchmark run, the client machines sent 1 million of requests to the SOAP service running in a dedicated machine with a dual-processor. We used the default configuration of Tomcat/Axis that allocates a JVM with 64Mb. This first run produced impressive results: this test took 31 minutes, and only 73.740 of the 1 million requests were processed (about 7.37% of the total). The remaining requests were not processed by the server due to "out of memory". It was observed that the reason for this failure was directly related with the occurrence of memory leaks in the Tomcat/Axis middleware.

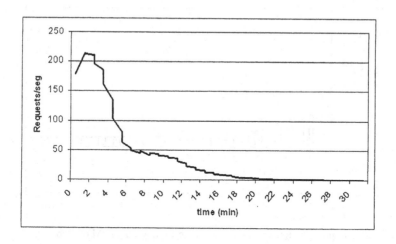

Figure 3.   Results for the first test run, with default-configuration

More interesting that this result is the type of failure that happened in the SUT server: the Tomcat processes did not crashed, they were left in a completely hang status that even the shutdown command of Tomcat was not able to restart the server. It was necessary to kill explicitly all the processes and restart the Tomcat server. This would be that type of failures that would require a human intervention in a production system. These failures are very expensive to maintain since they require human intervention. When the systems start growing in complexity the management will be almost virtually impossible [16]. The vision for autonomic computing defended by IBM researchers is entirely shared by the authors of this paper that recognize the strategic importance for creating self-healing Grid Services.

From the first test run was clear that the SOAP server was under-configured in terms of memory for the selected workload. So, in the second test run the memory of the Tomcat JVM was increased from 64Mb up to 1Gb. The results are presented in Figure 3. This time the SOAP server did not crash and executed all the 1 million requests. The total turnaround the execution was 737 minutes. Those peaks that show up in the graphic have to due with the execution of the garbage collector at the server side. We can conclude from the graphic that the SOAP service is maintained running but the throughput (requests-per-second) drops heavily over time, which ends in the observation: the SOAP service does not crash, but it runs slower and slower over time.

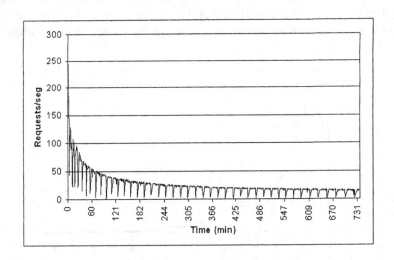

Figure 4.   Results for the second test run, with a JVM of 1Gb.

Once again the reason for this performance drop-out has to due with memory leakage in the SOAP middleware. One point of concern that we get even in this configuration scenario is the sharp decrease in the QOS level of the SOAP service: at the beginning it was able to sustain about 230 requests-per-second. At the end of the test run the throughput was less than 20 requests-per-second, so 10% of the initial throughput. This observation led us to think: how can we improve the throughput level of the SOAP service and maintain it at acceptable levels? How can we provide some self-healing mechanisms to this SOAP server? How can we prevent the SOAP server to fail and be left in a hang-status?

With these questions in mind we start thinking about applying some software-rejuvenation technique to increase the throughput of that SOAP service. And the decision was to implement a preventive rebooting to avoid a zombie crash (hang status) of the server but also to avoid that the server would fall down into a lower level of throughput: when the throughput level decrease down to 20% of the initial throughput the watchdog produced a restart of the Tomcat/Axis server. This restart was done in a clean way: the SOAP server closed the service to new requests and all the on-going requests were finished before applying the shutdown-restart to the Tomcat. At the end of the test run the correctness of the application was successfully verified.

In Figure 4 we present the results of this test run. Those deep peaks in the through-put level correspond to a restart event. Every shutdown-restart of the Tomcat took between 14 to 16 seconds, in average.

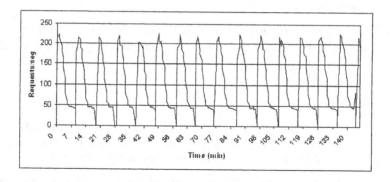

Figure 5. Results for the fourth test run with a preventive shutdown of the server

At first sight it seems that this technique would not produce interesting results, since it creates some seconds of downtime at the SOAP server. As can be seen in the Figure there was 15 preventive restarts and this may had resulted in 225 second of downtime in the overall. So this technique is not good from the point of view of availability metric. But the result obtained in the turnaround metric is quite interesting: the total turnaround the test run was 146 minutes. This means the SOAP service was 5 times faster when compared with the second test run. It is clear that this "wise-reboot" technique is a potential technique to increase the sustained throughput level of the SOAP server and to avoid the zombie crashes of the server that would normally require human intervention.

There are more results taken with the QUAKE tool, but these small set of results is clear representative of the interest of using dependability benchmarking to assess the robustness of SOAP services and Grid services.

5.   Conclusions and Current Status

We reviewed several available tools for software fault injection and dependability benchmarking tools for grids. We emphasized on the FAIL-FCI fault injector developed by INRIA, and on the QUAKE dependability benchmark developed by the University of Coimbra. The FAIL-FCI tool has so far only provided preliminary results on desktop grid middleware (XtremWeb) and P2P middleware (the FreePastry Distributed Hash Table). These results permitted to identify quantitative failure points in both tested middleware, as well as qualitative issues concerning the failure recovery of XtremWeb. With the QUAKE tool we have been conducting the following experimental studies: *(a)* assess the reliability of different middleware for client/server applications; *(b)* study the reliability of OGSA-DAI and other tools from GT4.

Acknowledgments

This research work is carried out in part under the FP6 Network of Excellence Core-GRID funded by the European Commission (Contract IST-2002-004265).

References

[1] P.Koopman, H.Madeira. "Dependability Benchmarking & Prediction: A Grand Challenge Technology Problem", Proc. 1st IEEE Int. Workshop on Real-Time Mis-sion-Critical Systems: Grand Challenge Problems; Phoenix, Arizona, USA, Nov 1999

[2] S Ghosh, AP Mathur, "Issues in Testing Distributed Component-Based Systems", 1st Int. ICSE Workshop on Testing Distributed Component-Based Systems, 1999

[3] H. Madeira, M. Zenha Rela, F. Moreira, and J. G. Silva. "Rifle: A general purpose pin-level fault injector". In European Dependable Computing Conference, pages 199-216, 1994.

[4] S. Dawson, F. Jahanian, and T. Mitton. "Orchestra: A fault injection environment for distributed systems". Proc. 26th International Symposium on Fault-Tolerant Comput-ing (FTCS), pages 404-414, Sendai, Japan, June 1996.

[5] D.T. Stott and al. "Nftape: a framework for assessing dependability in distributed systems with lightweight fault injectors". In Proceedings of the IEEE International Computer Performance and Dependability Symposium, pages 91-100, March 2000.

[6] R. Chandra, R. M. Lefever, M. Cukier, and W. H. Sanders. "Loki: A state-driven fault injector for distributed systems". In In Proc. of the Int.Conf. on Dependable Systems and Networks, June 2000.

[7] http://www.lri.fr/fci/GdX

[8] S. Lumetta and D. Culler. "The Mantis parallel debugger". In Proceedings of SPDT'96: SIGMETRICS Symposium on Parallel and Distributed Tools, pages 118-126, Philadelphia, Pennsylvania, May 1996.

[9] William Hoarau, and Sébastien Tixeuil. "A language-driven tool for fault injection in distributed applications". In Proceedings of the IEEE/ACM Workshop GRID 2005, page to appear, Seattle, USA, November 2005.

[10] M. Vieira and H. Madeira, "A Dependability Benchmark for OLTP Application Environments", Proc. 29th Int. Conf. on Very Large Data Bases (VLDB-03), Berlin, Ger-many, 2003.

[11] K. Buchacker and O. Tschaeche, "TPC Benchmark-c version 5.2 Dependability Benchmark Extensions", http://www.faumachine.org/papers/tpcc-depend.pdf, 2003

[12] D. Wilson, B. Murphy and L. Spainhower. "Progress on Deining Standardized Classes of Computing the Dependability of Computer Systems", Proc. DSN 2002, Workshop on Dependability Benchmarking, Washington, D.C., USA, 2002.

[13] A. Kalakech, K. Kanoun, Y. Crouzet and A. Arlat. "Benchmarking the Dependability of Windows NT, 2000 and XP", Proc. Int. Conf. on Dependable Systems and Net-works (DSN 2004), Florence, Italy, 2004.

[14] J. Durães, H. Madeira, "Characterization of Operating Systems Behaviour in the Presence of Faulty Drivers Through Software Fault Emulation", in Proc. 2002 Pa-cific Rim Int. Symposium Dependable Computing (PRDC-2002), pp. 201-209, Tsu-kuba, Japan, 2002.

[15] A. Brown, L. Chung, and D. Patterson. "Including the Human Factor in Dependability Benchmarks", Proc. of the 2002 DSN Workshop on Dependability Benchmarking, Washington, D.C., June 2002.

[16] A. Brown, L. Chung, W. Kakes, C. Ling, D. A. Patterson, "Dependability Bench-marking of Human-Assisted Recovery Processes", Dependable Computing and Communications, DSN 2004, Florence, Italy, June, 2004

[17] A Brown and D. Patterson, "Towards Availability Benchmarks: A Case Study of Software RAID Systems", Proc. of the 2000 USENIX Annual Technical Conference, San Diego, CA, June 2000

[18] J. Zhu, J. Mauro, I. Pramanick. "R3 - A Framework for Availability Benchmarking", Proc. Int. Conf. on Dependable Systems and Networks (DSN 2003), USA, 2003.

[19] J Zhu, J. Mauro, and I. Pramanick, "Robustness Benchmarking for Hardware Main-tenance Events", in Proc. Int. Conf. on Dependable Systems and Networks (DSN 2003), pp. 115-122, San Francisco, CA, USA, IEEE CS Press, 2003.

[20] J. Mauro, J. Zhu, I. Pramanick. "The System Recovery Benchmark", in Proc. 2004 Pacific Rim Int. Symp. on Dependable Computing, Papeete, Polynesia, 2004.

[21] S. Lightstone, J. Hellerstein, W. Tetzlaff, P. Janson, E. Lassettre, C. Norton, B. Ra-jaraman and L. Spainhower. "Towards Benchmarking Autonomic Computing Matur-ity", 1st IEEE Conf. on Industrial Automatics (INDIN-2003), Canada, August 2003.

[22] A.Brown, J.Hellerstein, M.Hogstrom, T.Lau, S.Lightstone, P.Shum, M.P.Yost, "Benchmarking Autonomic Capabilities: Promises and Pitfalls", Proc. Int. Conf. on Autonomic Computing (ICAC'04), 2004

[23] A. Brown and J. Hellerstein, "An Approach to Benchmarking Configuration Com-plexity", Proc. of the 11th ACM SIGOPS European Workshop, Leuven, Belgium, September 2004

[24] A.Brown, C.Redlin. "Measuring the Effectiveness of Self-Healing Autonomic Sys-tems", Proc. 2nd Int. Conf. on Autonomic Computing (ICAC'05), 2005

[25] J. Durães, M. Vieira and H. Madeira. "Dependability Benchmarking of Web-Servers", Proc. 23rd International Conference, SAFECOMP 2004, Potsdam, Germany, Sep-tember 2004. Lecture Notes in Computer Science, Volume 3219/2004

[26] William Hoarau, Sébastien Tixeuil, and Fabien Vauchelles. "Easy fault injection and stress testing with FAIL-FCI". Technical Report 1421, Laboratoire de Recherche en Informatique, Université Paris Sud, October 2005

USER MANAGEMENT FOR VIRTUAL ORGANIZATIONS

Jiří Denemark, Luděk Matyska, Miroslav Ruda
Institute of Computer Science, Masaryk University, Botanická 68a,
602 00 Brno, Czech Republic
{jirka,ludek,ruda}@ics.muni.cz

Michal Jankowski, Norbert Meyer, Pawel Wolniewicz
Poznań Supercomputing and Networking Center,ul. Noskowskiego 10,
61-704 Poznań, Poland
{jankowsk,meyer,pawelw}@man.poznan.pl

Abstract   Scalable and fine-grained Grid authorization requires moving away from a grid-mapfile based access control and 1-to-1 mappings to individual OS user accounts. This is recognized and addressed to by virtual organization (VO) authorization services, e. g. VOMS/LCAS and CAS. They, however,do not address user OS account management and isolation/sandboxing requirements, such as flexible pooling of accounts while maintaining auditing records. This paper describes some existing systems for user management for VOs and provides a list of requirements for a new user management system on which our current research is focused on.

Keywords: user management, virtual organization, accounting, authorization, authentication, encapsulation, logging, LCAS, LCMAPS, VOMS, VUS, Perun

1. Introduction

The main aim of the user management system is controlled, secure access to grid resources. Security requires authentication of the user and authorization based on combined security policy from the resource provider and virtual organization of the user. The second important thing is the possibility of logging user activities for accounting and auditing and then gathering these data both by the resource provider and virtual organization of the user. From the user's point of view, an important feature is single sign-on.

The problem of user management is a non-trivial one in an environment that includes a bulk number of computing resources, data, and hundreds or even thousands of users participating in lots of virtual organizations. The complexity rises from the point of view of time required for administration tasks and automation of these tasks. There are many solutions that attempt to fulfill these basic requirements and solve the mentioned problem, but none of them, to the best of our knowledge, solve the problem in a complex and satisfactory way.

2. Definitions

Virtual organization (VO) is a set of individuals and/or institutions that allows its members to share resources in a controlled manner, so that they may collaborate to achieve a shared goal [1].

We assume that virtual organizations may form hierarchies. The hierarchy of VO is useful for user management on the VO side (delegation of administrative burden to sub-organization in case of big organizations) and accounting (sub-organizations may refer to real institutions and departments who are responsible for paying the bills). The hierarchy forms a Directed Acyclic Graph (DAG) where the VOs are vertices and the edges represent relations between them (see [3], sub-organizations are called "groups").

The user may be a member of many VOs, and in particular, a member of a sub-organization is also a member of the parent organization.

The privileges the organization wants to grant the user, related to the tasks he is supposed to perform, are connected with *user roles*. The roles are defined across the hierarchy of VOs and managed in an independent structure, although the authorities of VOs are responsible for defining roles. One user may have multiple roles and he is responsible for selecting the required role while accessing the resource.

Any special rights to resources expressed, e. g., by ACL [2] are called *capabilities*. The capabilities may be used to express any rights to a specific user, e. g., some file is writable only by the owner.

Resource provider (RP) is an abstract entity that owns and offers some resources (e. g. services, CPU, disks, data, etc.) to the grid users.

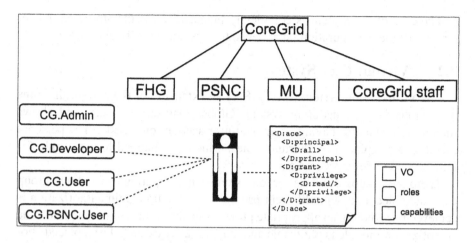

Figure 1. Hierarchy of Virtual Organizations, User Roles and Capabilities

By the *virtual environment* we understand encapsulation of user jobs in order to give it a limited set of privileges and be able to identify the user and organization on behalf of which the job acts. Example implementations are virtual accounts [8], virtual machines, and sandboxes [5].

3. Existing Solutions

In this section we provide a brief description of several systems trying to cope with user management in the context of virtual organizations.

3.1 Perun

Perun [9] provides a repository of complex authorization data, as well as tools to manage the data. The data are used to generate configuration of the authorization services themselves (starting from UNIX user accounts throught grid-mapfiles to the VOMS database). In turn, these services are used to enforce authorization policies.

Perun makes use of central configuration repository which models an *ideal world*, i.e. what the resources should look like. In this central repository all the necessary (and possibly very complex) integrity constraints are relatively easy to be enforced. The repository is complemented with a change propagation mechanism which detects the changes, generates consistent configuration snapshots of atomic pieces of managed systems, and tries to deliver them to their final destinations, appropriatelly dealing with resource or network failures. In this way, the *real world* is forced to follow the ideal one as closely as possible.

The core of the system is completely independent of the structure and semantics of the configuration data, hence the system is easily extensible.

3.2   Virtual User System

The Virtual User System (VUS) [8] is an extension of the system that runs
users' jobs (e.g. scheduling system, Globus Gatekeeper, etc.) and allows
running jobs without having a personal user account on a node. The personal
accounts are replaced by "virtual" ones, which are mapped to users only for
time needed to fully process a job.

There are groups of virtual accounts on each computing node. Each group
consists of accounts with different privileges, so the fine grain authorization is
achieved by selecting an appropriate group by an the authorization module. The
authorization module is pluggable and may be easily extended or replaced. For
example, the authorization decision may be based on VO-membership of the
user and the checking banned user list. The mapping user-account mechanism
assures that only one user is mapped to a particular account at any given time.
The history of user-account mappings is stored in a database, so that accounting
and tracking user activities are possible.

3.3   VOMS, LCAS and LCMAPS

The Virtual Organization Membership Service (VOMS) [2] contains a database
with information on the user's Virtual Organization and group (sub-organization)
membership, roles and capabilities. The service preserves it in a special format—
the VOMS credential. Before starting a job the user must acquire the VOMS
proxy certificate signed by his VO and valid for limited time. The extra authorization data is placed as a non-critical extension in the proxy, so it is compatible
with VOMS-non-aware services.

In order to take advantages of VOMS data, the Globus Gatekeeper was
extended by LCAS and LCMAPS. The Local Center Authorization System
(LCAS) is a service used on computing nodes in order to enforce local security
policies. Local Credential Mapping Service (LCMAPS) maps user to local credentials (AFS/Kerberos tokens, UNIX account and group), depending on user
proxy certificate and job description.

3.4   Virtual Workspaces, Runtime Environments, Dynamic
Virtual Environments

Very interesting work in the area was performed by researchers from the
Argonne National Lab and University of California [4–6]. They proposed and
implemented the Workspace Management Service, which allows to run user
jobs in the virtual environment (see section 2), using different technologies

(GRAM Gatekeeper, OGSI, WSRF). The virtual environments are implemented as dynamically created Unix accounts and virtual machines.

These works widely deal with problems connected with job encapsulation and provide some efficiency comparisons of different virtual environment implementations based on tests performed on prototype system and testbed. The authorization issues are addressed closer only by [4], where RSL-based policy language was proposed.

4. System Requirements

4.1 Authentication

The first step in obtaining access to a remote resource is authentication. From the user's point of view, the remote access should be as simple as possible and similar to the local access. This may be achieved by features like single sign-on, delegation, integration with local security solutions, user-based trust relationships (resources from different providers may be used together by the user without the need of any security configurations done amongst these RPs) [1]. The mentioned requirements are fulfilled by Globus Toolkit [10] to a great extent.

4.2 Authorization

The concept of virtual organizations allows for easier decentralization of user management (each VO is responsible for managing some group of users). On the contrary, in the classical solution each computing node must store user auhorisation information locally (e. g. in Globus grid-mapfile), which obviously is not scalable and brings a nightmare of synchronization. On the other hand, the resource provider must have full control on who and how uses his resources. Therefore, the security policy should be combined from two sources: VO and RP.

The second important issue is fine grained authorization [4] that allows limiting user access rights to specific resources. The authorization is based on the triplet VO, role, capabilities [2] and is done on the computing node. The RP policy defines privileges for given pair VO-role and interprets the capabilities. The RP policy may limit the privileges in any way, including denying access at all. The virtual environment should be able to enforce the (limited) privileges.

User's request should be self-contained so that RP does not need to contact any external entity to obtain any information (such as VO, role(s), capabilities) required to authorize the user. This additional information must be stored within the request in an expandable way.

The authorization module should be plug-in-based in order to allow flexible configuration (use a different set of plug-ins with different priorities) and easy integration with existing authorization systems, services or mechanisms.

In some applications (e. g. pre-paid systems) it may be required to suspend or delete a job after quotas expiration/overdraw. A related problem is estimation of resource usage before starting the job in order to avoid canceling jobs done in 90 %. The quota should be soft or it should be possible to suspend the job for some time.

4.3   Encapsulation of Jobs and Results

The system must assure that two different jobs will not interact in an unwanted and unpredictable way, e. g. overwriting each other's results. Moreover, it must be possible to identify when and who used specific resources, performed or attempted some actions. This is relevant from the security and accounting point of view. Usually it is not even enough to know the identity of a user, but it is important on whose (which VO) behalf he acted and in which role.

The basic model (default configuration) is that all jobs are encapsulated and thus isolated from one another. Final or partial results of a job are not available to other jobs until they are stored to the global space. However, in some situations (e. g. workflows of jobs that may share temporary files) some cooperation of jobs or access to the same resources may be required. It should be possible to specify if the job should run in an existing environment or in a new one. Possibly, the system should detect such situation and handle it automatically.

In a complex task it may be required that the user should have to use multiple roles or identities to gain access to multiple resources. It should be possible to separate subtasks pereformed with different privileges, identities (certificates) and on behalf of different VOs.

Files stored with some local privileges/IDs/tokens may be accessed later with a different ID (certificate) and a different local ID/token. Special access privileges may be required for VO authorities in order to control or even stop the user's jobs and to check the accounting data. Access to the virtual environment for other users, pointed by the user, may be required for interactive jobs that require cooperation.

Possibly, job encapsulation should provide a secure execution environment for jobs, in which no-one except authorized persons should be able to read and interpret the input and output data, even the RP.

4.4   Accounting and Logging Facilities

Any production grid, especially the commercial one, needs the accounting feature. The accounting data must be stored with a proper context (user, VO, role, capabilities, time) and then collected (possibly from several locations) by users, VOs and RPs. In numerous applications the standard system mechanisms (such as e. g. Unix accounting) offer enough information, but the system should also be capable of storing non-standard accounting data.

From the point of view of security, it is important to track user activities (e. g. by analyzing system logs) in order to detect any rule-breaking. It must be possible to identify the user who has performed a particular action.

Both of the above require proper encapsulation of jobs (as described in the previous section) and storing history of user-virtual environment mappings.

4.5   Other Requirements

There are also several other requirements that the user management system should met.

It should be possible to combine "classical" and "virtual" user management in some system.

The system architecture must be ready for lightweight virtual organizations (very dynamically created and removed after short time). This high dynamics shall not introduce much administrative burden or computational overhead.

Granting rights to the "long-lived" resources (like files) for users that changed certificates should be handled. CAs should track the history of issued certificates and associated physical users (i. e. proper *identity* management is necessary).

The architecture should be modular and flexible. It should give a chance for easy integration with the existing solutions and standards. The modularity embraces plug-in based authorization, a replaceable virtual environment module that allows different implementations of VEs.

Automatic registering of new users, issuing certificates and any special security considerations connected with this may be required in some solutions (e. g. application-on-demand).

While analyzing the existing solutions we realized that there are a number of tools that provide for at least part of the functionality mentioned in section 4 however none of them addresses all the issues. These tools are widely used in a number of projects and some of them become some kind of a standard, so it seems to be reasonable to be compatible with them. Moreover, it makes no sense to implement the existing functionality from scratch. Hence we propose to put them into a pluggable framework that will combine the features gaining the synergy effect.

The other important design assumption is being concordant with the existing standards and trends in the area of grid computing, especially the webservice (WS) approach. The WS-Stateful Resource [7] technology seems to be especially promising for our purpose, as it allows for easy modeling virtual environment and managing its life cycle.

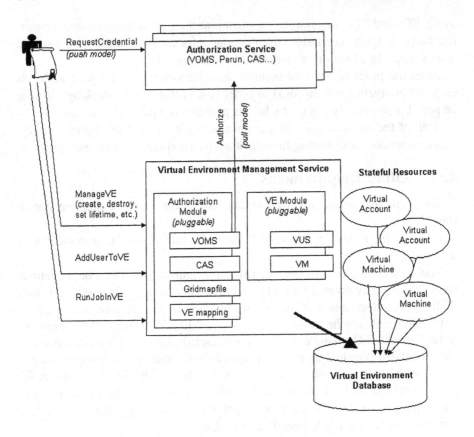

Figure 2.   Virtual Environment Management Service

5.   Proposed Solution

We propose a webservice responsible for managing virtual environments (Virtual Environment Management Service, Fig. 2), especially creating and destroying them as well as running jobs in them. In the background the service collects data on the virtual environments concerning time of creation and destruction, users mapped to the environment, accounting and logging information. These data will be available to different players on the scene like the users, managers of VOs, resource owners etc. via the second webservice called the Virtual Environment Information Service, Fig. 3.

5.1   Virtual Environment Management Service

The Virtual Environment Management Service consists of two main modules: the authorization module and the virtual environment module.

The authorization module first performs authenticationt. This may be based on the existing Globus GSI. The authorization is done by querying a set of authorization plugins. The set is configurable so that the administrator may tune the local authorization policy to the real Grid needs and abilities. We plan to implement plugins for the most frequently used authorization mechanisms and services like grid-mapfile (possibly dynamically updated by Perun), CAS, VOMS. The plugins play the role of policy decision points (PDP). The authorization decision itself may be done locally (in case of the push model of authorization which we prefer) or by querying remote authorization service (the pull model—not preferred, but possible). The plugins should not only answer the question if the user is allowed to perform the specified service action, but also give some hints for the parameters of the virtual environment, e.g. grid-mapfile plugin will tell the (virtual) account name, VOMS will expose ACL that will help with the creation of a virtual machine with specific limitation.

The special authorization plugin is VE mapping, introduced in order to satisfy requirements about loosening the isolation level of the VE. This plugin will check a special Access Control List for the VE. While the VE is created, the list will contain one user—owner (creator) of the VE—with full rights to the VE. Then, the owner can add users to the VE either with limited (e.g. read only access to files or job execution) or full (including VE life cycle management) privileges. Note that the user—the owner of VE—takes much responsibility for the added users, because while loosening the isolation level we also loosen the requirements for identifying user and context. The extent of this loosening depends on VE implementation; namely it is impossible to distinguish users if they run jobs in the same virtual account, but it is possible to distinguish them if they run jobs on different accounts of the same virtual machine.

The virtual environment module is responsible for the creation, deletion and communication with virtual environments, implemented as stateful resources. The module is also pluggable, so it is possible to use different implementations of VE. It is planned to implement the Virtual User System plugin and at least one plugin for a virtual machine. The module records all its relevant operations (especially like VE creation and deletion) to the Virtual Environment Database.

5.2 Virtual Environment Database

The records of VE operations together with the standard system logs and accounting data will provide complete information on user actions and resource usage. However these two sources must be combined and the result put to the database. This might be implemented as a database trigger that collects the logging and accounting data periodically or while the VE is destroyed. It must also be possible to put some non-standard data to the database (e.g. the usage time of laboratory equipment connected to the system).

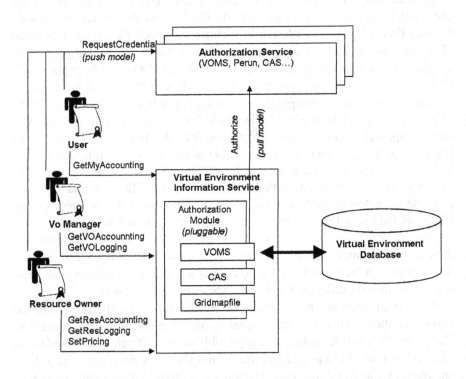

Figure 3.   Virtual Environment Information Service

For billing purposes the accounting information must be connected with prices. The price is computed depending on the pricing policy of the resource owner. In the simplest model the database contains a dynamic price list and the current price is put together with the accounting record.

This service is a front-end for the Virtual Environment Database. The access to the data must be authorized and depends on the user role:

- *Common users* who have run jobs—they should have rights to read the accounting data referring to themselves (e. g. in order to control their budget).

- *Managers of virtual organizations*—should be able to read logging and accounting data of all VO members to have full control on the budget and behavior of the users.

- *Owners of resources*—should be able to access all the data connected to the resource. In the simplest case, the resource is the whole local node or cluster on which the VE runs and the owner is the system administrator. In a more sophisticated case the resources may be differentiated and there can be more owners (e. g. usage of some software, owed by some local user may be a subject for the accounting). The owners should also have right to modify the pricing policy.

This service will require the authorization module with a set of plugins similar to the Virtual Environment Management Service, but they must take a slightly different decision, mainly based on the user role mentioned above.

6. Summary

In the paper we discussed detailed requirements for user management in the Grid environment with special respect to the Virtual Organization concept. Examples of the existing approaches to the problem were briefly described. As none of the existing approaches addresses all the requirements, but most of the requirements are addressed by some approach, we propose a system that will be a framework for the existing solutions, allowing combination of their features.

7. Acknowledgment

This work has been supported by the CESNET Research Intent (MSM-6383917201) and the EU CoreGRID NoE (FP6-004265).

References

[1] I.Foster, C.Kesselman, S.Tuecke, The Anatomy of the Grid: Enabling Scalable Virtual Organizations, International J. Supercomputer Applications, 15(3), 2001.

[2] R.Alfieri, R.Cecchini, V.Ciaschini, L.Dell'Agnello, A.Frohner, A.Gianoli, K.Lï¿½entey, F.Spataro, VOMS: an Authorization System for Virtual Organizations, 1st European Across Grids Conference, Santiago de Compostela, February 13-14, 2003.

[3] R.Alfieri, R.Cecchini, V.Ciaschini, L.dell'Angelo, A.Gianoli, F.Spataro, F.Bonnassieux, P.Broadfoot, G.Lowe, L.Cornwall, J.Jensen, D.Kelsey, A.Frohner, D.L.Groep, W.Som de Cerff, M.Steenbakkers, G.Venekamp, D.Kouril, A.McNab, O.Mulmo, M.Silander, J.Hahkala, K.Lorentey Managing Dynamic User Communities in a Grid of Autonomous Resources, Computing in High Energy and Nuclear Phisics, La Jolla, California, 24-28 March 2003.

[4] K.Keahey, V.Welch, S.Lang, B.Liu, S.Meder Fine-Grain Authorization Policies in the GRID: Design and Implementation 1st International Workshop on Middleware for Grid Computing, 2003.

[5] K.Keahey, K Doering, I.Foster, From Sandbox to Playground: Dynamic Virtual Environments in the Grid, 5th International Workshop in Grid Computing (Grid 2004), Pittsburgh, PA, November 2004

[6] K.Keahey, I.Foster, T.Freeman, X.Zhang, D.Garlon Wirtual Workspaces in the Grid, Europar 2005, Pisa, Italy, August, 2005.

[7] I.Foster, J.Frey, S.Graham, S.Tuecke, K.Czajkowski, D.Ferguson, F.Leymann, M.Nally, I.Sedukhin, D.Snelling, T.Storey, W.Vambenepe, S.Weerawarana Modeling Stateful Resources with Web Services, version 1.1 http://www-128.ibm.com/developerworks/library/specification/ws-resource/, March 2004.

[8] M.Jankowski, P.Wolniewicz, N.Meyer Virtual User System for Globus based grids, Cracow '04 Grid Workshop Proceedings, December 2004.

[9] Ales Křenek and Zora Sebestianová. Perun – Fault-Tolerant Management of Grid Resources, Cracow '04 Grid Workshop Proceedings, December 2004.

[10] Globus Toolkit Version 4: Software for Service-Oriented Systems. I. Foster. IFIP International Conference on Network and Parallel Computing, Springer-Verlag LNCS 3779, pp 2-13, 2005.

ON THE INTEGRATION OF PASSIVE AND ACTIVE NETWORK MONITORING IN GRID SYSTEMS

Sergio Andreozzi, Augusto Ciuffoletti, Antonia Ghiselli
INFN-CNAF
Viale Berti Pichat 6/2, 40126, Bologna, Italy
sergio.andreozzi@cnaf.infn.it
augusto@di.unipi.it
antonia.ghiselli@cnaf.infn.it

Demetres Antoniades, Michalis Polychronakis, Evangelos P. Markatos
Institute of Computer Science, Foundation for Research & Technology – Hellas
P.O. Box 1385, 71110, Heraklio, Greece
danton@ics.forth.gr
markatos@ics.forth.gr
mikepo@ics.forth.gr

Panos Trimintzios
European Network and Information Security Agency
P.O. Box 1309, 71001, Heraklio, Greece
panagiotis.trimintzios@enisa.eu.int

Abstract   This paper focuses on the integration of passive and active network monitoring techniques in Grid systems. We propose a number of performance metrics for assessing the quality of the connectivity, and describe the required measurement methods for obtaining these metrics. Furthermore, the issue of efficiently representing and publishing the measured values is considered. We show that it is important to have both active and passive monitoring strategies applied to Grid systems; and when we do have both strategies it is necessary to have an a priory hybrid design. Finally we depict the tradeoffs introduced by this approach and the description of the components for a domain oriented monitoring infrastructure that supports both passive and active monitoring tools in Grid systems.

Keywords: Grid connectivity, network monitoring, active monitoring, passive monitoring, connectivity performance metrics, distributed database.

1.   Introduction

The Grid computation system paradigm extends the traditional distributed computing approach towards the coordination and sharing of computing, application, data, storage, or network resources across dynamic and geographically dispersed organizations. In order to setup an optimal execution environment for a Grid application, knowledge about the status, characteristics and composition of the various resources is required. In current systems, monitoring and understanding of characteristics, status and availability of computing and storage resources has been extensively explored (e.g., see [1]) and working solutions on large-scale systems exist (e.g., see [11]). In contrast, monitoring of communication resources is at an early stage, mainly due to the complexity of the infrastructure to monitor and of the monitoring activity.

Monitoring the network infrastructure of a Grid has a vital role in the management and the utilization of the Grid itself. While it gives to maintenance activities the basic information for identifying network problems and diagnosing the cause, thus contributing to Grid fault tolerance, it also provides to Grid-aware applications the ability to undertake actions in order to improve performance and resource utilization. In the latter category we also include accounting activities that are important when Grid resources are shared by different administrative authorities.

According to the Grid Monitoring Architecture (GMA) [3], defined in the context of the Global Grid Forum (GGF) [8], the overall network infrastructure monitoring can be divided into three distinct phases: the *production* of observations, their *publication*, and their *utilization*. The three activities tightly interoperate based on carefully designed interfaces among them, although each of them uses different tools. Network monitoring tools are used for the *production*, powerful databases and publication services following different delivery and data models are used for the *publication*, and various other techniques, such as administration and workflow analysis visualization tools, are used for the *utilization*.

In this paper, we focus on network monitoring from the Grid viewpoint, and we concentrate on tools related to the *production* and *publication* activities of observations. For the *production* activity, we propose a number of metrics related to the quality of the Grid connectivity. We also describe the monitoring techniques that are required for obtaining these metrics. We qualitatively discuss both the accuracy with which we can derive each metric, as well as the complexity and overhead induced by the measurement process. For the *publication* activity, we are mainly interested in the efficient representation of both active and passive monitoring metrics. Our primary concern is the scalability when producers are increasing in number and monitoring data output. In order to limit the quantity of observations that need to be published, we also propose a *domain-oriented* overlay network.

The rest of this paper is organized as follows. In Section 2, we classify existing network monitoring tools and techniques. Section 3 describes the proposed network monitoring architecture, comprising passive sensors distributed at ingress and egress points of Grid resources, and presents performance metrics that can be derived using single or pairs of passive monitoring sensors. Section 4 presents the current Grid connectivity monitoring architecture based on active network monitoring. In Section 5 we describe the issues and potential approaches for the integration of passive network monitoring into the *publication* infrastructure, which currently supports *only* metrics derived using active monitoring, such as the Round Trip Time (RTT). Section 6 addresses security and privacy concerns related to our integrated monitoring architecture. Finally, Section 7 concludes the paper.

2. Classification of Network Monitoring Techniques

In this section, we classify network monitoring approaches based on two different criteria. We first look into the distinction between *path-* and *link-* oriented monitoring. Then, we classify network monitoring approaches based on whether they use *active* monitoring or *passive* monitoring strategies.

2.1 Link versus Path Monitoring

An important issue that emerges when considering network monitoring is related to the monitoring granularity. We consider two main alternatives: (1) *Single link* is appropriate for maintainers that require a fine-grained view of the network in order to localize problems; nevertheless, it is not suitable for most of the Grid-aware applications, since they require end-to-end observations and typically cannot derive the necessary information from the correlation of measurements regarding multiple single links; (2) *End-to-end path* gives a view of the system that is filtered through routing; this may be sometimes confusing for maintainers, but is appropriate for Grid-aware applications.

The scalability of the two approaches is dramatically different. Let N be the number of resources in the system. A link oriented monitoring system grows with $O(N)$, since a Grid can be assimilated to a bounded degree graph. On the other side, an end-to-end (or path-oriented) approach, grows with $O(N^2)$, since, as a general rule, each resource has a distinct path to any other resource. This consideration would exclude the adoption of an end-to-end path approach, but there are issues to be considered with the single-link approach. First, the edges of each link are often black boxes containing proprietary software; there may be no way to add sensors for monitoring purposes, or even to simply access the stored data. Second, deriving an end-to-end path performance metric from single-link observations requires two critical steps: to reconstruct the link sequence, and, even more problematic, to obtain time correlated path performance compositions from single-link observations.

From the considerations given above, it is obvious that no single approach is the most appropriate for all monitoring purposes. We propose to complement the two strategies in order to limit their drawbacks. Our strategy is to introduce an overlay network that clusters networked services into *domains*, and restricts monitoring to inter-domain paths. This approach, which resembles the inter/intra domain routing dichotomy in the Internet, strikes a balance between the two extreme design strategies outlined below:

- An *end-to-end path strategy* offers to Grid oriented applications a valuable insight of the path connecting two resources. However, this insight does not include the performance of the local network, which usually outperforms inter-domain paths, and the address space is still $O(N^2)$. Nevertheless, it must be considered that N now stands for the number of domains, which should be significantly smaller than the number of resources.

- A *single link strategy* provides maintainers with a reasonable localization of a problem. Regarding accounting, as long as domains are mapped to administrative entities, it gives sufficient information to account resource utilization.

In essence, a *domain-oriented* approach limits the complexity of the address space into a range that is already managed by routing algorithms, avoids path reconstruction, and has a granularity that is compatible with relevant tasks. The implied overlay view cannot be derived from a pre-existent structure. For instance, the Domain Name System (DNS) is not adequate to map monitoring domains, since the same DNS subnetwork may in principle contain several monitoring domains, and a domain may overlap with several DNS subnetworks. Thus, the overlay network, or *domain partition*, must be separately designed, maintained, and made available to users, as explained in Section 5.

2.2 Passive versus Active Monitoring

Another classification scheme that is often used when dealing with network monitoring distinguishes between active and passive monitoring techniques. The definition itself is rather slippery, and often a matter of discussion. For this work, we adopt the following classification criterion: a monitoring tool is classified as *active* if it induces traffic into the network, otherwise it is classified as *passive*.

Passive monitoring is more appropriate for monitoring gross connectivity metrics like link throughput; it is also needed for accounting purposes. Passive network monitoring techniques analyze network traffic by capturing and examining individual packets passing through the monitored link, allowing for fine-grained operations, such as deep packet inspection. The main benefit of passive monitoring approaches, compared to active monitoring, is its non-intrusive nature. Active network monitoring techniques incur an unavoidable network overhead due to the injected probe packets, which compete with user traffic. In contrast, passive network monitoring techniques passively observe the current traffic of the monitored link, without introducing any network overhead

Active monitoring is more effective for observing the network sanity and is suitable for application oriented observations, such as jitter, when related to multimedia applications. On the other side, this approach implies an unavoidable network overhead due to the injected probe packets which compete with user traffic.

Passive monitoring tools can give an extremely detailed view of the network's performance, while active tools return a response that combines several performance figures. As a general rule, effective network monitoring should exploit both techniques. In the following two sections we discuss both passive and active monitoring in the context of the data *production* for Grid infrastructures.

3. Passive Network Monitoring for Grid Infrastructures

Passive traffic monitoring has become increasingly vital for network management as well as for supporting a growing number of automated control mechanisms needed to make IP-based networks more robust, efficient, and secure. Besides monitoring a single link, emerging applications can benefit from monitoring data gathered at multiple observation points across a network. Such a distributed monitoring infrastructure [15] can be extended outside the border of a single organization and span multiple administrative domains across the Internet. In such an environment, the processing and correlation of the data gathered at each sensor gives a broader perspective of the state of the monitored network, in which related events become easier to identify.

Figure 1 illustrates a high-level view of such a distributed passive network monitoring infrastructure. Monitoring sensors are distributed across several domains, with each domain operating one or more monitoring sensors. Each sensor may monitor the link between the domain and the Internet (as in domain 1 and 3), or an internal link of a local sub-network (as in domain 2). An authorized user, who may not be located in any of the participating domains, can run monitoring applications that require the involvement of an arbitrary number of the available monitoring sensors.

A passive network monitoring infrastructure, either local or distributed, can be used to derive several performance metrics useful to Grid applications for

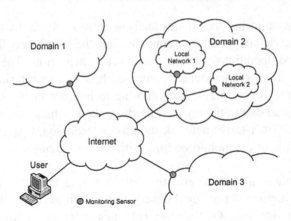

Figure 1. A high-level view of a distributed passive network monitoring infrastructure.

assessing the status of the Grid infrastructure connectivity and taking effective balancing decisions. Although some of these metrics could be measured using active monitoring techniques, passive techniques have the benefit of not injecting any additional traffic into the network. Furthermore, there are also several metrics measurable by passive monitoring techniques that cannot be measured using active monitoring. In the following sections we enlist several of these metrics, classified based on the number of passive monitoring observation points required to derive them.

3.1 Metrics based on a Single Observation Point

In this section, we present basic metrics that can be measured using passive monitoring from single observation point. This observation point can be located usually at the link that connects the domain with the rest of the Grid infrastructure.

3.1.1 Network-level Round-Trip Time.
The network Round-Trip Time (RTT) is the time taken for a packet to traverse the network from the source to the destination and back. RTT is one of the simplest network connectivity metrics, and can be easily measured using active monitoring tools like for example ping. However, it is also possible to measure RTT using solely passive monitoring techniques. One such technique is based on monitoring the TCP connections that pass through a link [10]. RTT can be estimated more accurately based on the time difference between the SYN and ACK packets exchanged during the three-way handshake of a TCP connection.

3.1.2 Application-level Round-Trip Time.
Besides the network RTT time, passive monitoring allows for measuring the RTT time at the service

level, i.e., the time that a client has to wait in order to receive a response from a remote service for a particular request. For example, Web server response time, as perceived by the end user, can be measured by monitoring the traffic between the user and the Web server. By inspecting the contents of the packets, one can distinguish a request for a particular page and the relevant reply, and then compute the service response time based on their time difference. Similar techniques are used in EtE [7], which measures service performance characteristics using passive monitoring.

Note that the application-level RTT is composed by the network-level RTT plus the delay in the server. Both these metrics could be measured: the first by pings or using the technique in Section 3.1.1; the second by means of host-based resource availability tools. Nevertheless, the composed metric will not be as accurate as the direct approach since the latter does not have to deal with time correlation aspects.

3.1.3 Throughput.

Passive monitoring can provide traffic throughput metrics at varying levels of granularity. The aggregate throughput provides an indication for the current utilization of the monitored link. Based on the current conditions, (i.e., the throughput seen by the active connections) this metric may provide the means to estimate the future aggregate throughput. Consequently, as a proportion of the total link capacity, it provides an estimate for the available bandwidth of the link.

Besides aggregate throughput, fine-grained per-flow measurements can be used to observe the throughput achieved by specific applications. This metric can be measured using the appropriate filters based on known ports, specified IP addresses, or both. Even for applications that do not use predefined ports, protocol-inspection techniques can be used to identify the traffic they produce, and quantify it [13].

3.1.4 Retransmitted Packets.

In case that packet loss cannot be measured (e.g., because only one observation point is available, see Section 3.2.2), the amount of retransmitted packets provides a good indication of the quality of the route towards their destination.

Packet loss ratio can be measured using a single monitor by tracking the packets that are sent multiple times during a given time window. However, storing all the outgoing packets that passed through the link during the time window is a highly resource-consuming task, especially for high speed links.

Furthermore, comparing each new packet to the already captured packets for finding duplicates is a very computationally-intensive task. Techniques similar to those used in trajectory sampling [6] can be used in order to keep only digests of the packets, reduce the space requirements, and search them more efficiently.

3.1.5   Packet Reordering.   Packet reordering, as reported in [12], can play a significant role in degrading application throughput, even in small occurrence. In order to measure the percentage of reordered packets, a single passive monitor can observe the sequence field of incoming TCP packets. Since this kind of monitoring uses only header-level information, it would be computationally inexpensive, and also could help to avoid highly reordering links in order to achieve maximum application throughput.

3.2   Metrics based on Multiple Observation Points

In this section, we discuss metrics that can be derived using either a pair of passive monitoring observation points, each located at the link that connects the domain to the rest of the Grid infrastructure, or more monitoring points distributed across several domains.

3.2.1   One-Way Delay and Jitter.   The one-way delay is the time taken for a packet to traverse the path from the source to the destination. The asymmetric routing that commonly occurs within the Internet makes this metric important for some applications. The one-way delay can be measured using two passive monitors located at the source and destination network domains. When the same packet passes through both monitors, the one-way delay can be measured from the difference in the time each monitor observed the packet. For such measurements, the clocks of the monitors have to be synchronized, e.g., using the Network Time Protocol (NTP) or synchronizing with the Global Positioning System (GPS), depending on the required accuracy.

A closely related metric is the *variation* in the one-way delay of successive packets, commonly referred to as jitter. Jitter is particularly important for real-time applications, since it predetermines the sizes of the relevant stream buffers.

Note that both these metrics can be measured with active monitoring techniques, which suffer from the trade-off between accuracy and amount of additional test traffic injected into the network. The passive monitoring approach discussed here does not add any additional traffic, while it is as accurate as the synchronized clocks in the monitoring observation points.

3.2.2   Packet Loss Ratio.   Packet loss occurs when correctly transmitted packets from a source never arrive at the intended destination. Packets are usually lost due to congestion, e.g., at the queue of some router; they can also be lost due to routing system problems, or due to poor network conditions that may result to damages in the datagram. The packet loss ratio is a very important metric, since it affects data throughput performance and overall end-to-end quality.

In passive monitoring observation points, packet loss can be measured using two cooperating monitors at the source and destination network domains. The two sensors will track the packets that have been sent from the source network, but have not arrived to the destination after a timeout period. The timeout period must be greater than the one-way delay between the domains, though to be on the safe side for extreme delays, values greater than RTT should be used.

3.2.3   Service Availability.
The domain and service availability metric is a major concern for Grid users. For example, in the case where a SYN packet does not have a SYN-ACK response, meaning that the domain is not available. By passively counting the unestablished connections, both in network and application level, can give us an indication of the availability of a particular domain or service. Correlating the results from several monitoring points can be a good measurement of the availability.

4.   Active Network Monitoring for Grid Infrastructures

Active tools induce test traffic into the Grid connectivity infrastructure and observe the behavior of the network. As a general rule, one end (the 'probe') generates a specific traffic pattern, while the other end (the 'target') cooperates by returning some kind of feedback. The ping tool is a well known representative of this category.

Disregarding the characteristics of the benchmark, an active monitoring tool reports a view of the network that is near to the needs of the application: for instance, a ping message that uses the Internet Control Message Protocol (ICMP) gives an indication of raw transmission times, useful for applications like multimedia streaming. A ping that uses UDP packets or a short ftp session may be used to gather the necessary information for optimal file transfers. Since active tools report the same network performance that the application would observe, their results are readily usable by Grid-aware applications that want to optimize their performance.

The coordination activity associated to active monitoring is minimal. This is a relevant property for a dynamic entity, such as a Grid where join and leave events are frequent. A new resource that joins the Grid enters the monitoring activity simply by starting its probe and target related activities. However, join and leave activities introduce security problems, which are further addressed in Section 6.

Most of the statistics collected by active tools have a local relevance and need not be transmitted elsewhere. As a general rule, they are used by applications that run in the domain where the probe resides. A distributed publication engine may take advantage of that, exporting to the global view only those observations that are requested by remote consumers.

Network performance statistics that can be observed using active monitoring techniques can be divided into two categories: (1) 'packet oriented', related to the behavior induced by single packet transmissions between the measurement points; (2) 'Stream oriented', related to the behavior induced by a sequence of packets with given characteristics such as the timing and the length of the packet stream or the content of individual packets.

In the first category, we find RTT, TCP connection setup characteristics and one-way figures of packet delay and packet delay variation. In the second category, we find ftp transfer of a randomly generated file of given length, or a back-to-back sequence of UDP packets.

A relevant feature shared by active monitoring tools is the ability to detect the presence of a resource, disregarding if it is used or not, since they require an active participation of all actors (probe, target and network). This not only helps fault tolerance, but may also simplify the maintenance of the Grid layout, which is needed by Grid-aware applications. Since active monitoring consumes some resources, security rules should limit the impact of malicious uses of such tools (this issue is also covered in Section 6).

5. The Domain Overlay Database

The domain overlay database is a cornerstone of a domain-based architecture. The structure of this architecture reflects a view of a Grid focusing on network performance, and its implementation addresses performance and scalability.

The GlueDomains [5, 4] prototype serves as a starting point for our study. GlueDomains supports the network monitoring activity of the prototype Grid infrastructure of INFN, the Italian National Institute for Nuclear Physics [9]. GlueDomains follows a domain-oriented approach, as defined in Section 2.1. The measured values are published using the Globus Monitoring and Discovery Service (MDS) [14]. MDS is the information services component of the Globus Toolkit that provides information about the available resources on a Grid and their status. This service is the official information service of a large-scale Grid such as the LHC Computing Grid [11]. The published information is rendered through GridICE [2], a Grid monitoring tool.

The domain overlay maps Grid resources into domains and introduces concepts specific to the task of representing the monitoring activity. We illustrate this overlay view using the Unified Model Language (UML) class diagram presented in Figure 2. The classes that represent Grid resources are the following: 'Edge Service', that is a superclass representing a resource that does not consist of connectivity, but is reached through connectivity; 'Network Service', representing the interconnection between two Domains; its attributes include a class, corresponding to the offered service class, and a statement of expected connectivity; 'Theodolite Service', it monitors a number of Network Elements; in GlueDomains, theodolites perform active network monitoring.

The following classes represent aggregation of services: 'Domain', that is a representation of partitions that compose a Grid; its attributes include the service

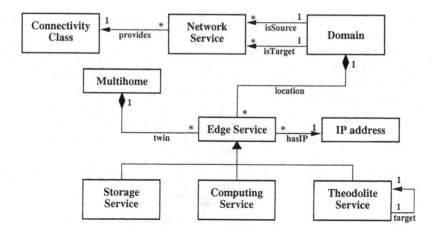

Figure 2. The UML class diagram of the topology database with domain partitioning

class offered by its fabric; 'Multihome', that aggregates Edge Services sharing the same hardware support, but being accessible through distinct interfaces.

The description of the overlay network using the above classes is made available through a 'topology database' which is used by the 'publication' engine in order to associate observations to network services.

Integration with passive monitoring. The *domain-oriented* database approach within GlueDomains was designed having in mind metrics only *produced* with active monitoring tools. It is clear though that this approach also smoothly fits with the performance metrics structure described in Sections 3.1-3.2. All measurement data collected by passive monitoring traffic observers can be associated to a specific network service and domain, since basic attributes (e.g., source and destination IP address, service class) are typically provided by such devices. The knowledge of theodolites as hosts relevant from the viewpoint of network monitoring may indicate the devices performing passive monitoring which packets are more significant, thus opening the way to the cooperation between theodolites and passive traffic observers.

5.1   Monitoring Activities Description

The description of the monitoring activity is relevant to its management. In order to limit human intervention in the design and deployment of the network monitoring infrastructure, such a description should be available to devices that contribute to this task, also considering the possibility of self-organization of such an activity.

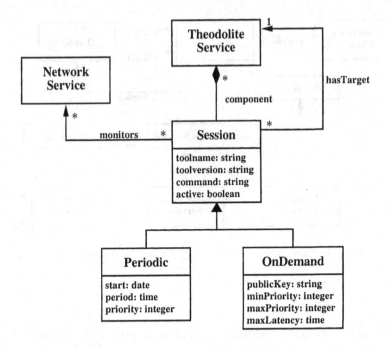

Figure 3.   The UML class diagram of the monitoring database

In GlueDomains, theodolite services are agents of monitoring configuration. The UML model shown in Figure 3 is centered around such entity and describes the structure of the monitoring database.

In GlueDomains, active monitoring is organized into monitoring 'sessions'. Each session is associated to a theodolite which runs the monitoring tool, and to a monitored network service. The description of each session contains details of the monitoring tool and details about the injected traffic.

The 'monitoring database' is accessed infrequently by 'producers' that download the description of their monitoring tasks. This may happen once during a monitoring session, or periodically. Updates are bound to some kind of topology change. Both read and update activities should be restricted to authorized producers, and limited to the records that describe its activity.

Integration with passive monitoring.   Passive monitoring fits into the schema of the monitoring database either as a new session class, where the theodolite instructs the remote passive monitoring device about the required activity, or as a new service class, with associated 'passive monitoring' sessions. In the former case, an authentication mechanism should be introduced to avoid unauthorized use of passive monitoring devices.

6. Security and Privacy Issues

A large-scale network monitoring infrastructure is exposed to several threats. Each component should be able to ensure an appropriate degree of security, depending on the role it plays. Monitoring sensors may become targets of co-ordinated Denial of Service (DoS) attacks, aiming to prevent legitimate users from receiving a service with acceptable performance, or sophisticated intrusion attempts, aiming to compromise the monitoring hosts. Being exposed to the public Internet, monitoring sensors should have a rigorous security configuration in order to preserve the confidentiality of the monitored network, and resist to attacks that aim to compromise them.

The security enforcement strategy is slightly different for active and for passive monitoring tools. In the case of passive monitoring tools, the monitoring host should ensure the identity and the capabilities associated with a host submitting a request. Such a request may consist in activating a given packet filter, or in returning the results of the monitoring activity. Each passive sensor should be equipped with a firewall, configured using a conservative policy that selectively allows inbound traffic according with accepted requests, and dropping inbound traffic from any other source. An option is to consider that only theodolite services, whose credentials (for instance their public keys) are recorded in the monitoring database, are able to access passive sensor configuration, and therefore dynamically configure its firewall. Theodolite capabilities may vary according to a specific monitoring strategy.

In the case of active monitoring tools, the target is exposed to DoS attacks, consisting in submitting benchmark traffic from unauthorized, and possibly malicious, sources. One should distinguish between tools that are mainly used for discovery, and those that are used for monitoring purposes. The former should be designed as lightweight as possible, for instance consisting of a predetermined ping pattern: probe's firewall should not mask such packets, unless their source is reliably detected as threatening. The latter might consist in rather resource consuming patterns, and the probe should filter packets according to an IP based strategy: such configuration would be based on the content of the monitoring database.

Both passive and active monitoring tools have in common the need of ensuring an adequate degree of confidentiality. In fact, data transfers through TCP are unprotected against eavesdropping from third-parties that have access to the transmitted packets, since they can reconstruct the TCP stream and recover the transferred data. This would allow an adversary to record control messages, forge them, and replay them in order to access a monitoring sensor and impersonate a legitimate user. For protection against such threats, communication between the monitoring applications and a remote sensors is encrypted using the Secure Sockets Layer protocol (SSL). Furthermore, in a distributed monitoring infrastructure that promotes sharing of network packets and statistics between different parties, sensitive data should be anonymized before made publicly available, due to security, privacy, and business competition concerns that may arise between the collaborating parties.

From this picture emerges the role of the monitoring database as a kind of certification authority, which is also used as a repository of public keys used by the actors of the monitoring activity: the publication engine, the monitoring tools, and the theodolite services. Its distributed implementation is challenging, yet tightly bound to the scalability of the monitoring infrastructure.

7.   Summary and Conclusions

In this paper, we explore the issues arising from the integration of passive and active monitoring techniques when used for Grid network infrastructure monitoring. Our proposal is related to the monitoring of the *production* and *publication* activities as defined by the GGF.

For the production activity, we propose a number of interesting performance metrics related to the quality of the connectivity of the Grid infrastructure, and the related network monitoring techniques that are required for obtaining these metrics. We qualitatively discuss both the accuracy with which we can measure each metric, as well as the complexity and overhead induced by the monitoring activity. We also look at the impact of the induced information that various measurement metrics may have on the modules of other actors in a Grid monitoring infrastructure.

For the publication activity, which is deployed in the form of databases, we are mainly interested in the efficient representation of both the active and passive monitoring metrics. The issues of interest in this case is the induced complexity when the various monitoring producers are increasing in size and the monitoring data output is growing in volume. Scalability is also one of our main concerns. Being able to extend the monitoring coverage of a Grid to hundreds of nodes requires the careful design of a distributed hierarchical publication database architecture. In this work, we propose as a starting point the per-domain architecture, where the Grid infrastructure is divided into domains. In our future endeavors, we will try to look into making the information in database available in distributed fashion among many domains.

This work is a first approach towards studying the issues behind the integration of passive and active monitoring. Our target is to reach an integrated system for monitoring the network infrastructure with a Grid-specific point of view. Our second target is to perform a further analysis of the scalability issues of the integrated architecture. In future activities, we aim at making a quantitative scalability assessment and analysis identifying potential bottlenecks. Based on the results of this assessment, we plan to investigate ways to reduce the impact of these bottlenecks. Potential avenues for solving the scalability issues are to use the publish/subscribe model, the threshold crossing/alarming ideas, the 'divide and conquer' principle, and techniques from peer-to-peer systems communication.

References

[1] S. Andreozzi, S. Burke, L. Field, S. Fisher, B. Kónya, M. Mambelli, J.M. Schopf, M. Viljoen, and A. Wilson. GLUE Schema Specification - Version 1.2, Dec 2005.

[2] Sergio Andreozzi, Natascia De Bortoli, Sergio Fantinel, Antonia Ghiselli, Gian Luca Rubini, Gennaro Tortone, and Vistoli Cristina. GridICE: a Monitoring Service for Grid Systems. *Future Generation Computer Systems Journal, Elsevier*, 21(4):559–571, 2005.

[3] Ruth Aydt, Dan Gunter, Warren Smith, Martin Swany, Valerie Taylor, Brian Tierney, and Rich Wolski. A Grid Monitoring Architecture. Recommendation GWD-I (Rev. 16, jan. 2002), Global Grid Forum, 2000.

[4] Augusto Ciuffoletti. The Wandering Token: Congestion Avoidance of a Shared Resource. Technical Report TR-05-13, Universitá di Pisa, Largo Pontecorvo - Pisa -ITALY, May 2005.

[5] Augusto Ciuffoletti, Tiziana Ferrari, Antonia Ghiselli, and Cristina Vistoli. Architecture of Monitoring Elements for the Network Element Modeling in a Grid Infrastructure. In *Proceedings of Workskop on Computing in High Energy and Nuclear Physics (CHEP2003)*, La Jolla (California), March 2003.

[6] Nick G. Duffield and Matthias Grossglauser. Trajectory Sampling for Direct Traffic Observation. In *Proceedings of the conference on Applications, Technologies, Architectures, and Protocols for Computer Communication (SIGCOMM)*, pages 271–282, 2000.

[7] Yun Fu, Ludmila Cherkasova, Wenting Tang, and Amin Vahdat. EtE: Passive End-to-End Internet Service Performance Monitoring. In *Proceedings of the USENIX Annual Technical Conference*, pages 115–130, 2002.

[8] Global Grid Forum, 2006. http://www.ggf.org.

[9] INFN – Istituto Nazionale di Fisica Nucleare, 2006. http://www.infn.it.

[10] Hao Jiang and Constantinos Dovrolis. Passive Estimation of TCP Round-Trip Times. *SIGCOMM Comput. Commun. Rev.*, 32(3):75–88, 2002.

[11] LCH Computing Grid, 2006. http://www.cern.ch/lcg.

[12] Laor Michael and Gendel Lior. The Effect of Packet Reordering in a Backbone Link on Application Throughput. *Network, IEEE*, 16(5):28–36, 2002.

[13] Michalis Polychronakis, Kostas G. Anagnostakis, Evangelos P. Markatos, and Arne Øslebø. Design of an Application Programming Interface for IP Network Monitoring. In *Proceedings of the 9th IFIP/IEEE Network Operations and Management Symposium (NOMS'04)*, pages 483–496, April 2004.

[14] The Globus Toolkit 4.0 Documentation. *GT Information Services: Monitoring & Discovery System (MDS)*, 2006. Available at: http://www.globus.org/toolkit/mds/.

[15] Panos Trimintzios, Michalis Polychronakis, Antonis Papadogiannakis, Michalis Foukarakis, Evangelos P. Markatos, and Arne Øslebø. DiMAPI: An Application Programming Interface for Distributed Network Monitoring. In *Proceedings of the 10th IEEE/IFIP Network Operations and Management Symposium (NOMS)*, April 2006.

SENSOR ORIENTED GRID MONITORING INFRASTRUCTURES FOR ADAPTIVE MULTI-CRITERIA RESOURCE MANAGEMENT STRATEGIES

Piotr Domagalski and Krzysztof Kurowski and
Ariel Oleksiak and Jarek Nabrzyski
Poznań Supercomputing and Networking Center,
Noskowskiego 10, 60-688 Poznań, Poland
piotrdom@man.poznan.pl
krzysztof.kurowski@man.poznan.pl
ariel@man.poznan.pl
naber@man.poznan.pl

Zoltán Balaton and Gábor Gombás and Péter Kacsuk
MTA SZTAKI,
Budapest, H-1528 P.O.Box 63, Hungary
balaton@sztaki.hu
gombasg@sztaki.hu
kacsuk@sztaki.hu

Abstract   In a distributed multi-domain environment, where conditions of resources, services as well as applications change dynamically, we need reliable and scalable management capabilities. The quality of management depends on many factors among which distributed measurement and control primitives are particularly important. By exploiting the extensible monitoring infrastructure provided at the middleware level in a grid meta-scheduling service, in particular integration between GRMS (Grid Resource Management System) and Mercury (Grid Monitoring System), it is possible to perform analysis and then make intelligent use of grid resources. These provide the basis to realize dynamic and adaptive resource management strategies, as well as automatic checkpointing, opportunistic migration, rescheduling and policy-driven management, that has attracted attention of many researchers for the last few years. In this paper we present the current status of our ongoing research in this field together with an example of sensor oriented grid monitoring capabilities facilitating efficient remote control of applications and resources.

Keywords: grid resource management, distributed monitoring, monitoring control, multicriteria analysis

1.   Introduction

Recently developed grid middleware services[1] [2] [3] allow us to connect resources (machines, storage devices, etc.) such as computing clusters with local queuing systems to establish a virtual multi-domain grid environment where various calculations and data processing tasks can be performed in a more efficient way. Unfortunately, efficient and flexible remote management of distributed applications and resources is still an issue that must be addressed today. Note, that management is already complex with existing queuing systems and their complexity is expected to reach a new dimension with multi-domain grid environment. Applications submitted to various resources are usually run under the full control of a queuing system running on a gateway node (front-end machine). Internal nodes of these systems are often inaccessible from the out-side due to private IP addresses (using NAT) or firewalls and queuing systems often provide only basic operations that can be used to control applications remotely. Furthermore, in many grid systems relatively simple, script-based solutions[3] have been adopted to expose capabilities offered by queuing systems what in fact limit the allowed monitoring and control/steering operations that can be performed on jobs running within local clusters to the minimum set of starting/cancelling a job and finding out its status, see Fig. 1.

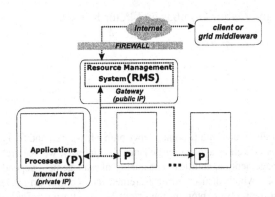

Figure 1.   A general architecture of many local resource management systems (i.e. local batch scheduler, local queuing system)

There is also a lack of flexible monitoring mechanisms enabling dynamic configuration and reconfiguration of information providers and monitoring tools in case of adding or removing resources. As a step towards better management of grid environments, in this paper we present a set of advanced metrics and sensor oriented features, provided by Mercury monitoring system, which can be exploited by the grid middleware. We believe that new application steering and control routines will help to build more efficient and adaptive resource management strategies suitable for many real scenarios.

2. Motivation

One of the main motivations of our research was to facilitate efficient and dynamic adaptive resource management in distributed environments by a tight integration between grid middleware services, in particular GRMS[4], a meta-scheduling system, and Mercury[5], a grid monitoring system providing reliable distributed measurement of resources, hosts and applications. The second objective was to make use of new monitoring capabilities, in particular embedded non-intrusive application sensors and actuators, and provide a grid middleware with more efficient remote application steering and control mechanisms. We have proposed some extensions to push mechanisms in Mercury enabling clients to configure and dynamically reconfigure certain measurement conditions for applications and resources. In this way, clients or grid middleware services can be automatically notified when these conditions are met. Finally, we have established a distributed testing environment connecting a few geographically distributed clusters to evaluate the performance of remote application steering and sensor oriented monitoring mechanisms and also to prove the concept of using these capabilities for more efficient and adaptive resource management in distributed environments.

All aforementioned objectives are addressed in this paper within the next sections. In Sect. 3 related works and various distributed monitoring infrastructures are presented. In Sect. 4 we present example controls and metrics which can be embedded in distributed applications for more efficient remote control. An additional component to Mercury for flexible event or rule based monitoring of applications and resources is discussed in Sect. 5. Example adaptive multi-criteria resource management strategies and potential benefits of using advanced monitoring capabilities are presented in Sect. 6. Finally, Sect. 7 summarizes our research efforts and shows preliminary results.

3. Related Works and Activities

Monitoring is a very broad term and different grid middleware services and tools are often considered in this category. Specifically grid information systems (e.g. Globus MDS and R-GMA), infrastructure monitoring services (Hawkeye, Ganglia), network (e.g. NWS) and application monitoring tools (e.g. OCM-G) all grouped together under this umbrella, although the functionalities they realize and provide for specific problems are very different. The APART2 project published a white paper[10] containing a directory of existing performance monitoring and evaluation tools with the aim to help grid users, developers and administrators in finding an appropriate tool according to their requirements. Another collection and comparison of several grid monitoring systems can be found in [11].

The Grid Monitoring Architecture (GMA), a recommendation of the Global Grid Forum (GGF), describes the basic characteristics of a grid monitoring system. According to the GMA, data is made available by *producers* and is used by *consumers*. Information discovery is supported by utilizing a *directory service*. Data is transmitted from the producer to the consumer as a series of time-stamped events. The GMA also defines the most important interactions between producers, consumers and the directory service. The GMA however makes no recommendations about the data model or protocols.

In this paper we discuss remote management of distributed applications and resources for which a reliable and efficient monitoring infrastructure is a crucial component which has to support both monitoring and controlling of grid resources as well as applications running on them.

The Mercury Grid Monitoring System is a general purpose grid monitoring system developed by the GridLab project. It has been designed to satisfy requirements of grid performance monitoring: it provides monitoring data represented as metrics and also supports steering by controls. It supports monitoring of different grid entities such as resources, services and running applications in a generic, extensible and scalable way. Mercury features a modular design with emphasis on simplicity, efficiency, portability and low intrusiveness on the monitored system. It follows recommendations of the Grid Monitoring Architecture defined by GGF. The input of the monitoring system consists of measurements generated by sensors. A Local Monitor (LM, see Fig. 2) runs on every machine and manages sensors embedded into it or in application processes (P) and also acts as a producer which forwards collected data to a Main Monitor. Note here that many application processes can simultaneously send and receive messages to/from LM. The Main Monitor (MM), which is preferably situated on a gateway, receives requests from a client (consumer) and routes them to Local Monitors, eventually gathering all answers and forwarding them back to the client.

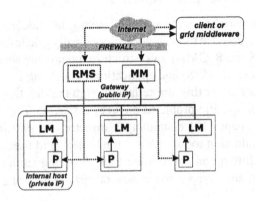

Figure 2.　A general Mercury monitoring system architecture

4. Embedding Sensors in Applications - MPI Example

In addition to basic monitoring features, Mercury also allows sensors to be embedded in applications by enabling applications to register their own metrics and controls in order to both publish application specific information and receive steering signals via Mercury. Application specific metrics and controls can be accessed in the same way as any other metric/control. As it is presented in Fig. 3, a direct two-way communication channel can be established between applications/processes (P) and Local Monitors (LM) of Mercury thus external clients, for example a management system, can interact with the application via a Main Monitor (MM) located on a gateway machine.

Three parameters are associated with every application that is using an embedded sensor to provide a way to uniquely identify a process in a multi-threaded or parallel (e.g. MPI) application:

program name this parameter can be used for the human-readable identification of a particular process or thread in a multi-process or multi-threaded application,

tid this parameter is a machine-readable identification number of processes, e.g. the thread identifier of a multi-threaded application or process' rank in an MPI application; the tid should be unique for every process of the same job,

jobid a global job identification usually given by a grid service (such as a scheduler), the local queuing system or operating system (see the RMS component in Fig. 3).

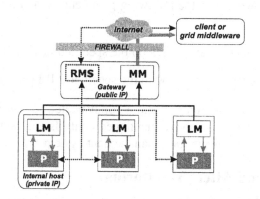

Figure 3. Two-way communication channels between distributed applications and Mercury Local Monitors

Once a communication channel is established between P and LM, embedded sensors can be used to interact dynamically with remote applications/processes.

Technically speaking, applications must be recompiled with non-intrusive and portable Mercury libraries.

Initially, we have implemented and tested the following metrics and controls for MPI applications:

progress every process in MPI groups works independently; this metric indicates its status, for example as 0-100% value,

jobsize this metric provides the maximum MPI rank identifier, so the external control entity knows how to independently access every running processes,

whereami it is crucial to know which process is run on which local host, so this metric provides MPI rank and hostname for each process in MPI group,

checkpoint this control should be interpreted by a master process in an MPI process group. Therefore, it should act properly and inform other processes using MPI to shutdown and write down their status files. This can be used by GRMS to dynamically reschedule the execution of the application and migrate it if necessary,

resource usage metrics these metrics provide a detailed view of resources (e.g. memory usage, CPU load, free disk quota) consumed by the application.

To access mentioned metrics and controls, a client of Mercury, in our case a management system, has to simply query the Main Monitor by using a metric name (e.g. progress) and appropriate parameters specifying an application identity (jobid). Moreover, the following parameters may also be added in the query:

host to limit the query to processes on the specified host in cluster,

tid to limit the query to process with the specified MPI process' rank.

In the next section we present more sophisticated monitoring capabilities which are in fact based on above mentioned controls and metrics but provide flexible control mechanisms for a management system.

5.   Event and Altert Monitoring

Mercury provides push mechanisms for event-like measurements (e.g. a state change) and basic support for generating periodic events to enable monitoring of continous metrics (e.g. processor load). One of the useful features from the management point of view however, is a generation of events based on processing monitoring data. Since this capability is not strictly part of the monitoring system and in fact needs knowledge about the semantics of the monitored data we have proposed an external module to Mercury called Event Monitor (EM). In a nutshell, EM implements more sophisticated push mechanisms as it is highlighted in Fig. 4. Event Monitors allow clients dynamic management and control of event-like metrics as very useful information providers for clients or management systems. We see many real scenarios in which an external client wants to have access to metrics described in the previous section (regardless of their type) and additionally, often due to performance reasons, does not want to constantly monitor their values.

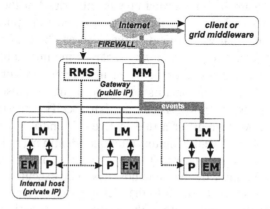

Figure 4. Event Monitors as external Mercury modules for event-like monitoring of resources and applications

Nowadays, policy-driven change and configuration management that can dynamically adjust the size, configuration, and allocation of resources are becoming extremely important issues. In many real use cases, a resource management system may want to take an action according to predefined management rules or conditions. For example, when application progress reaches a certain level, the process memory usage becomes too high or dedicated disc quota is exceeded. Event Monitor was developed to facilitate such scenarios. Its main functionality is to allow an external client to register a metric in Event Monitor for receiving appropriate notifications when certain conditions are met. Strictly speaking, clients can setup an appropriate frequency (a default one has been set to 5 seconds) of Event Monitor requests to LM. They can also use a predefined standard relational operator (greater than, less than, etc.) and different values of metrics to define various rules and conditions. Example EM rules for fine-grained enforcement of resource usage or application control are presented below:

- Example *application oriented* rules in Event Monitor:

```
app.priv.jobid.LOAD(tid) > 0.8
```

```
app.priv.jobid.MEMORY(tid) > 100MB
app.priv.jobid.PROGRESS(tid) > 90
```

- Example *host oriented* rules in Event Monitor:

```
host.loadavg5(host) > 0.5
host.net.total.error(host, interface) > 0
```

When the condition is fulfilled Event Monitor can generate an event-like message and forward it to interested clients subscribed at the Mercury Main Monitor component - MM. Note that any metric, host or application specific, that returns a numerical value or a data type that can be evaluated to a simple numerical value (e.g. a record or an array) can be monitored this way.

In fact, four basic steps must be taken in order to add or remove a new rule/condition to Event Monitor. First of all, the client must discover a metric in Mercury using its basic features. Then it needs to specify both a relation operator and a value in order to register a rule in Event Monitor. After successfully registering the rule in Event Monitor, a unique identifier (called *Event ID*) is assigned to the monitored metric. To start the actual monitoring, the commit control of Event Monitor on the same host has to be executed. Eventually, the client needs to subscribe to listen to the metric (with no target host specified) through Main Monitor and wait for the event with the assigned *Event ID* to occur.

6.   Example Adaptive Multi-criteria Resource Management Strategie

The efficient management of jobs before their submission to remote domains often turns out to be very difficult to achieve. It has been proved that more adaptive methods, e.g. rescheduling, which take advantage of a migration mechanism may provide a good way of improving performance[6] [7] [8]. Depending on the goal that is to be achieved using the rescheduling method, the decision to perform a migration can be made on the basis of a number of events. For example the rescheduling process in the GrADS project consists of two modes: migrate on request (if application performance degradation is unacceptable) and opportunistic migration (if resources were freed by recently completed jobs)[6]. A performance oriented migration framework for the Grid, described in[8], attempts to improve the response times for individual applications. Another tool that uses adaptive scheduling and execution on Grids is the GridWay framework[7]. In the same work, the migration techniques have been classified into the application-initiated and grid-initiated migration. The former category contains the migration initiated by application performance degradation and the change of application requirements or preferences (self-migration).

The grid-initiated migration may be triggered by the discovery of a new, better resource (opportunistic migration), a resource failure (failover migration), or a decision of the administrator or the local resource management system. Recently, we have demonstrated that checkpointing, migration and rescheduling methods could shorten queue waiting times in the Grid Resource Management System (GRMS) and, consequently, decrease the application response times[9]. We have explored a migration that was performed due to the insufficient amount of free resources required by incoming jobs. Application-level checkpointing has been used in order to provide full portability in the heterogeneous Grid environment. In our tests, the amount of free physical memory has been used to determine whether there are enough available resources to submit the pending job. Nevertheless, the algorithm is generic, so we have easily incorporated other measurements and new Mercury monitoring capabilities described in previous two sections. Based on new sensor-oriented features provided by Event Monitor we are planning to develop a set of tailor-made resource management strategies in GRMS to facilitate the management of distributed environments.

7. Preliminary Results and Future Work

We have performed our experiments in a real testbed connecting two clusters over the Internet located in different domains. The first one consists of 4 machines (Linux 2-CPU Xeon 2,6GHz), and second consists of 12 machines (Linux 2-CPU Pentium 2,2 GHz). The average network latency time between these two clusters was about 70ms.

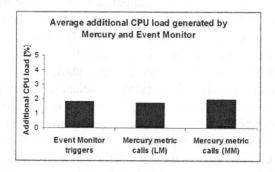

Figure 5. Performance costs of Mercury and Event Monitor

In order to test capabilities as well as performance costs of Mercury and Event Monitors running on testbed machines we have developed a set of example MPI applications and client tools. As it is presented in Fig. 5 all control, monitoring and event-based routines do not come at any significant performance. Additional CPU load generated during 1000 client requests per minute did not exceed ca. 3% and in fact was hard to observe on monitored hosts.

Additional memory usage of Mercury and Event Monitor was changing from 2 to 4 MB on each host.

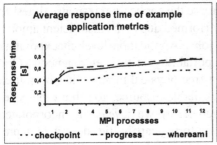 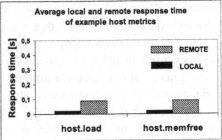

Figure 6.   Response times of basic monitoring operations performed on Mercury and Event Monitor

In our tests we have been constantly querying Mercury locally from many client tools and the average response time of all host metrics monitored on various hosts was stable and equaled approximately 18 ms. Remote response times as we expected were longer due to network delays (70ms). The next figure shows us results of application oriented metrics which have been added in various testing MPI applications. The important outcome is that the response time (less than 1 second) did not increase significantly when more MPI processes were used, what is important especially to adopt monitoring capabilities for large scale experiments running on much bigger clusters.

All these performance tests have proved efficiency, scalability and low intrusiveness of both Mercury and Event Monitor and encouraged us for further research and development. Currently, as it was mentioned in Sect. 5, Event Monitor works as an external application as far as Mercury's viewpoint is concerned but this does not restrict its functionality. However, in the future it may become more tightly integrated with the Mercury system (e.g. as a Mercury module) due to performance and maintenance reasons. To facilitate integration of Mercury and Event Monitor with external clients or grid middleware services, in particular GRMS, we have also developed the JEvent-monitor-client package in Java which provides a higher level interface as a simple wrapper based on the low-level metric/control calls provided by Mercury API. Additionally, to help application developers we have developed easy-to-use libraries which connect applications to Mercury and allow them to take advantage of mentioned monitoring capabilities.

Acknowledgments

Most of presented work has been done in the scope of CoreGrid project. This project is founded by EU and aims at strengthening and advancing scientific and technological excellence in the area of Grid and Peer-to-Peer technologies.

References

[1] http://www.gridlab.org

[2] http://glite.web.cern.ch/glite/

[3] http://www.globus.org

[4] http://www.gridlab.org/grms/

[5] G. Gombás and Z. Balaton. "A Flexible Multi-level Grid Monitoring Architecture", In Proceedings of 1st European Across Grids Conference, Santiago de Compostela, Spain, 2003. Volume 2970 of Lecture Notes in Computer Science, p. 214-221

[6] K. Cooper et al., "New Grid Scheduling and Rescheduling Methods in the GrADS Project", In Proceedings of Workshop for Next Generation Software (held in conjunction with the IEEE International Parallel and Distributed Processing Symposium 2004), Santa Fe, New Mexico, April 2004

[7] E. Huedo, R. Montero and I. Llorente, "The GridWay Framework for Adaptive Scheduling and Execution on Grids", In Proceedings of AGridM Workshop (in conjunction with the 12th PACT Conference, New Orleans (USA)), Nova Science, October 2003

[8] S. Vadhiyar and J. Dongarra, "A Performance Oriented Migration Framework For The Grid", In Proceedings of CCGrid, IEEE Computing Clusters and the Grid, CCGrid 2003, Tokyo, Japan, May 12-15, 2003

[9] "Improving Grid Level Throughput Using Job Migration and Rescheduling Techniques in GRMS. Scientific Programming", Krzysztof Kurowski, Bogdan Ludwiczak, Jarosław Nabrzyski, Ariel Oleksiak, Juliusz Pukacki, IOS Press. Amsterdam The Netherlands 12:4 (2004) 263-273

[10] M. Gerndt et al., "Performance Tools for the Grid: State of the Art and Future", Research Report Series, Lehrstuhl fuer Rechnertechnik und Rechnerorganisation (LRR-TUM) Technische Universitaet Muenchen, Vol. 30, Shaker Verlag, ISBN 3-8322-2413-0, 2004

[11] Serafeim Zanikolas and Rizos Sakellariou, "A Taxonomy of Grid Monitoring Systems in Future Generation Computer Systems", volume 21, p.163-188, 2005, Elsevier, ISSN 0167-739X

TOWARDS SEMANTICS-BASED RESOURCE DISCOVERY FOR THE GRID*

William Groleau†
Institut National des Sciences Appliquées de Lyon (INSA),
Lyon, France
william.groleau@insa-lyon.fr

Vladimir Vlassov
Royal Institute of Technology (KTH),
Stockholm, Sweden
vlad@it.kth.se

Konstantin Popov
Swedish Institute of Computer Science (SICS),
Kista, Sweden
kost@sics.se

Abstract   We present our experience and evaluation of some of the state-of-the-art software tools and algorithms available for building a system for Grid service provision and discovery using agents, ontologies and semantic markups. We believe that semantic information will be used in every large-scale Grid resource discovery, and the Grid should capitalize on existing research and development in the area. We built a prototype of an agent-based system for resource provision and selection that allows locating services that semantically match the client requirements. Services are described using the Web service ontology (OWL-S). We present our prototype built on the JADE agent framework and an off-the-shelf OWL-S toolkit. We also present preliminary evaluation results, which in particular indicate a need for an incremental classification algorithm supporting incremental extension of a knowledge base with many unrelated or weakly-related ontologies.

Keywords: Grid computing, resource discovery, Web service ontology, semantics.

*This research work is carried out under the FP6 Network of Excellence CoreGRID funded by the European Commission (Contract IST-2002-004265).
†The work was done when the author was with the KTH, Stockholm, Sweden.

1.   Introduction

The Grid is envisioned as an open, ubiquitous infrastructure that allows treating all kinds of computer-related services in a standard, uniform way. Grid services need to have concise descriptions that can be used for service location and composition. The Grid is to be become large, decentralized and heterogeneous. These properties of the Grid imply that service location, composition and inter-service communication needs to be sufficiently flexible since services being composed are generally developed independently of each other [4, 3], and probably do not match perfectly. This problem should be addressed by using semantic, self-explanatory information for Grid service description and inter-service communication [3], which capitalizes on the research and development in the fields of multi-agent systems and, more recently, web services [1].

We believe that basic ontology- and semantic information handling will be an important part of every Grid resource discovery, and eventually – service composition service [2, 6, 20]. W3C contributes the basic standards and tools, in particular the Resource Description Framework (RDF), Web Ontology Language (OWL) and Web service ontology (OWL-S) [21]. RDF is a data model for entities and relations between them. OWL extends RDF and can be used to explicitly represent the meaning of entities in vocabularies and the relations between those entities. OWL-S defines a standard ontology for description of Web services. Because of the close relationship between web- and Grid services, and in particular - the proposed convergence of these technologies in the more recent Web Service Resource Framework (WSRF), RDF, OWL and OWL-S serve as the starting point for the "Semantic Grid" research.

In this paper we present our practical experience and evaluation of the state-of-the-art semantic-web tools and algorithms. We built an agent-based resource provision and selection system that allows locating available services that semantically match the client requirements. Services are described using the Web service ontology (OWL-S), and the system matches descriptions of existing services with service descriptions provided by clients. We extend our previous work [12] by deploying semantic reasoning on service descriptions. We attempted to implement and evaluate matching of both descriptions of services from the functional point of view (service "profiles" in the OWL-S terminology), and descriptions of service structure (service "models"), but due to technical reasons succeeded so far only with the first.

The remainder of the paper is structured as follows. Section 2 presents some background information about semantic description of Grid services and matchmaking of services. The architecture of the agent-based system for Grid service provision and selection is presented in Section 3. Section 4 describes implementation of the system prototype, whereas Section 5 discusses evaluation of the prototype. Finally, our conclusions and future work are given in Section 6.

2. Background

2.1 Semantic Description of Grid Services

The Resource Description Framework (RDF) is the foundation for OWL and OWL-S. RDF is a language for representing information about resources (metadata) on the Web. RDF provides a common framework for expressing this information such that it can be exchanged without loss. "Things" in RDF are identified using Web identifiers (URIs) and described in terms of simple properties and property values. RDF provides for encoding binary relations between a subject and an object. Relations are "things" on their own, and can be described accordingly. There is an XML encoding of RDF.

RDF Schema can be used to define the vocabularies for RDF statements. RDF Schema provides the facilities needed to describe application-specific classes and properties, and to indicate how these classes and properties can to be used together. RDF Schema can be seen as a type system for RDF. RDF Schema allows to define class hierarchies, and declare properties that characterize classes. Class properties can be also sub-typed, and restricted with respect to the domain of their subjects and the range of their objects. RDF Schema also contains facilities to describe collections of entities, and to state information about other RDF statements.

OWL [13] is a semantic markup language used to describe ontologies in terms of classes that represent concepts or/and collection of individuals, individuals (instances of classes), and properties. OWL goes beyond RDF Schema, and provides means to express relations between classes such as "disjoint", cardinality constraints, equality, richer typing of properties etc. There are three versions of OWL: "Lite", "DL" , and "Full"; the first two provide computationally complete reasoning. In this work we need the following OWL elements:

- *owl:Class* defines a concept in the ontology (e.g. *<owl:Class rdf:ID="Winery"/>*);

- *rdfs:subClassOf* relates a more specific class to a more general class;

- *rdfs:equivalentClass* defines a class as equivalent to another class.

OWL-S [14] defines a standard ontology for Web services. It comprises three main parts: the profile, the model and the grounding. The service profile presents "what the service does" with necessary functional information: input, output, preconditions, and the effect of the service. The service model describes "how the service works", that is all the processes the service is composed of, how these processes are executed, and under which conditions they are executed. The process model can hence be seen as a tree, where the leaves are the atomic processes, the interior nodes are the composite processes, and the root node is the process that starts execution of the service.

```
<ions:LangInput rfd:ID="InputLanguage">
    <process:parameterType rdf:resource=
        "http://www.mindswap.org/2004/owl-s/1.1/BabelFishTranslator" />
</ions:LangInput>
```

Figure 1. Definition of an OWL-S service parameter.

An example definition of an OWL-S service input parameter is shown in Figure 1. In this example, the concept attached to the parameter *InputLanguage* is *SupportedLanguage*, found in the ontology http://www.mindswap.org/2004/owl-s/1.1/BabelFishTranslator.owl. The class of the parameter is *LangInput*, which has been defined as a subclass of *Input* (predefined in the OWL-S ontology) in the namespace *ions*.

Few basic OWL-S elements need to be considered by matchmakers:

- *profile:Profile* defines the service profile that includes a textual description of the service, references to the model, etc., and a declaration of the parameters:

    – *profile:hasInput* / *profile:hasOutput*

- *process:Input* / *process:Output* defines the parameters previously declared in the profile, and mostly contains the following elements:

    – *process:parameterType* which defines the type of the parameter.

Note that inputs can be defined by *process:input* or *process:output* or by any subclass of input or output, as in our example Figure 1. Moreover a profile can also be defined by a subclass of *profile:Profile*.

2.2 Matching Services

Matchmaking is a common notion in multi-agent systems. It denotes the process of identifying agents with similar capabilities [11]. Matchmaking for Web Services is based on the notion of *similar* services [16] since it is unrealistic to expect services to be *exactly* identical. The matchmaking algorithms proposed in [19, 8, 16] calculate a degree of resemblance between two services.

Services can be matched by either their OWL-S profiles or OWL-S models [17]. In this work we consider only matching service profiles leaving matching of service models to our future work. Matching service profiles can include matching (1) service functionalities and (2) functional attributes. The latter is exemplified by the ATLAS matchmaker [17]. We focus on matching service functionalities as, in our view, it is more important than matching functional attributes. The idea of matching capabilities of services described in OWL-S using the profiles has been approached first in [16] and refined in [19, 8]. We use the latter extension in our work as it allows more precise matchmaking by taking into account more elements of OWL-S profiles. Other solutions such as the ATLAS matchmaker [17], are more focused in matching functional attributes and do not appear to be as complete as the one we use.

Our profile matchmaker compares inputs and outputs of request and advertisement service descriptions, and includes matching of the *profile types*. A service profile can be defined as an instance of a subclass of the class *Profile*, and included in a concept hierarchy (the OWL-S ServiceCategory element is not used in our prototype). When two parameters are being matched, the relation between the concepts linked to the parameters is evaluated (sub/super-class, equivalent or disjoint). This relation is called "concept match". In the example in Figure 1, *SupportedLanguage* would be the concept to match. Next, the relation existing between the parameter property classes is evaluated (sub/super-property, equivalent, disjoint or unclassified). This relation is called "property match". In the example in Figure 1, *LangInput* would be the property to match. The final matching score assigned for two parameters is the combination of the scores obtained in the concept and property matches, as shown in Table 1. Finally, the matching algorithm computes aggregated scores for outputs and inputs, as shown below for outputs:

$$min(max(scoreMatch(outputAdv, outputReq)$$
$$|outputAdv \in AdvOutputs)$$
$$|outputReq \in ReqOutputs)$$

scoreMatch is the combination score of the "concept match" and "property match" results (see Table 1); *AdvOutputs* is the list of all outputs parameters of the provided service; *reqOutputs* is the list of all outputs parameters of the requested service (requested outputs). The algorithm identifies outputs in the provided service that match outputs of the requested service with the maximal score, and finally determines the pair of outputs with the worst maximal score. For instance, the score will be sub-class if all outputs of the advertised service perfectly match the requested outputs, except for one output which is a sub-class of its corresponding output in the requested service (if we neglect the "property match" score). A similar aggregated score is computed also for inputs.

The final comparison score for two services is the weighted sum of outputs-, inputs- and profile matching scores. Typically, outputs are considered most important ([16]) and receive the largest weight. The profile matchmaker returns all matching services sorted by the final scores.

When a requestor does not want to disclose to providers too much information about the requested service, the requestor can specify only the service category.

Table 1.   Rankings for the matching of two parameters.

Rank	Property-match result	Concept-match result
0	Fail	Any
	Any	Fail
1	Unclassified	Invert Subsumes
2		Subsumes
3		Equivalent
4	Subproperty	Invert Subsumes
5		Subsumes
6		Equivalent
7	Equivalent	Invert Subsumes
8		Subsumes
9		Equivalent

3.   Architecture

The architecture of the first system prototype was presented in [12]. In Figure 2, the highlighted "Virtual Organization Registry" is obsolete and replaced by the indexing services of the Globus Toolkit 4 [5]. In the first prototype, a requested service is assumed to be described in GWSDL where properties are defined in Service Data Elements. In the system prototype reported in this article, a requested service is described by the user in an OWL-S document.

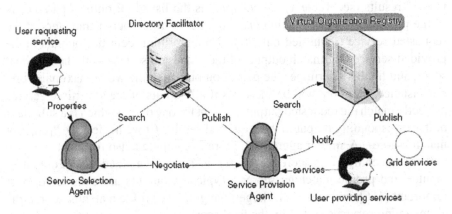

Figure 2.   Architecture of the Agent-Based System for Grid Service Provision and Selection.

The UML sequence diagram in Figure 3 shows how our platform works, and highlights the matchmaking parts. A service provider specifies URLs of its services to a Service Provision Agent, which registers (if not yet) to the Directory facilitator. A user selecting a service performs the following steps:

1 Instantiation of a Service Selection Agent (SSA);

2 Getting the list of available providers (a.k.a Service Provision Agents, SPA) via the Directory Facilitator (DF);

3 Searching for a matching service, in three steps:

  (a) Sending a description of the requested service as an OWL-S file to the available providers, obtained in Step 1;

  (b) On the provision side, each SPA computes possible matches in parallel;

  (c) The SPAs asynchronously send their results to the requesting SSA;

4 Result treatment, i.e. in our case presenting the matching services to the user.

As we can see, the matchmaking processes occur in the red-marked zone of the diagram, on the provision side. The algorithms implemented at this level are of course either the profile or the model matchmakers.

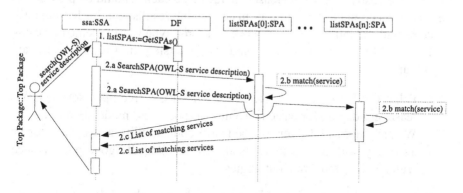

Figure 3. Selecting services.

The use of the category matchmaker (not considered here) is justified in the "secure mode" when a requestor provides only category rather than a detailed description of the service.

The dataflow in the system is depicted in Figure 4. If services are described in GWSDL or in WS-RF, the system should provide WSDL-to-QWL-S or/and WS-RF-to-OWL-S translator like the one used in the first system prototype [12].

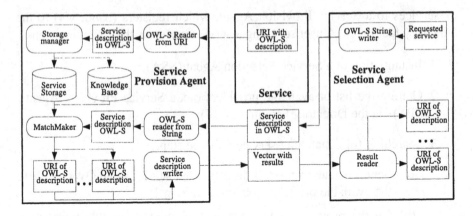

Figure 4.   Information flow in the system.

4.   Implementation

The first system prototype was reported in [12]. We have upgraded the overall system faithfully to the system specification described in Section 3. We implemented the profile matchmaker detailed in Section 2. The trickiest part was the implementation of the inference engine where one should be vigilant about limiting the costly calls to the reasoner. Ideally, a cache should be provided to remember all computed relations or matchmaking results, but this has not been implemented and left to our future work. The prototype was implemented using Java 1.4 and the Jade multi-agent platform [7], using the following software and libraries:

- Pellet OWL Reasoner, v. 1.2, [18], which is a free open-source OWL reasoner adapted for basic reasoning purposes and moderate ontologies. We have used Pellet for its good Java compatibility and mostly for its adequacy with our basic needs and for its allegedly good performance with small to moderate ontologies.

- OWL-S API, [15]. This API is one of the available APIs which has no particular advantages (apart supporting the latest OWL-S version). The API has been chosen because it is compatible with the Pellet reasoner.

- Jena v.2.2 [10] – a framework required by the Pellet reasoner.

- Jade [7]. Multi-agent platform on which the system works. We kept Jade which was used in the previous system [12], as this seams to be an efficient platform.

- Jdom v. 1.0 [9]

As mentioned above, the prototype supports only profile matching; we intend to add the matchmaking mechanism for model matching. GUIs have been developed for the providers (letting the possibility to add and remove services) and for the requesters (letting the possibility to search services and modify various search parameters: results collection time, number of providers to contact, specification of the request OWL-S document). A system prototype is available from the authors on request.

5. Evaluation

The implemented prototype has been evaluated using sample services and ontologies found at http://www.mindswap.org, http://www.aktors.org/ontology/portal and http://protege.stanford.edu. In this article we focus only on the evaluation of the profile matchmaker described in section 2.2. We ran the prototype on a Pentium M 1.6GHz with 512MB of RAM. In our experiments, initially the knowledge base in the SPA is loaded with base service ontologies and ontologies of provisioned services. In our evaluation experiments we have considered the following four activities during matchmaking:

- *Parsing services.* We measure the time spent in parsing OWL-S documents in order to store the service descriptions in the API internal representation.

- *Knowledge base classification* (computing subclass relations between all the named classes), which is necessary for efficient determining of relations between classes during matchmaking. Classification is performed once concepts from a pattern service description are added to the knowledge base.

- *Getting a class in the ontology.* We measure the time spent obtaining a reference to a class in the knowledge base, given its URI. Reference to classes are used in particular when the knowledge base is queried about relations between profile types and concepts of service parameters.

- *Determining relations between classes.* We measure the time spent computing the relations (sub/super-class, equivalent, disjoint) between two service parameters. This computation is requested by the matchmaker when it compares two parameters. Relations are inferred by the Pellet reasoner. Note that this reasoning is performed on ontology concepts only (so-called TBox reasoning), and in particular does not depend on the number of OWL class instances.

In order to estimate the relative importance of each of these activities during matchmaking, we calculate the total time taken by an activity as a measured time of one invocation multiplied by the number of invocations. For example, 2 classes need to be fetched in the ontology in order to infer one relation; at worst 6 relations need to be inferred (3 for the concept match and 3 for the property match) in order to match 2 parameters. Our estimates show that in order to match a typical service with 2 inputs and 2 outputs against a provided service, 1 service description is parsed and added to the knowledge base, 1 knowledge base classification is performed, and in the worst case 56 classes are fetched from the knowledge base and 28 relations between classes are computed. Resulting time partitioning in the matchmaking process is shown in Figure 5.

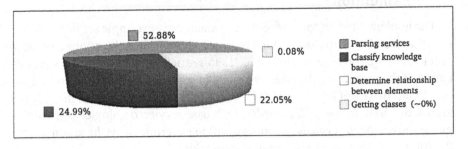

Figure 5.   Time partitioning in the matchmaking process.

We studied the scalability of the system wrt the size of the knowledge base in the SPA. Since parsing OWL-S documents does not depend on the size of the knowledge base, and getting classes in the ontology is very inexpensive, we focused on scalability of the remaining two operations - knowledge base classification and determining relations between classes.

We evaluated the scalability of the classification algorithm by incremental loading of additional ontologies into the knowledge base. Execution time as a function of the knowledge base size is presented in Figure 6. The test program run out of memory as we attempted to load larger ontologies. Note that there are no OWL class instances (i.e. the reasoner's ABox is empty) in this test. For each knowledge base size, we also evaluated the cost of classification after loading an OWL-S service description document into the base, which mimics the operation of an SPA. The execution time of this second classification is presented in Figure 7. We assume that the significant increase in classification time in the latter case is due to OWL class instances in the OWL-S document. Clearly, classification of larger ontologies measured in minutes makes the application hardly usable. An incremental classification algorithm could solve this problem.

We also partially evaluated the scalability of the "is-subclass-of" reasoning used for determining relations between classes.   First, we took the http://www.aktors.org/ontology/portal ontology and an OWL-S service descrip-tion, and measured and averaged the "is-subclass-of" execution time between 5 randomly chosen but fixed pairs of concepts from the "portal" ontology. Then, we repeated the measurements with knowledge bases containing additional un-related to "portal" ontologies, as presented in Figure 8. Note that the execution time is given in nanoseconds. The results confirmed that the reasoning time is not affected by additional unrelated information present in the knowledge base.

As a future work, we plan to find a set of related ontologies and evaluate the scalability of the "is-subclass-of" reasoning with a sequence of experiments, such that in each experiment concepts are randomly chosen from the experiment's entire knowledge base.

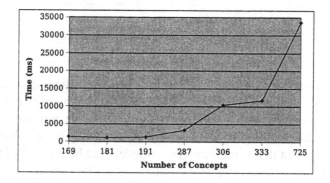

Figure 6. Cost of classification as a function of knowledge base size.

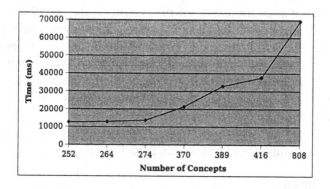

Figure 7. Cost of classification after loading an OWL-S document.

6. Conclusions and Future Work

We presented our experience and evaluation of some of the state-of-the-art semantic-web tools and algorithms. We built an agent-based resource provision and selection system that allows to locate services that semantically match the client requirements. We conducted the research since we believe that basic ontology- and semantic information handling will be an important part of every

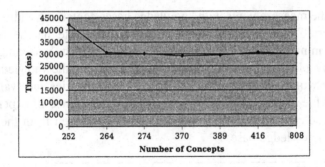

Figure 8.   Scalability of "is-subclass-of" inference.

Grid resource discovery, and eventually – service composition service. In our system prototype we have implemented the matchmaking algorithm proposed in [19]. The algorithm compares a requested service profile with provided service profiles to find a better match(es), if any. Alternatively or complementary, a matching algorithm that compares service models can be used. We intend to consider service model matching in our future work. Our system prototype allows a "secure" mode in which a requester provides only information on service category, and a category matching is done by the providers, whereas profile or model matchmaking is done by the requester.

We have presented an evaluation of the system prototype. We have estimated contribution of different parts of the system to the overall performance. Our evaluation results indicate that the system performance is very sensitive to the performance of the knowledge base and the reasoner which can become a bottleneck with larger knowledge bases. In particular, an incremental classification algorithm is required to support incremental extension of a knowledge base with many unrelated or weakly-related ontologies.

Our future work includes improvements of the reasoning performance, research on service composition, and service model matchmaking.

Acknowledgments

This work was supported by Vinnova, Swedish Agency for Innovation Systems (GES3 project 2003-00931). This research work is carried out under the FP6 Network of Excellence CoreGRID funded by the European Commission (Contract IST-2002-004265). The authors would like to acknowledge the anonymous reviewers for their constructive comments and suggestions.

References

[1] T. Berners-Lee, J. Hendler, and O. Lassila. The semantic web. *Sci.American*, May 2001.

[2] J. Brooke, D. Fellows, K. Garwood, and C.A. Goble. Semantic matching of grid resource descriptions. In *Proceedings of The 2nd European Across Grids Conference*, 2004.

[3] D. de Roure, N. R. Jennings, and N. Shadbolt. The semantic Grid: Past, present and future. *Proceedings of the IEEE*, 93, 2005.

[4] I. Foster, N.R. Jennings, and C. Kesselman. Brain meets brawn: Why grid and agents need each other. In *Third International Joint Conference on Autonomous Agents and Multiagent Systems (AAMAS'04)*. IEEE, 2004.

[5] The Globus Alliance. www.globus.org.

[6] F. Heine, M. Hovestadt, and O. Kao. Towards ontology-driven P2P Grid resource discovery. In *5th IEEE/ACM International Workshop on Grid Computing*, November 2004.

[7] Telecom italia lab. jade 3.1. http://jade.tilab.com/.

[8] M. Jaeger, G. Rojec-Goldmann, G. Mühl, C. Liebetruth, and K. Geihs. Ranked matching for service descriptions using OWL-S. *Kommunikation in verteilten Systemen*, Feb 2005.

[9] The JDOM project. jdom 1.0. http://jdom.org/.

[10] HP Labs, Jena 2.2. http://www.hpl.hp.com/semweb/jena.htm.

[11] M. Klusch and K. Sycara. Brokering and matchmaking for coordination of agent societies: a survey. In *Coordination of Internet agents: models, technologies, and applications*, pages 197–224. Springer, 2001.

[12] G. Nimar, V. Vlassov, and K. Popov. Practical experience in building an agent system for semantics-based provision and selection of gridservices. In *Proceedings of PPAM 2005: Sixth International Conference on Palel Processing and Applied Mathematics*, Poznan, Poland, September 11-14, 2005, Revised Selected Papers, volume 3911 of LNCS, Springer 2006.

[13] OWL web ontology language overview. W3C Recommendation, http://www.w3.org/TR/owl-features/, February 10 2004.

[14] OWL-S: Semantic markup for web services. http://www.daml.org/services/owl-s/1.1/overview.

[15] OWL-S API. http://www.mindswap.org/2004/owl-s/api/.

[16] M. Paolucci, T. Kawamura, T.R. Payne, and K.P. Sycara. Semantic matching of web services capabilities. In *ISWC '02: Proceedings of the First International Semantic Web Conference on The Semantic Web*, pages 333–347, London, UK, 2002. Springer-Verlag.

[17] T. Payne, M. Paolucci, and K. Sycara. Advertising and matching DAML-S service descriptions. In *Position papers of the first Semantic Web Working Symposium (SWWS'2001)*, pages 76–78, Stanford, USA, July 2001.

[18] E. Sirin, B. Parsia, B. Grau, A. Kalyanpur, and Y. Katz. Pellet: A practical OWL-DL reasoner. Submitted for publication to Journal of Web Semantics. See alo http://www.mindswap.org/2003/pellet/index.shtml, 2006.

[19] S. Tang. Matching of web service specifications using DAML-S descriptions. Master thesis, Dept. of Telecommunication Systems, Berlin Technical University, March 18 2004.

[20] H. Tangmunarunkit, S. Decker, and C. Kesselman. Ontology-based resource matching in the Grid – the Grid meets the semantic web. In *2nd International International Semantic Web Conference (ISWC2003)*, 2003.

[21] World Wide Web Consortium (W3C). www.w3c.org.

SCHEDULING WORKFLOWS
WITH BUDGET CONSTRAINTS*

Rizos Sakellariou and Henan Zhao
School of Computer Science
University of Manchester
U.K.

rizos@cs.man.ac.uk

hzhao@cs.man.ac.uk

Eleni Tsiakkouri and Marios D. Dikaiakos
Department of Computer Science
University of Cyprus
Cyprus

cstsiak@cs.ucy.ac.cy

mdd@cs.ucy.ac.cy

Abstract   Grids are emerging as a promising solution for resource and computation demanding applications. However, the heterogeneity of resources in Grid computing, complicates resource management and scheduling of applications. In
addition, the commercialization of the Grid requires policies that can take into
account user requirements, and budget considerations in particular. This paper
considers a basic model for workflow applications modelled as Directed Acyclic
Graphs (DAGs) and investigates heuristics that allow to schedule the nodes of
the DAG (or tasks of a workflow) onto resources in a way that satisfies a budget
constraint and is still optimized for overall time. Two different approaches are
implemented, evaluated and presented using four different types of basic DAGs.

Keywords: Workflows, Scheduling, Budget Constrained Scheduling, DAG Scheduling.

---

*This work was supported by the CoreGRID European Network of Excellence, part of the European Com-
mission's IST programme #004265

1.   Introduction

In the context of Grid computing, a wide range of applications can be represented as workflows many of which can be modelled as Directed Acyclic Graphs (DAGs) [9, 12, 2, 7]. In this model, each node in the DAG represents an executable task (it could be an application component of the workflow). Each directed edge represents a precedence constraint between two tasks (data or control dependence). A DAG represents a model that helps build a schedule of the tasks onto resources in a way that precedence constraints are respected and the schedule is optimized. Virtually all existing work in the literature [1, 8, 10, 11] aims to minimize the total execution time (length or makespan) of the schedule.

Although the minimization of an application's execution time might be an important user requirement, managing a Grid environment is a more complex task which may require policies that strike a balance between different (and often conflicting) requirements of users and resources. Existing Grid resource management systems are mainly driven by system-centric policies, which aim to optimize system-wide metrics of performance. However, it is envisaged that future fully deployed Grid environments will need to guarantee a certain level of service and employ user-centric policies driven by economic principles [3, 6]. Of particular interest will be the resource access cost, since different resources, belonging to different organisations, may have different policies for charging. Clearly, users would like to pay a price which is commensurate to the budget they have available.

There has been little work examining issues related to budget constraints in a Grid context. The most relevant work is available in [4–5], where it is demonstrated, through Grid simulation, how a scheduling algorithm can allocate jobs to machines in a way that satisfies constraints of Deadline and Budget at the same time. In this simulation, each job is considered to be a set of independent Gridlets (objects that contain all the information related to a job and its execution management details such as job length in million instructions, disk I/O operations, input and output file sizes and the job originator) [4]. Workflow types of applications, where jobs have precedence constraints, are not considered.

In this paper, we consider workflow applications that are modelled as DAGs. Instead of focussing only on makespan optimisation, as most existing studies have done [2, 8, 10], we also consider that a budget constraint needs to be satisfied. Each job, when running on a machine, costs some money. Thus, the overall aim is to find the schedule that gives the shortest makespan for a given DAG and a given set of resources *without* exceeding the budget available. In this model, our emphasis is placed on the heuristics rather than the accurate modelling of a Grid environment; thus, we adopt a fairly static methodology in defining execution costs of the tasks of the DAG. However, as indicated by studies on workflow scheduling [2, 7, 12], it appears that heuristics performing best in a static environment (e.g., HBMCT [8]) have the highest potential to perform best in a more accurately modelled Grid environment.

In order to solve the problem of scheduling optimally under a budget constraint, we propose two basic families of heuristics, which are evaluated in the paper. The idea in both approaches is to start from an assignment which has good performance under one of the two optimization criteria considered (that is, makespan and budget) and swap tasks between machines trying to optimize as much as possible for the other criterion. The first approach starts with an assignment of tasks onto machines that is optimized for makespan (using a standard algorithm for DAG scheduling onto heterogeneous resources, such as HEFT [10] or HBMCT [8]). As long as the budget is exceeded, the idea is to keep swapping tasks between machines by choosing first those tasks where the largest savings in terms of money will result in the smallest loss in terms of schedule length. We call this approach as LOSS. Conversely, the second approach starts with the cheapest assignment of tasks onto resources (that is, the one that requires the least money). As long as there is budget available, the idea is to keep swapping tasks between machines by choosing first those tasks where the largest benefits in terms of minimizing the makespan will be obtained for the smallest expense. We call this approach GAIN. Variations in how tasks are chosen result in different heuristics, which we evaluate in the paper.

The rest of the paper is organized as follows. Section 2 gives some background information about DAGs. In Section 3 we present the core algorithm proposed along with a description of the two approaches developed and some variants. In Section 4, we present experimental results that evaluate the two approaches. Finally, Section 5 concludes the paper.

2. Background

Following similar studies [2, 12, 9], the DAG model we adopt makes the following assumptions. Without loss of generality, we consider that a DAG starts with a single entry node and has a single exit node. Each node connects to other nodes with edges, which represent the node dependencies. Edges are annotated with a value, which indicates the amount of data that need to be communicated from a parent node to a child node. For each node the execution time on each different machine available is given. In addition, the time to communicate data between machines is given. Using this input, traditional studies from the literature aim to assign tasks onto machines in such a way that the overall schedule length is minimized and precedence constraints are met. An example of a DAG and the schedule length produced using a well-known heuristic, HEFT [10], is shown in Figure 1. A number of other heuristics could

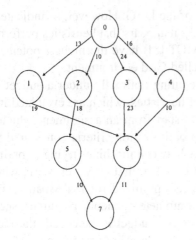

task	m0	m1	m2
0	17	28	17
1	26	11	14
2	30	13	27
3	6	25	3
4	12	2	12
5	7	8	23
6	23	16	29
7	12	14	11

(b) the computation cost of nodes
on three different machines

machines	time for a data unit
m0 - m1	1.607
m1 - m2	0.9
m0 - m2	3.0

(a) an example graph

(c) communication cost between the
machines

node	start time	finish time
0	0	17
1	17	43
2	33.07	46.07
3	43	49
4	46.07	48.07
5	48.07	56.07
6	64.14	87.14
7	87.14	99.14

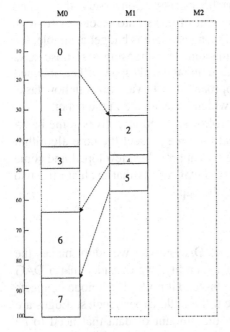

(e) the start time and finish time of
each node in (d)

(d) the schedule derived using the
HEFT algorithm

Figure 1.   An Example of HEFT scheduling in a DAG workflow.

be used too (see [8], for example). It is noted that in the example in the figure
no task is ever assigned to machine M2. This is primarily due to the high

communication; since HEFT assigns tasks onto the machine that provides the earliest finish time, no task ever satisfies this condition.

The contribution of this paper relates to the extension of the traditional DAG model with one extra condition: the usage of each machine available costs some money. As a result, an additional constraint needs to be satisfied when scheduling the DAG, namely, that the overall financial cost of the schedule does not exceed a certain budget. We define the overall (total) cost as the sum of the costs of executing each task in the DAG onto a machine, that is,

$$TotalCost = \sum C_{ij}, \tag{1}$$

where C_{ij} is the cost of executing task i onto machine j and is calculated as the product of the execution time required by the task on the machine that has been assigned to, times the cost of this machine, that is,

$$C_{ij} = MachineCost_j \times ExecutionTime_{ij}, \tag{2}$$

where $MachineCost_j$, is the cost (in money units) per unit of time to run something on machine j and $ExecutionTime_{ij}$ is the time task i takes to execute on machine j. Throughout this paper, we assume that the value of $MachineCost_j$, for all machines, is given.

3. The Algorithm

3.1 Outline

The key idea of the algorithm proposed is to satisfy the budget constraint by finding the *best affordable assignment* possible. We define the "best assignment" as the assignment whose execution time is the minimum possible. We define "affordable assignment" as the assignment whose cost does not exceed the budget available. We also assume that, on the basis of the input given, the budget available is higher than the cost of the cheapest assignment (that is, the assignment where tasks are allocated onto the machine where it costs the least to execute them); this guarantees that there is at least one solution within the budget available. We also assume that the budget available is less than the cost of the schedule that can be obtained using a DAG scheduling algorithm that aims to minimize the makespan, such as HEFT or HBMCT. Without the latter assumption, there would be no need for further investigation: since the cost of the schedule produced by the DAG scheduling would be within the budget available, it would be reasonable to use this schedule.

The algorithm starts with an initial assignment of the tasks onto machines (schedule) and computes for each reassignment of each task to a different machine, a weight value associated with that particular change. Those weight values are tabulated; thus, a weight table is created for each task in the DAG and each machine. Two alternative approaches for computing the weight values are proposed, depending on the two choices used for the initial assignment: either optimal for makespan (approach called LOSS — in this case, the initial assignment would be produced by an efficient DAG scheduling heuristic [10, 8]), or cheapest (approach called GAIN — in this case, the initial assignment would be produced by allocating tasks to the machines where it costs the least in terms of money; we call this as the cheapest assignment); the two approaches are described in more detail below. Using the weight table, tasks are repeatedly considered for possible reassignment to a machine, as long as the cost of the current schedule exceeds the budget (in the case that LOSS is followed), or, until all possible reassignments would exceed the budget (in the case of GAIN). In either case, the algorithm will try to reassign any given pair of tasks only once, so when no reassignment is possible the algorithm will terminate. We illustrate the key steps of the algorithm in Figure 2.

3.2   The LOSS Approach

The LOSS approach uses as an initial assignment the output assignment of either HEFT [10] or HBMCT [8] DAG scheduling algorithms. If the available budget is bigger or equal to the money cost required for this assignment then this assignment can be used straightaway and no further action is needed. In all the other cases that the budget is less than the cost required for the initial assignment, the LOSS approach is invoked. The aim of this approach is to make a change in the schedule (assignment) obtained through HEFT or HBMCT, so that it will result in the minimum loss in execution time for the largest money savings. This means that the new schedule has an execution time close to the time the original assignment would require but with less cost. In order to come up with such a re-assignment, the LOSS weight values for each task to each machine are computed as follows:

$$LossWeight(i, m) = \frac{T_{new} - T_{old}}{C_{old} - C_{new}} \qquad (3)$$

where T_{old} is the time to execute task i on the machine assigned by HEFT or HBMCT, T_{new} is the time to execute Task i on machine m. Also, C_{old} is the cost of executing task i on the machine given by the HEFT or HBMCT assignment and C_{new} is the cost of executing task i on machine m. If C_{old} is less than or equal to C_{new} the value of $LossWeight$ is considered zero. The algorithm keeps trying re-assignments by considering the smallest values of the $LossWeight$ for all tasks and machines (step 4 of the algorithm in Figure 2).

Input: A DAG (workflow) G with task execution time and communication
A set of machines with cost of executing jobs
A DAG scheduling algorithm H
Available Budget B

Algorithm: (two options: LOSS and GAIN)
1) If LOSS
then generate schedule S using algorithm H
else generate schedule S by mapping each task onto the cheapest machine
2) Build an array A[number_of_tasks][number_of_machines]
3) for each Task in G
for each Machine
if, according to Schedule S, Task is assigned to Machine
then A[Task][Machine] ← 0
else Compute the Weight for A[Task][Machine]
endfor
endfor
4) if LOSS
then condition ← (Cost of schedule S > B)
else condition ← (Cost of schedule S ≤ B)
While (condition and not all possible reassignments have been tried)
if LOSS
then find the smallest non-zero value from A, A[i][j]
else find the biggest non-zero value from A, A[i][j]
Re-assign Task i to Machine j in S and calculate new cost of S.
if (GAIN and cost of S > B)
then invalidate previous reassignment of Task i to Machine j.
endwhile
5) if (cost of schedule S > B)
then use cheapest assignment for S.
6) Return S

Figure 2. The Basic Steps of the Proposed Algorithm

3.3 The GAIN Approach

The GAIN approach uses as a starting assignment the assignment that requires the least money. Each task is initially assigned to the machine that executes the task with the smallest cost. This assignment is called the Cheapest Assignment. In this variation of the algorithm, the idea is to change the Cheapest Assignment by keeping re-assigning tasks to the machine where there is going to be the biggest benefit in makespan for the smallest money cost. This is repeated until there is no more money available (budget exceeded). In a way similar to Equation 3, weight values are computed as follows. It is noted that tasks are considered for reassignment starting with those that have the largest

GainWeight value.

$$GainWeight(i, m) = \frac{T_{old} - T_{new}}{C_{new} - C_{old}} \qquad (4)$$

where T_{old}, T_{new}, C_{new}, C_{old} have exactly the same meaning as in the LOSS approach. Furthermore, if T_{new} is greater than T_{old} or C_{new} is equal to C_{old} we assign a weight value of zero.

3.4 Variants

For each of the two approaches above, we consider three different variants which relate to the way that the weights in Equations 3 and 4 are computed; these modifications result in slightly different versions of the heuristics. The three variants are:

- LOSS1 and GAIN1: in this case, the weights are computed exactly as described above.

- LOSS2 and GAIN2: in this case, the values of T_{old}, T_{new}, and C_{new}, C_{old} in Equations 3 and 4 refer to the benefit in terms of the overall makespan and the overall cost for the schedule and not the benefit associated with the individual tasks being considered for reassignment.

- LOSS3 and GAIN3: in this case, the weights, computed as shown by Equations 3 and 4, are recomputed each time a reassignment is made by the algorithm.

4. Experimental Results

4.1 Experiment Setup

The algorithm described in the previous section was incorporated in a tool developed at the University of Manchester, for the evaluation of different DAG scheduling algorithms [8–9]. In order to evaluate each version of both approaches we run the algorithm proposed in this paper with four different types of DAGs used in the relevant literature [8–9]: FFT, Fork-Join (denoted by FRJ), Laplace (denoted by LPL) and Random DAGs, generated as indicated in [13, 8]. All DAGs contain about 100 nodes each and they are scheduled on 3 different machines. We run the algorithm proposed in the paper 100 times for each type of DAG and both approaches and their variants, and we considered the average values. In each case, we considered nine values for the possible budget, B, as follows:

$$B = C_{cheapest} + k \times (C_{DAG} - C_{cheapest}), \qquad (5)$$

where C_{DAG} is the total cost of the assignment produced by the DAG scheduling heuristic used for the initial assignment (that is, HEFT or HBMCT) when the LOSS approach is considered and $C_{cheapest}$ is the cost of the cheapest assignment. The value of k varies between 0.1 and 0.9. Essentially, this approach allows us to consider values of budget that lie in ten equally distanced points between the money cost for the cheapest assignment and the money cost for the schedule generated by HEFT or HBMCT. Clearly, values for budget outside those two ends are trivial to handle since they indicate that either there is no solution satisfying the given budget, or HEFT and/or HBMCT can provide a solution within the budget.

4.2 Results

Average Normalized Difference metric: In order to compare the quality of the schedule produced by the algorithm for each of the six variants and each type of DAG, and since 100 experiments are considered in each case, we normalize the schedule length (makespan) using the following formula:

$$\frac{T_{value} - T_{cheapest}}{T_{DAG} - T_{cheapest}}, \tag{6}$$

where T_{value} is the makespan returned by our algorithm, $T_{cheapest}$ is the makespan of the cheapest assignment and T_{DAG} is the makespan of HEFT or HBMCT. As a general rule, the makespan of the cheapest assignment, $T_{cheapest}$, is expected to be the worst (longest), and the makespan of HEFT or HBMCT, T_{DAG}, the best (shortest). As a result, the formula above is expected to return a value between 0 and 1 indicating how close the algorithm was to each of the two bounds (note that since HEFT or HBMCT are greedy heuristcs, occasional values which are better than the values obtained by those two heuristics may occur). Hence, for comparison purposes, larger values in Equation 6 indicate a shorter makespan. Since for each case we take 100 runs, the average value of the quantity above produces the *Average Normalized Difference* (AND) from the worst and the best, that is,

$$AND = \frac{1}{100} \sum_{i=1}^{100} \left(\frac{T_{value}^i - T_{cheapest}^i}{T_{DAG}^i - T_{cheapest}^i} \right), \tag{7}$$

where the superscript i denotes the i-th run.

Results showing the AND for each different type of DAG, variant, and budget available (shown in terms of the value of k — see Equation 5) are presented in Figures 3, 4 and 5. Each figure groups the results of a different approach: LOSS starting with HEFT, LOSS starting with HBMCT, and GAIN (in the latter case, a DAG scheduling heuristic would not make any difference, since the initial schedule is built on the basis of assigning tasks to the machine with the least cost). The graphs show the difference of the two approaches. The LOSS variants have a generally better makespan than the GAIN variants and they are capable of

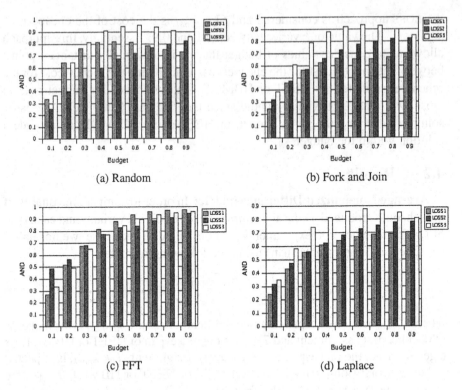

Figure 3. Average normalized difference for the three variants of LOSS when HEFT is used to generate the initial schedule.

performing close to the baseline performance of HEFT or HBMCT (that is, the value 1 in Figures 3 and 4) for different values of the budget. This is due to the fact that the starting basis of the LOSS approach is a DAG scheduling heuristic, which already produces a short makespan. Instead, the GAIN variants starts from the Cheapest Assignment whose makespan is typically long. However, from the experimental results we notice that in a few, limited, cases where the budget is close to the cheapest budget, the AND of the first variant of the GAIN approach is higher than the AND of the LOSS approaches.

Running Time for the Algorithm: To evaluate the performance of each version of the algorithm, using both the LOSS and GAIN approaches, we extracted from the experiments we carried out before, the running time of the algorithm. It appears that the results have little difference between different types of DAGs, so we include here only the results obtained for FFT graphs. Two graphs are presented in Figure 6; one graph assumes that the starting point for LOSS is HEFT and the other graph assumes that the starting point for LOSS is HBMCT. Same as before, the execution time is the average value from 100 runs. It can be

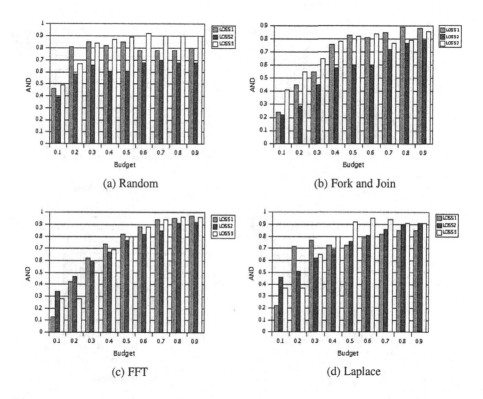

Figure 4. Average normalized difference for the three variants of LOSS when HBMCT is used to generate the initial schedule.

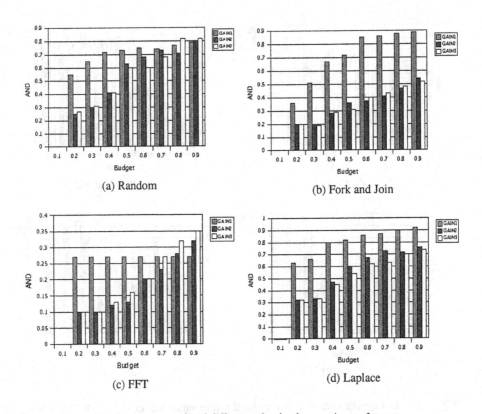

(a) Random

(b) Fork and Join

(c) FFT

(d) Laplace

Figure 5.   Average normalized difference for the three variants of GAIN.

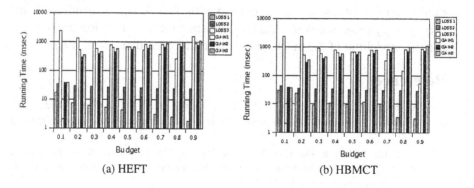

Figure 6. Average running time for each variant of the algorithm, using FFT DAGs.

seen that the GAIN approaches, generally, take longer than the LOSS approaches (the exception seems to arise in cases where the budget is close to the cheapest assignment and the GAIN approaches are quick in identifying a solution). Also, as expected, the third variant of LOSS, which involves re-computation of the weights after each reassignment of tasks, takes longer than the other two.

Summary of observations: The above experiments indicate that the algorithm proposed in this paper is able to find affordable assignments with better makespan when the LOSS approach is applied, instead with the GAIN approach. The LOSS approach applies re-assignment to an assignment that is given by a good DAG scheduling heuristic, whereas in the GAIN approach the cheapest assignment is used to build the schedule; this may have the worst makespan. However, in cases where the available budget is close to the cheapest budget, GAIN1 gives better makespan than LOSS1 or LOSS2. This observation can contribute to the optimization in the performance of the algorithm.

Regarding the running time, it appears that the LOSS approach takes more time as we move towards a budget close to the cost of the cheapest assignment; the opposite happens with the GAIN approach. This is correlated with the starting basis of each of the two approaches.

5. Conclusion

We have implemented an algorithm to schedule DAGs onto heterogeneous machines under budget constraints. Different variants of the algorithm were modelled and evaluated. The main conclusion is that starting from an optimized schedule, in terms of its makespan, pays off when trying to satisfy the budget constraint. As for future work: (i) other types of DAGs that correspond to workflows of interest in the Grid community could be considered (e.g., [2, 12]); (ii) more sophisticated models to charge for machine time could be incorporated (although relevant research in the context of the Grid is still in its infancy); and, (iii) more dynamic scenarios and environments for the execution of the DAGs and the modelling of the machine time could be considered (e.g., [9]).

References

[1] O. Beaumont, V. Boudet, and Y. Robert. A realistic model and an efficient heuristic for scheduling with heterogeneous processors. In *11th Heterogeneous Computing Workshop*, 2002.

[2] J. Blythe, S. Jain, E. Deelman, Y. Gil, K. Vahi, A. Mandal, and K. Kennedy. Resource Allocation Strategies for Workflows in Grids In *IEEE International Symposium on Cluster Computing and the Grid (CCGrid 2005)*.

[3] R. Buyya, D. Abramson, and S. Venugopal. The Grid Economy. In *Proceedings of the IEEE*, volume 93(3), pages 698–714, March 2005.

[4] R. Buyya. *Economic-based Distributed Resource Management and Scheduling for Grid Computing*. PhD thesis, Monash University, Melbourne, Australia, http://www.buyya.com/thesis, April 12 2002.

[5] R. Buyya, D. Abramson, and J. Giddy. An economy grid architecture for service-oriented grid computing. In *10th IEEE Heterogeneous Computing Workshop (HCW'01)*, San Fransisco, 2001.

[6] C. Ernemann, V. Hamscher and R. Yahyapour. Economic Scheduling in Grid Computing. In *Proceedings of the 8th Workshop on Job Scheduling Strategies for Parallel Processing*, Vol. 2537 of Lecture Notes in Computer Science, Springer, pages 128–152, 2002.

[7] A. Mandal, K. Kennedy, C. Koelbel, G. Marin, J. Mellor-Crummey, B. Liu and L. Johnson. Scheduling Strategies for Mapping Application Workflows onto the Grid. In *IEEE International Symposium on High Performance Distributed Computing (HPDC 2005)*, 2005.

[8] R. Sakellariou and H. Zhao. A hybrid heuristic for DAG scheduling on heterogeneous systems. In *13th IEEE Heterogeneous Computing Workshop (HCW'04)*, Santa Fe, New Mexico, USA, April 2004.

[9] R. Sakellariou and H. Zhao. A low-cost rescheduling policy for efficient mapping of workflows on grid systems. In *Scientific Programming*, volume 12(4), pages 253–262, December 2004.

[10] H. Topcuoglu, S. Hariri, and M. Wu. Performance-effective and low-complexity task scheduling for heterogeneous computing. In *IEEE Transactions on Parallel and Distributed Systems*, volume 13(3), pages 260–274, March 2002.

[11] L. Wang, H. J. Siegel, V. P. Roychowdhury, and A. A. Maciejewski. Task matching and scheduling in heterogeneous computing environments using a genetic-algorithm-based approach. *Journal of Parallel and Distributed Computing*, 47:8–22, 1997.

[12] M. Wieczorek, R. Prodan and T. Fahringer. Scheduling of Scientific Workflows in the ASKALON Grid Environment. In *SIGMOD Record*, volume 34(3), September 2005.

[13] H. Zhao and R. Sakellariou. An experimental investigation into the rank function of the heterogeneous earliest finish time scheduling algorithm. In *Euro-Par 2003*. Springer-Verlag, LNCS 2790, 2003.

INTEGRATION OF ISS INTO THE VIOLA META-SCHEDULING ENVIRONMENT

Vincent Keller, Ralf Gruber, Michela Spada, Trach-Minh Tran
École Polytechnique Fédérale de Lausanne
CH-1015 Lausanne, Switzerland
{vincent.keller, ralf.gruber, trach-minh.tran, michela.spada}@epfl.ch

Kevin Cristiano, Pierre Kuonen
École d'Ingénieurs et d'Architectes
CH-1705 Fribourg, Switzerland
{kevin.cristiano , pierre.kuonen}@eif.ch

Philipp Wieder
Forschungszentrum Jülich GmbH,
D-52425, Germany
ph.wieder@fz-juelich.de

Wolfgang Ziegler, Oliver Wäldrich
Fraunhofer Gesellschaft, Institute SCAI
D-53754 St. Augustin, Germany
{wolfgang.ziegler, oliver.waeldrich}@scai.fraunhofer.de

Sergio Maffioletti , Marie-Christine Sawley, Nello Nellari
Swiss National Supercomputer Centre,
CH-1015 Manno, Switzerland
{sergio.maffioletti , sawley, nello.nellari}@cscs.ch

Abstract   The authors present the integration of the Intelligent (Grid) Scheduling System into the VIOLA meta-scheduling environment which itself is based on the UNI-CORE Grid software. The goal of the new, integrated environment is to enable the submission of jobs to the Grid system best-suited for the application workflow. For this purpose a cost function is used that exploits information about the type of application, the characteristics of the system architectures, as well as the availabilities of the resources. This document presents an active collaboration between Ecole Polytechnique Fédérale de Lausanne (EPFL), Ecole d'Ingénieurs et d'Architectes (EIF) de Fribourg, Forschungszentrum Jülich, Fraunhofer Institute SCAI, and Swiss National Supercomputing Centre (CSCS).

Keywords: Intelligent Grid Scheduling System, VIOLA, UNICORE, meta-scheduling, cost function, Γ model

1.   Introduction

The UNICORE middleware has been designed and implemented in various projects world-wide, for example the German UNICORE Plus project [1], the EU projects EUROGRID [2] and UniGrids [3], or the Japanese NaReGI project [4]. A recently developed extension to UNICORE, the VIOLA Meta-Scheduling Service, strongly increases its functionalities by adding capabilities needed to schedule arbitrary resources in a co-ordinated fashion. This meta-scheduling environment provides the software basis for the VIOLA testbed [5] and offers the opportunity to include proprietary scheduling solutions. The Intelligent (Grid) Scheduling System (ISS) [6] is such a scheduling system. It uses historical runtime data of an application to schedule a well suited computational resources for execution based on the performance requirements of the user. The goal of the work presented here is to integrate the ISS into the meta-scheduling environment to realise a Grid system satisfying the requirements of the SwissGRID. The Intelligent Scheduling System will add a data repository, a broker and an information service to the resulting Grid system. The scheduling algorithm used to calculate the best-suited system is based on a cost function that takes the data collected during previous executions into account describing inter alia the type of the application, its performance on the different machines in the Grid, and their availability.

In the following section, the functions of UNICORE and the Meta-Scheduling Service are shortly presented. Then, the ISS model is introduced followed by a description of the overall architecture which illustrates the integration of the ISS concept into the VIOLA environment (Sections 3 and 4). Section 5 then outlines the processes that will be executed to schedule application workflows in the meta-scheduling environment. Subsequent to the generic process description an ORB5 application example that runs on machines with over 1000 processors is discussed in Section 6. We conclude this document with a summary and a brief outlook on future work.

2.   UNICORE and the Meta-scheduling Service

The basic Grid environment we use for our work comprises the UNICORE Grid system and the Meta-Scheduling Service developed in the VIOLA project. It is not the purpose of this document to introduce these systems in detail, but a short characterisation of both is given in the following two sections. Descriptions of UNICORE's models and components can be found in other publications [1, 7], respective in publications covering the Meta-Scheduling Service [8–10].

2.1 UNICORE

A workflow is in general submitted to a UNICORE Grid via the UNICORE Client (see Fig. 1) which provides means to construct, monitor and control workflows. In addition the client offers extension capabilities through a plug-in interface, which has for example been used to integrate the Meta-Scheduling Service into the UNICORE Grid system. The workflow then passes the security Gateway and is mapped to the site-specific characteristics at the UNICORE Server before being transferred to the local scheduler.

The concept of resource virtualisation manifests itself in UNICORE's Virtual Site (Vsite) that comprises a set of resources. These resources must have direct access to each other, a uniform user mapping, and they are generally under the same administrative control. A set of Vsites is represented by a UNICORE Site (Usite) that offers a single access point (a unique address and port) to the resources of usually one institution.

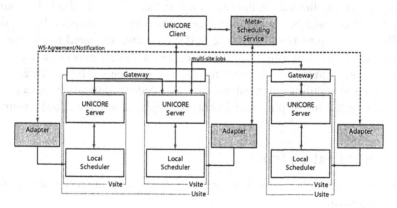

Figure 1. Architecture of the VIOLA Meta-scheduling Environment

2.2 Meta-Scheduling Service

The meta-scheduler is implemented as a Web Service receiving a list of resources preselected by a resource selection service (a broker for example, or a user) and returning reservations for some or all of these resources. To achieve this, the Meta-Scheduling Service first queries selected local scheduling systems for the availability of these resources and then negotiates the reservations across all local scheduling systems. In the particular case of the meta-scheduling environment the local schedulers are contacted via an adapter which provides a generic interface to these schedulers. Through this process the Meta-Scheduling Service supports scheduling of arbitrary resources or services for dedicated times. It offers on one hand the support for workflows where the agreements about resource or service usage (aka reservations) of consecutive parts should be made in advance to avoid delay during the execution of the workflow. On the other hand the Meta-Scheduling Service also supports co-allocation of resources or services in case it is required to run a parallel distributed application which needs several resources with probably different characteristics at the same time. The meta-scheduler may be steered directly by a user through a command-line interface or by Grid middleware components like the UNICORE client through its SOAP interface (see Fig. 1). The resulting reservations are implemented using the WS-Agreement specification [11].

3.   Intelligent Scheduling System Model

The main objective of the Intelligent GRID Scheduling System (ISS) project [6] is to provide a middleware infrastructure allowing optimal positioning and scheduling of real life applications in a computational GRID. According to data collected on the machines in the GRID, on the behaviour of the applications, and on the performance requirements demanded by the user, a well suited computational resource is detected and allocated to execute the application. The monitoring information collected during execution is put into a database and reused for the next resource allocation decision. In addition to providing scheduling information, the collected data allows to detect overloaded resources and to pin-point inefficient applications that could be further optimised.

3.1   Application types

The Intelligent Scheduling System model is based on the following application type system:

- **Single Processor Applications** These applications do not need any internode communication. They may benefit from backfilling strategies.

- **Embarrassingly parallel applications** This kind of applications requires a client-server concept. The internode communication network is not important. Seti@Home is an example of an embarrassingly parallel application for which data is sent over the Web.

- **Point-to-point applications** Point-to-point communications typically appear in finite element or finite volume methods when a huge 3D domain is decomposed in sub-domains and an explicit time stepping method or an iterative matrix solver is applied. If the number of processors grows with the problem size, and the size of a sub-domain is fixed, the local problem size is fix. Hence, that kind of applications can run well on a cluster with a relatively slow and cost-effective communication network that scales with the number of processors.

- **Multicast communications applications** The parallel 3D FFT algorithm is a typical example of an application that is dominated by multicast operations. The internode communication increases with the number of processors. Such an application needs a faster switched network such as Myrinet, Quadrics, or Infiniband. If thousands of processors are needed, special-purpose machines such as RedStorm or BlueGene might be required.

- **Multi components applications** Such applications consist of well-separable components, each one being a parallel job with little inter-component interaction. The different components can be submitted to different machines. An example is presented in [13].

The ISS concept is straight-forward: if a scheduler is able to differentiate between the types of applications presented above, it can decide where to run an application. For this purpose the so-called Γ model has been developed which is described in the following.

3.2 The Γ model

In the Γ model described in [12], it is supposed that each component of the application is ideally parallelised, i.e. each task of a component takes the same CPU and communication times.

The most important parameter Γ is a measure of the ratio of the computation over the communication times of each component. An application component adapted parallel machine should have a $\Gamma > 1$. Specifically, $\Gamma = 1$ means that communication and computation times are equal.

4. Resulting Grid Middleware Architecture

The overall architecture of the ISS integration into the meta-scheduling environment is depicted in Fig. 2 and the different modules and services are presented in this section. Please note that it is assumed that the executables of the application components already exist before execution.

4.1 Meta-Scheduling Service

The Meta-Scheduling Service (MSS) receives from the Resource Broker (RB) the resource requirements of an application, namely the number of nodes (or a set of numbers of nodes in case of a distributed parallel application) and the planned or estimated execution time. The MSS queries for the availability of known resources and selects a suited machine by optimising an objective function composed by the Γ model (described above) and the evaluation of costs. The MSS tries to reserve the proposed resource(s) for the job. The result of the reservation is sent back to the RB to check whether the final reservation

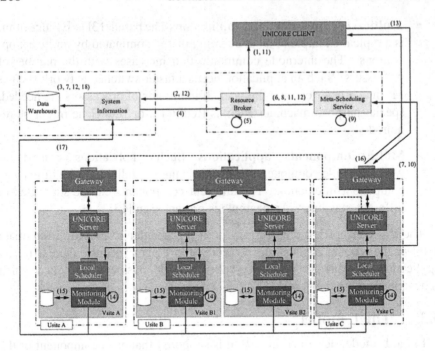

Figure 2.   Integration of ISS into the meta-scheduling environment.

matches the initial request. In case of a mismatch the reservation process will be re-iterated.

4.2   Resource Broker

The Resource Broker receives requests from the UNICORE Client (UC), collects the necessary information to choose the set of acceptable machines in the prologue phase.

4.3   Data Warehouse

We assume that information about application components exists at the Data Warehouse (DW) module. It is also assumed that at least one executable of all the application components exists.

The DW is the database that keeps all the information related to the application components, to the resources, to the services provided by the Vsites, to monitoring, and to other parameters potentially used to calculate the cost function.

Specifically, the Data Warehouse module contains the following information:

1 **Resources** Application independent hardware quantities.

2 **Services** The services a machines provides (software, libraries installed, etc.).

3 **Monitoring** Application dependent hardware quantities collected after each execution.

4 **Applications** Γ model quantities computed after each execution of an application component.

5 **Other** Other information needed in the cost function such as cost of one hour engineering time.

4.4 System Information

The System Information (SI) module manages the DW, accesses the Vsite-specific UNICORE information service periodically to update the static data in the DW, receives data from the Monitoring Module (MM) and the MSS, and interacts with the RB.

4.5 Monitoring Module

The Monitoring Module collects the application relevant data per Vsite during the runtime of an application. Specifically, it collects dynamic resource information (like CPU usage, network packets number and size, memory usage, etc.), and sends it to the SI.

5. Detailed Scheduling Scenario

Fig. 2 also shows the processes which are executed after a workflow is submitted to the Grid system we have developed. The 18 steps are broken down into three different phases: prologue, scheduling/execution, and epilogue.

First phase: Prologue

(1) The user submits a workflow to the RB through the UNICORE Client.

(2) The RB asks SI for systems able to run each workflow components (in terms of cost, amount of memory, parallel paradigm, etc...)

(3) The SI request the information from the DW

(4) The SI sends the information back to the RB.

(5) According to the information obtained in (3) the RB selects resources that might be used to run the job.

(6) The RB sends the list of resources together with further information (like number of nodes, expected run-time, etc.) and a user certificate to the MSS.

(7) The MSS collects information across all pre-selected resources about availability (e.g. of the compute nodes or of necessary licenses), user-related policies (like access rights), and cost-related parameters.

(8) The MSS notifies the RB about the completion of the prologue phase.

Second phase: Optimal Scheduling and execution

(9) The MSS can now choose among a number of acceptable machines that could execute the workflow. To select a well suited one, it uses con-solidated information about each Vsite, e.g. the number of nodes, the memory size per node M_{Vsite}, or the cost for 1 CPU hour per node. The MSS then calculates the cost function to find a well suited resource for the execution of the workflow. Knowing the amount of memory needed by the application, M_a, the MSS can determine the number of nodes P ($P > M_a/M_{Vsite}$) and compute the total time T:
$$Total\ time\ T\ =\ Waiting\ Time\ T_w\ +\ Computation\ Time\ T_c$$
needed in the cost function. The MSS chooses the machine(s).

(10) The MSS contacts the local scheduling system(s) of the selected re-source(s) and tries to obtain a reservation.

(11) If the reservation is confirmed the MSS creates an agreement, sends it to the UNICORE Client via the RB.

(12) The MSS then forwards the decision made in (9) via the RB to the SI which puts the data into the DW.

(13) The UNICORE Client creates the workflow based on the agreement and submits it to the UNICORE Gateway. Subsequent parts of the workflow are handled by the UNICORE Server of the submission Usite.

(14) During the workflow execution, application characteristics, such as CPU usage, network usage, number and size of MPI and NFS messages, and the amount of memory used, are collected by the MM.

(15) The MM stores the information in a local database.

(16) The result of the computation is sent back to the UNICORE Client.

Third phase: Epilogue

(17) Once the workflow execution has finished, the MM sends data stored during the computation to the SI.

(18) The SI computes the Γ model parameters and writes the relevant data into the DW.

The user only has to submit the workflow, the subsequent steps including the selection of well suited resource(s) are transparent to him. Only if an application is executed for the first time, the user has to give some basic information since no application-specific data is present in the DW.

There is a number of uncertainties in the computation of the cost model. The parameters used in the cost function are those that were measured in a previous execution of the same application. However, this previous execution could have used a different input pattern. Additionally, the information queried from the different resources by the MSS is based on data that has been provided by the application (or the user) before the actual execution and may therefore be rather imprecise. In future, by using ISS, such estimations could be improved.

During the epilogue phase data is also collected for statistical purpose. This data can provide information about reasons for a resource's utilisation or a user's satisfaction. If this is bad for a certain HPC resource, for instance because of overfilled waiting queues, other machines of this type should be purchased. If a resource is rarely used it either has a special architecture or the cost charged using it is too high. In the latter case one option would be to adapt the price.

6. Application Example: Submission of ORB5

Let us follow the data flow of the real life plasma physics application ORB5 that runs on parallel machines with over 1000 processors. ORB5 is a particle in cell code. The 3D domain is discretised in $N_1 x N_2 x N_3$ mesh cells in which move p charged particles. These particles deposit their charges in the local cells. Maxwell's equation for the electric field is then solved with the charge density distribution as source term. The electric field accelerates the particles during a short time and the process repeats with the new charge density distribution. As a test case, $N_1 = N_2 = 128$, $N_3 = 64$, $p = 2'000'000$, and the number of time steps is $t = 100$. These values form the ORB5 input file.

Two commodity clusters at EPFL form our test Grid, one having 132 single processor nodes interconnected with a full Fast Ethernet switch (Pleiades), the other has 160 two processor nodes interconnected with a Myrinet network (Mizar).

The different steps in decision to which machine the ORB5 application is submitted are:

(1) The ORB5 execution script and input file are submitted to the RB through a UNICORE client.

(2) The RB requests information on ORB5 from the SI.

(3) The SI selects the information from the DW (memory needed 100 GB, $\Gamma = 1.5$ for Pleiades, $\Gamma = 20$ for Mizar, 1 hour engineering time cost SFr. 200.-, 8 hours a day).

(4) SI sends back to RB the information.

(5) RB selects Mizar and Pleiades.

(6) RB sends the information on ORB5 to MSS

(7) MSS collects machine information from Pleiades and Mizar:

- **Pleiades:** 132 nodes, 2 GB per node, SFr. 0.50 per node*h, 2400 h*node job limit, availability table (1 day for 64 nodes), user is authorised, executable ORB5 exist.
- **Mizar:** 160 nodes, 4 GB per node, SFr. 2.50 per node*h, 32 nodes job limit, availability table (1 hour for 32 nodes), user is authorised, executable ORB5 exist.

(8) Prologue is finished.

(9) MSS computes the cost function values using the estimated execution time of 1 day:

- **Pleiades:** Total costs = Computing costs (24*64*0.5=SFr. 768.-) + Waiting time ((1+1)*8*200=SFr. 3200.-) = SFR 3968.-
- **Mizar:** Total costs = Computing costs (24*32*2.5=SFr.1920.-) + Waiting time ((1+8)*200=SFr. 1800.-) = SFR 3720.-

MSS decides to submit to Mizar.

(10) MSS requests the reservation of 32 nodes for 24 hours from the local scheduling system of Mizar.

(11) If the reservation is confirmed the MSS creates the agreement, sends it to UC. Otherwise the broker is notified and the selection process will start again.

(12) MSS sends the decision to use Mizar to SI via the RB.

(13) UC submits the ORB5 job to the UNICORE gateway.

(14) Once the job is executed on the 32 nodes the execution data is collected by MM.

(15) MM sends execution data to local database.

(16) Results of job are sent to UC.

(17) MM sends the job execution data stored in the local database to the SI.

(18) SI computes Γ model parameters (e.g. $\Gamma = 18.7$, $M = 87\,GB$, Computing time=21h 32') and stores them into DW.

7. Conclusion

The ISS integration into the VIOLA Meta-scheduling environment is part of the SwissGRID initiative and will be realised in a co-operation between CoreGRID partners. It is planned to install the resulting Grid middleware by the end of 2007 to guide job submission to all HPC machines in Switzerland.

Acknowledgments

Some of the work reported in this paper is funded by the German Federal Ministry of Education and Research through the VIOLA project under grant #01AK605F. This paper also includes work carried out jointly within the CoreGRID Network of Excellence funded by the European Commission's IST programme under grant #004265.

References

[1] D. Erwin (ed.), *UNICORE plus final report – uniform interface to computing resource*, Forschungszentrum Jülich, ISBN 3-00-011592-7, 2003.

[2] The EUROGRID project, web site. 1 July 2006 <http://www.eurogrid.org/>.

[3] The UniGrids Project, web site. 1 July 2006 <http://www.unigrids.org/>.

[4] The National Research Grid Initiative (NaReGI), web site. 01 July 2006 <http://www.naregi.org/index_e.html>.

[5] VIOLA – Vertically Integrated Optical Testbed for Large Application in DFN, web site. 1 July 2006 <http://www.viola-testbed.de/>.

[6] R. Gruber, V. Keller, P. Kuonen, M.-Ch. Sawley, B. Schaeli, A. Tolou, M. Torruella, and T.-M. Tran, Intelligent Grid Scheduling System, In *Proc. of Conference on Parallel Processing and Applied Mathematics PPAM 2005*, Poznan, Poland, 2005, to appear.

[7] A. Streit, D. Erwin, Th. Lippert, D. Mallmann, R. Menday, M. Rambadt, M. Riedel, M. Romberg, B. Schuller, and Ph. Wieder, UNICORE - From Project Results to Production Grids. In *Grid Computing: The New Frontiers of High Performance Processing (14)*, L. Grandinetti (ed.), pp. 357-376, Elsevier, 2005. ISBN: 0-444-51999-8.

[8] G. Quecke and W. Ziegler, MeSch – An Approach to Resource Management in a Distributed Environment, In *Proc. of 1st IEEE/ACM International Workshop on Grid Computing (Grid 2000)*. Volume 1971 of Lecture Notes in Computer Science, pages 47-54, Springer, 2000.

[9] A. Streit, O. Wäldrich, Ph. Wieder, and W. Ziegler, On Scheduling in UNICORE - Extending the Web Services Agreement based Resource Management Framework, In *Proc. of Parallel Computing 2005 (ParCo2005)*, Malaga, Spain, 2005, to appear.

[10] O. Wäldrich, Ph. Wieder, and W. Ziegler, A Meta-Scheduling Service for Co-allocating Arbitrary Types of Resources. In *Proc. of the Second Grid Resource Management Work-

shop (GRMWS'05) in conjunction with Parallel Processing and Applied Mathematics: 6th International Conference, PPAM 2005, Lecture Notes in Computer Science, Volume 3911, Springer, R. Wyrzykowski, J. Dongarra, N. Meyer, and J. Wasniewski (eds.), pp. 782-791, Poznan, Poland, September 11-14, 2005. ISBN: 3-540-34141-2.

[11] A. Andrieux et. al., Web Services Agreement Specification, July, 2006. Online: <https://forge.gridforum.org/sf/docman/do/downloadDocument/projects.graap-wg/docman.root.current_drafts/doc13652>.

[12] Ralf Gruber, Pieter Volgers, Alessandro De Vita, Massimiliano Stengel, and Trach-Minh Tran, Parameterisation to tailor commodity clusters to applications, *Future Generation Comp. Syst.*, 19(1), pp. 111-120, 2003.

[13] P. Manneback, G. Bergère, N. Emad, R. Gruber, V. Keller, P. Kuonen, S. Noël, and S. Petiton, Towards a scheduling policy for hybrid methods on computational Grids, submitted to CoreGRID Integrated Research in Grid Computing workshop Pisa, November, 2005.

MULTI-CRITERIA GRID RESOURCE MANAGEMENT USING PERFORMANCE PREDICTION TECHNIQUES

Krzysztof Kurowski, Ariel Oleksiak, and Jarek Nabrzyski
Poznań Supercomputing and Networking Center
{krzysztof.kurowski,ariel,naber}@man.poznan.pl

Agnieszka Kwiecień, Marcin Wojtkiewicz, and Maciej Dyczkowski
Wrocław Center for Networking and Supercomputing,
Wrocław University of Technology
{agnieszka.kwiecien, marcin.wojtkiewicz, maciej.dyczkowski}@pwr.wroc.pl

Francesc Guim, Julita Corbalan, Jesus Labarta
Computer Architecture Department,
Universitat Politècnica de Catalunya
{fguim,juli,jesus}@ac.upc.edu

Abstract   To date, many of existing Grid resource brokers make their decisions concerning selection of the best resources for computational jobs using basic resource parameters such as, for instance, load. This approach may often be insufficient. Estimations of job start and execution times are needed in order to make more adequate decisions and to provide better quality of service for end-users. Nevertheless, due to heterogeneity of Grids and often incomplete information available the results of performance prediction methods may be very inaccurate. Therefore, estimations of prediction errors should be also taken into consideration during a resource selection phase. We present in this paper the multi-criteria resource selection method based on estimations of job start and execution times, and prediction errors. To this end, we use GRMS [28] and GPRES tools. Tests have been conducted based on workload traces which were recorded from a parallel machine at UPC. These traces cover 3 years of job information as recorded by the LoadLeveler batch management systems. We show that the presented method can considerably improve the efficiency of resource selection decisions.

Keywords: Performance Prediction, Grid Scheduling, Multicriteria Analysis, GRMS, GPRES

1.   Introduction

In computational Grids intelligent and efficient methods of resource management are essential to provide easy access to resources and to allow users to make the most of Grid capabilities. Resource assignment decisions should be made by Grid resource brokers automatically and based on user requirements. At the same time the underlying complexity and heterogeneity should be hidden. Of course, the goal of Grid resource management methods is also to provide a high overall performance. Depending on objectives of the Virtual Organization (VO) and preferences of end-users Grid resource brokers may attempt to maximize the overall job throughput, resource utilization, performance of applications etc.

Most of existing available resource management tools use general approaches such as load balancing ([25]), matchmaking (e.g. Condor [26]), computational economy models (Nimrod [27]), or multi-criteria resource selection (GRMS [28]). In practice, the evaluation and selection of resources is based on their characteristics such as load, CPU speed, number of jobs in the queue etc. However, these parameters can influence the actual performance of applications in various ways. End users may not know a priori accurate dependencies between these parameters and completion times of their applications. Therefore, available estimations of job start and run times may significantly improve resource broker decisions and, consequently, the performance of executed jobs.

Nevertheless, due to incomplete and imprecise information available, results of performance prediction methods may be accompanied by considerable errors (to see examples of exact error values please refer to [3–4]). The more distributed, heterogeneous, and complex environment the bigger predictions errors may appear. Thus, they should be estimated and taken into consideration by a Grid resource broker for evaluation of available resources.

In this paper, we present a method for resource evaluation and selection based on a multi-criteria decision support method that uses estimations of job start and run times. This method takes into account estimated prediction errors to improve decisions of the resource broker and to limit their negative influence on the performance.

The predicted job start- and run-times are generated by the Grid Prediction System (GPRES) developed within the SGIgrid [30] and Clusterix [31] projects. The multi-criteria resource selection method implemented in the Grid Resource Management System (GRMS) [23, 28] has been used for the evaluation of knowledge obtained from the prediction system. We used a workload trace from UPC.

Sections of the paper are organized as follows. In Section 2, a brief description of activities related to performance prediction and its exploitation in Grid scheduling is given. In Section 3 the workload used is described. The prediction system and algorithm used for generation of predictions is included in Section 4. Section 5 presents the algorithm for the multicriteria resource evaluation and utilization of the knowledge from the prediction system. Experiments, which we performed, and preliminary results are described in Section 6. Section 7 contains final conclusions and future work.

2. Related work

Prediction techniques can be applied in a wide area of problems related to Grid computing: from the short-term prediction of the resource performance to the prediction of the queue wait time [5]. Most of these predictions are oriented to the resource selection and job scheduling.

Prediction techniques can be classified into statistical, AI, and analytical. Statistical approached are based on applications that have been previously executed. Among the most common techniques there are time series analysis [6–8] and categorization [4, 1, 2, 22]. In particular, correlation and regression have been used to find dependencies between job parameters. Analytical techniques construct models by hand [9] or using automatic code instrumentation [10]. AI techniques use historical data and try to learn and classify the information in order to predict the future performance of resources or applications. AI techniques include, for instance, classification (decision trees [11], neural networks [12]), clustering (k-means algorithm [13]), etc.

Predicted times are used to guide scheduling decisions. This scheduling can be oriented to load balancing when executing in heterogeneous resources [14–15], applied to resource selection [5, 22], or used when multiple requests are provided [16]. For instance, in [17] authors use the 10-second ahead predicted CPU information provided by NWS [18, 8]. Many local scheduling policies, such as Least Work First (LWF) or Backfilling, also consider user provided or predicted execution time to make scheduling decisions [19, 20,21].

3. Workload

The workload trace file was obtained from a IBM SP2 System placed at UPC. This system has two different configurations: the IBM RS-6000 SP with 8*16 Nighthawk Power3 @375Mhz with 64 GB RAM, and the IBM P630 9*4 p630 Power4 @1Ghz with 18 GB RAM. A total performance of 336Gflops and 1.8TB of storage are available. All nodes are connected through an SP Switch2 operating at 500MB/sec. The operating system that they are running is an AIX 5.1 with the queue system Load Leveler.

The workload was obtained from Load Leveler history files that contained information about job executions during around last three years (178183 jobs). Through the Load Leveler API, we converted the workload history files that were in a binary format, to a trace file whose format is similar to those proposed in [21]. The workload contains fields such as: job name, group, username, memory consumed by a job, user time, total time (user+system), tasks created by a job, unshared memory in the data segment of a process, unshared stack size, involuntary context switches, voluntary context switches, finishing state, queue, submission date, dispatch time, and completion date. More details on the workload can be found in [29].

Analyzing the trace file we can see that total time for parallel jobs is approximately an order of magnitude bigger than the total time for sequential jobs, which means that in median they are consuming around 10 times more of CPU time. For both kind of jobs the dispersion of all the variables is considerable big, however for parallel jobs is also around an order of magnitude bigger. Parallel jobs use around 72 times more memory than the sequential applications. The IQR value also is bigger[1]. In general these variables are characterized by a significant variance what can make their prediction difficult.

Users submit jobs that have various levels of parallelism. However, there is an important amount of jobs that are sequential (23%). The relevant parallel jobs that are consuming a big amount of resources belong to three main number of processor usage intervals: 5-16 processors (31% of the total jobs), 65-128 processors (29% of the total jobs) and 17-32 processors (13% of the total jobs).

In median all the submitted LoadLeveler scripts used to be executed only once using the same number of tasks. This fact might imply that the number of tasks would be not significant to be used for prediction. However, those jobs that where executed with 5-16 and 65-128 processors are executed in general more than 5 times with the same number of tasks, and represent the 25 % of the submitted jobs. This suggests that this variable might be relevant.

4.   Prediction System

This section provides a description of the prediction system that has been used for estimating start and completion times of the jobs. Grid Prediction System (GPRES) is constructed as an advisory expert system for resource brokers managing distributed environment, including computational Grids.

4.1   Architecture

The architecture of GPRES is based on the architecture of expert systems. With this approach the process of knowledge acquisition can be separated from the prediction. The Figure 1 illustrates the system architecture and how its components interact with each other.

---

[1]The IRQ is defined as IQR=Q3-Q1, where: Q1 is a value such that only exactly 25% of the observations have a value of considered parameter less than Q1, and the Q3 is a value such that exactly 25% of the observations have value of considered parameter greater than Q3.

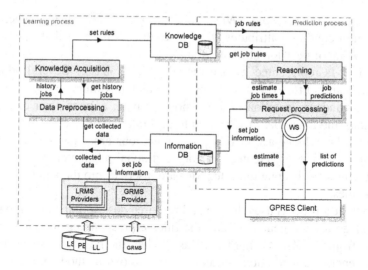

Figure 1.   Architecture of GPRES system

Data Providers are small components distributed in the Grid. They gather information about historical jobs from logs of GRMS and local resource management systems (LRMS, e.g. LSF, PBS, LL) and insert it into Information data base. After the information is gathered the Data Preprocessing module prepares data for a knowledge acquisition. Jobs' parameters are unified and joined (if the information about one job comes from several different sources, e.g. LSF and GRMS). Such prepared data are used by the Knowledge Acquisition module to generate rules. The rules are inducted into the Knowledge Data Base. When an estimation request comes to GPRES the Request Processing module prepares all the incoming data (about a job and resources) for the reasoning. The Reasoning module selects rules from the Knowledge Data Base and generates the requested estimation.

4.2   Method

As in previous works [1, 2, 3, 4] we assumed that the information about historical jobs can be used to predict time characteristics of a new job. The main problem is to define the similarity of the jobs and to select appropriate parameters to evaluate it.

GPRES system uses a template-based approach. The template is a subset of job attributes, which are used to evaluate jobs' "similarity". The attributes for templates are generated from the historical information after tests.

The knowledge in the Knowledge Data Base is represented as rules:

IF $A_1 op v_1$ *AND* $A_2 op v_2$ *AND... AND* $A_n op v_n$ *THEN* d $=d_i$, where $A_i \in$ A, the set of condition attributes, v_i – values of condition attributes, $op \in \{=, <, >\}$, d_i – value of decision attribute, i, n $\in$ N.

One rule is represented as one record in a database. Several additional parameters are set for every rule: a minimum and maximum value of a decision attribute, standard deviation of a decision attribute, a mean error of previous predictions and a number of jobs used to generate the rule.

During the knowledge acquisition process the jobs are categorized according to templates. For every created category additional parameters are calculated. When the process is done the categories are inserted into the Knowledge Data Base as rules.

The prediction process uses the job and resource description as the input data. Job's categories are generated and the rules corresponding to categories are selected from the Knowledge Data Base. Then the best rule is selected and used to generate a prediction. Actually there are two methods of selecting the best rule available in GPRES. The first one prefers the most specific rule, with the best matching to condition attributes of the job. The second strategy prefers a rule generated from the highest number of history jobs. If both methods don't give the final selection, the rules are combined and the arithmetic mean of the decision attribute is returned.

5.   Multi-criteria prediction-based resource selection

Knowledge acquired by the prediction techniques described above can be utilized in Grids, especially by resource brokers. Information concerning job run-times as well as a short-time future behavior of resources may be a significant factor in improving the scheduling decisions. A proposal of the multi-criteria scheduling broker that takes the advantage of history-based prediction information is presented in [22].

One of the simplest algorithms which requires the estimated job completion times is the Minimum Completion Time (MCT) algorithm. It assigns each job from a queue to resources that provide the earliest completion time for this job.

Algorithm MCT

- *For each job J_i from a queue*

    – *For each resource R_j, at which this job can be executed*

        * *Retrieve estimated completion time of job $C_{Ji,Rj}$*
        * *Assign job J_i to resource R_{best} so that*
        * $C_{J_i,R_{best}} = \min_{R_j} \left(C_{J_i,R_j} \right)$

Nevertheless, apart from predicted times, the knowledge about potential prediction errors is needed. The knowledge coming from a prediction system shouldn't be limited only to the mean times of previously executed jobs that fit to a template. Therefore, we also consider a maximum value, standard deviation, and estimated error (as explained in Section 4.2). These parameters should be taken into account during a selection of the most suitable resources. Of course, the mean time is the most important criterion, however, relative importance of all parameters depends on user preferences and/or characteristics of applications. For instance, certain applications (or user needs) may be very sensitive to delays, which can be caused by incorrectly estimated start and/or run times. In such case a standard deviation, maximum values become important. Therefore, a multi-criteria resource selection is needed to accurately handle these dependencies. General use of multi-criteria resource selection methods in Grids was described in [23].

In our case we used the functional model for aggregation of preferences. That means that we used a utility function and we ranked resources based on its values. In detail, criteria are aggregated for job J_i and resource R_j by the weighted sum given according to the following formula:

$$F_{J_i,R_j} = \frac{1}{\sum\limits_{k=1}^{n} kw} \sum_{k=1}^{n} kw * kc \tag{1}$$

where the set of criteria C *(n=4)* consists of the following metrics:
C_1 – mean completion time ($time_{Ji,Rj,}$)
C_2 – standard deviation of completion time ($stdev_{Ji,Rj}$)
C_3 – maximum value of completion time ($max_{Ji,Rj}\text{-}min_{Ji,Rj}$)
C_4 – estimated error of previous predictions ($err_{Ji,Rj}$)
and weights w_k that define the importance of the corresponding criteria.

This method can be considered as a modification of the MCT algorithm to a multi-criteria version. In this way possible errors and inaccuracy of estimations are taken into consideration in MCT. Instead of selection of a resource, at which a job completes earliest, the algorithm chooses resources characterized by the best values of the utility function $F_{Ji,Rj}$.

Multi-criteria MCT algorithm

- *For each job J_i from a queue*

    – *For each resource R_j, at which this job can be executed*

    * *Retrieve estimated completion time of job $C_{Ji,Rj}$ and $err_{Ji,Rj}$, $stdev_{Ji,Rj}$, $max_{Ji,Rj}$*

* Calculate the utility function F_{J_i,R_j}

* Assign job J_i to resource R_{best} so that

* $F_{J_i,R_{best}} = \max_{R_j} \left(F_{J_i,R_j} \right)$

6.   Preliminary Results

There are two main hypothesis of this paper defined. First, use of knowledge about estimated job completion times may significantly improve resource selection decisions made by resource broker and, in this way, the performance of both particular applications and the whole VO. Nevertheless, estimated job completion times may be insufficient for effective resource management decisions. Therefore, the second hypothesis is that results of these decisions may be further improved by taking the advantage of information about possible uncertainty and inaccuracy of prediction.

In order to check these hypotheses we performed two major experiments. First, we compared results obtained by the MCT algorithm with a common approach based on the matchmaking technique (job was submitted to the first resource that met user's requirements). In the second experiment, we studied improvement of results of the prediction-based resource evaluation after application of knowledge about possible prediction errors. For both experiments the following metrics were compared: mean, worst, and best job completion time. The worst and best job completion values were calculated in the following way. First, for each application the worst/best job completion times have been found. Second, an average of these values was taken as the worst and best value for comparison.

5000 jobs from the workload were used to acquire knowledge by GPRES. Then 100 jobs from the workload were scheduled to appropriate queues using methods presented in Section 5.

The results of the comparison are presented in Figure 2. In general, it shows noticeable improvement of mean job completion times when the performance prediction method was used.

The least enhancement was obtained for the best job completion times. The multi-criteria MCT algorithm turned out to be the most useful for improvement of the worst completion times. Further study is needed to test the influence of relative importance of criteria on final results.

7.   Conclusion

In this paper we proposed the multi-criteria resource evaluation method based on knowledge of job start- and run-times obtained from the prediction system. As a prediction system the GPRES tool was used. We exploited the method of multi-criteria evaluation of resources implemented in GRMS.

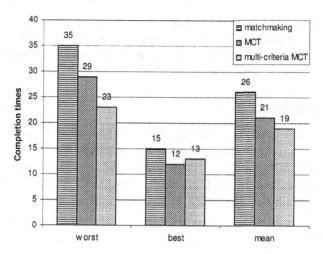

Figure 2. Comparison of job completion times for matchmaking, MCT, and multi-criteria MCT algorithms

The hypotheses assumed in the paper have been verified. Exploitation of the knowledge about performance prediction allowed a resource broker to make more efficient decisions. This was visible especially for mean values of job completion times.

Exploitation of knowledge about possible prediction errors brought another improvement of results. As we had supposed it improved mainly the worst job completion times. Thus, taking the advantage of knowledge about prediction errors we can limit number of job completion times that are significantly worst than estimated values. Moreover, we can tune the system by setting appropriate criteria weights depending on how reliable results we need and how sensitive to delays application are. For instance, certain users may accept "risky" resources (i.e. only the mean job completion time is important for them) while others may expect certain reliability (i.e. low ratio of strongly delayed jobs).

The advantage of performance prediction methods is less visible for strongly loaded resources because many jobs have to be executed at worse resources. This drawback could be partially eliminated by scheduling a set of jobs at the same time. This approach will be a subject of further research. Of course, information about possible prediction errors is the most useful in case of inaccurate predictions. If a resource broker uses high quality predictions, knowledge of estimated errors becomes less important.

Although a substantial improvement of the performance was shown, these results are rather still far from users' expectations. This is caused by, among others, a quality of available information. Most of workloads (including the LoadLeveler workload used for our study) do not contain such essential information as number of jobs in queues, size of input data, etc. Exploitation of more detailed and useful historical data is also foreseen as the future work on improving efficiency of Grid resource management based on performance prediction.

Acknowledgments

This work has been supported by the CoreGrid, network of excellence in "Foundations, Software Infrastructures and Applications for large scale distributed, Grid and Peer-to-Peer Technologies" the Spanish Ministry of Science and Education under contract TIN2004-07739-C02-01, and SGIgrid and Clusterix projects funded by the Polish Ministry of Science.

References

[1] Allen Downey. Predicting Queue Times on Space-Sharing Parallel Computers. In *International Parallel Processing Symposium*, 1997.

[2] Richard Gibbons. A Historical Application Profiler for Use by Parallel Schedulers. Lecture Notes on Computer Science, pages 58-75, 1997.

[3] Warren Smith, Valerie Taylor, Ian Foster. Using Run-Time Predictions to Estimate Queue Wait Times and Improve Scheduler Performance. In *Proceedings of the IPPS/SPDP '99 Workshop on Job Scheduling Strategies for Parallel Processing*.

[4] Warren Smith, Valerie Taylor, Ian Foster. Predicting Application Run-times Using Historical Information. In *Proceedings IPPS/SPDP '98 Workshop on Job Scheduling Strategies for Parallel Processing*, 1998.

[5] I. Foster and C. Kesselman. Computational grids. In I. Foster and C. Kesselman, editors, *The Grid: Blueprint for a New Computing Infrastructure*, pages 15–52. Morgan Kaufmann, San Francisco, California, 1986.

[6] R. Wolski, N. Spring, and J. Hayes. Predicting the CPU availability of time-shared unix systems. Submitted to SIGMETRICS '99 (also available as UCSD Technical Report Number CS98-602), 1998.

[7] P. Dinda. Online prediction of the running time of tasks. In *Proc. 10th IEEE Symp. on High Performance Distributed Computing* 2001

[8] R. Wolski, N. Spring, and J. Hayes. The network weather service: A distributed resource performance forecasting service for metacomputing. *Future Generation Computer Systems*, 15 (5-6):757-768 1999

[9] J. Schopf and F. Berman. Performance prediction in production environments. In *Proceedings of IPPS/SPDP*, 1998.

[10] V. Taylor, X. Wu, J. Geisler, X. Li, z. Lan, M. Hereld, I. Judson, and R. Stevens. Prophesy: Automating the modeling process. In *Proc. Of the Third International Workshop on Active Middleware Services*, 2001.

[11] J.R. Quinlan. Induction of decision trees. *Machine Learning*, pages 81-106, 1986

[12] D.E.Rumelhart, G.E. Hinton, and R.J. Williams. Learning representations by back propagating errors. *Nature*, 323:533-536, 1986

[13] C.Darken, J.Moody: Fast adaptive K-Means Clustering: some Empirical Results, *Proc. International Joint Conference on Neural Networks* Vol II, San Diego, New York, IEEE Computer Scienc Press, pp.233-238, 1990.

[14] H.J.Dail. A Modular Framework for Adaptive Scheduling in Grid Application Development Environments. Technical report CS2002-0698, Computer Science Department, University of California, San Diego, 2001

[15] S.M. Figueira and F. Berman. Mapping Parallel Applications to Distributed Heterogeneous Systems, Department of Computer Science and Engineering, University of California, San Diego, TR - UCSD - CS96-484, 1996

[16] K. Czajkowski, I. Foster, C. Kesselman, S. Martin, W. Smith, and S. Tuecke. A resource management architecture for metacomputing systems. Technical report, Mathematics and Computer Science Division, Argonne National Laboratory, Argonne, Ill., JSSPP Whorskshop. LNCS #1459 pages 62-68. 1997.

[17] C. Liu, L. Yang, I. Foster, D. Angulo. Design and Evaluation of a Resource selection Framework for Grid Applications. In *Proceedings of the Eleventh IEEE International Symposium on High-Performance Distributed Computing* (HPDC 11), 2002

[18] R. Wolski. Dynamically Forecasting Network Performance to Support Dynamic Scheduling Using the Network Weather Service. In *6th High-Performance Distributed Computing*, Aug. 1997.

[19] D. Lifka. The ANL/IBM SP scheduling system. In *Job Scheduling Strategies for Parallel Processing*, D. G. Feitelson and L. Rudolph (eds.), pp. 295–303, Springer-Verlag, 1995. Lect. Notes Comput. Sci. vol. 949

[20] D. G. Feitelson and A. Mu'alem Weil. Utilization and predictability in scheduling the IBM SP2 with backfilling. In *Proc. 12th Int'l. Parallel Processing Symp.*, pages 542–546, Orlando, March 1998.

[21] D.G.Feitelson. Parallel Workload Archive. http://www.cs.huji.ac.il/labs/parallel/workload

[22] K. Kurowski, J. Nabrzyski, J. Pukacki. Predicting Job Execution Times in the Grid. In *Proceedings of the 1st SGI 2000 International User Conference*, Kraków, 2000

[23] K. Kurowski, J. Nabrzyski, A. Oleksiak, and J, Węglarz,. Multicriteria Aspects of Grid Resource Management. In *Grid Resource Management* edited by J. Nabrzyski, J. Schopf, and J. Węglarz, Kluwer Academic Publishers, Boston/Dordrecht/London, 2003.

[24] Kurowski, K., Ludwiczak, B., Nabrzyski, J., Oleksiak, A., Pukacki, J. Improving Grid Level Throughput Using Job Migration and Rescheduling Techniques in GRMS. *Scientific Programming. IOS Press.* Amsterdam The Netherlands 12:4 (2004) 263-273

[25] B. A. Shirazi, A. R. Husson, and K. M. Kavi. Scheduling and Load Balancing in Parallel and Distributed Systems. IEEE Computer Society Press, 1995.

[26] Condor project. http://www.cs.wisc.edu/condor.

[27] D. Abramson, R. Buyya, and J. Giddy. A computational economy for Grid computing and its implementation in the Nimrod-G resource broker. *Future Generation Computer Systems*, 18(8), October 2002.

[28] Grid Resource Management System (GRMS), http://www.gridlab.org/grms.

[29] F.Guim, J. Corbalan, J. Labarta. Analyzing LoadLeveler historical information for performance prediction. In *Proc. Of Jornadas de Paralelismo 2005*. Granada, Spain

[30] SGIgrid project. http://www.wcss.wroc.pl/pb/sgigrid/en/index.php

[31] Clusterix project. http://www.clusterix.pcz.pl

A PROPOSAL FOR A GENERIC
GRID SCHEDULING ARCHITECTURE*

Nicola Tonellotto
Institute of Information Science and Technologies, 56100 Pisa, Italy
Information Engineering Department, University of Pisa, 56100 Pisa, Italy
nicola.tonellotto@isti.cnr.it

Ramin Yahyapour
Robotics Research Institute, University of Dortmund, 44221 Dortmund, Germany
ramin.yahyapour@udo.edu

Philipp Wieder
Research Centre Jülich, 52425 Jülich, Germany
ph.wieder@fz-juelich.de

Abstract   In the past years, many Grids have been deployed and became commodity systems in production environments. While several Grid scheduling systems have already been implemented, they still provide only "ad hoc" and domain-specific solutions to the problem of scheduling resources in a Grid. However, no common and generic Grid scheduling system has emerged yet. In this work we identify generic features of three common Grid scheduling scenarios, and we introduce a single entity called scheduling instance that can be used as a building block for the scheduling solutions presented. We identify the behaviour that a scheduling instance must exhibit in order to be composed with other instances, and we describe its interactions with other Grid services. This work can be used as a foundation for designing common Grid scheduling infrastructures.

Keywords: Grid computing, Resource management, Scheduling, Grid middleware.

---

*This paper includes work carried out jointly within the CoreGRID Network of Excellence funded by the European Commission's IST programme under grant #004265.

1.   Introduction

The allocation and scheduling of applications on a set of heterogeneous, dynamically changing resources is a complex problem. There are still no common Grid scheduling strategies and systems available which serve all needs. The available implementations of scheduling systems depend on the specific architecture of the target computing platform and the application scenarios. The complexity of the applications and the user requirements, and the system heterogeneity do not permit to efficiently perform manually any scheduling procedure.

The task of scheduling a job, a workflow, or an application, something which we call a *scheduling problem*, does not only include the search for a suitable set of resources to run applications with regard to some user-dependent Quality of Service (QoS) requirements. Moreover the scheduling system may be in charge of the coordination of time slots allocated on several different resources to run the application. In addition dynamic changes of the status of resources must be considered. It is the task of the scheduling system to take all those aspects into account to efficiently run an application. Moreover, the scheduling system must execute these activities while balancing several optimisation functions: those provided by the user with her objectives (e.g. cost, response-time) as well as those objectives defined by the resource providers (e.g. throughput, profit).

These tasks increase the complexity of the scheduling problem and the resource allocation . Note that Grid scheduling significantly differs from the conventional job scheduling on parallel computing systems. Several Grid schedulers have been implemented in order to reduce the complexity of the problem for particular application scenarios. However, no common and generic Grid scheduler yet exists, and probably there will never be one as the particular scenarios will require dedicated scheduling strategies to run efficiently. Nevertheless several common aspects can be found examining existing Grid schedulers, which leads to the assumption that a generic architecture may be conceivable not only to simplify the implementation of different schedulers but also to provide an infrastructure for the interaction between these different systems. Ongoing work [1] in the Global Grid Forum [2] is describing those common aspects, and starting from this analysis we propose a generic Grid Scheduling Architecture (GSA) and describe how a generic Grid scheduler should behave.

In Section 2 we analyse three common Grid scheduling scenarios, namely Enterprise Grids, High Performance Computing Grids, and Global Grids. In Section 3 we identify the generic characteristics of the previous scenarios and their interactions with other Grid entities or services. In Section 4 we introduce a single entity that we call *scheduling instance* that can be used as a building block for the scheduling architectures presented and we identify the behaviour

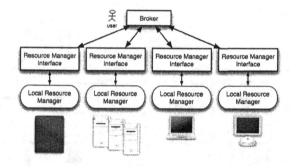

Figure 1. Example of a scheduling infrastructure for Enterprise Grids

that this scheduling instance must exhibit in order to be composed with other instances to build the Grid scheduling systems discussed.

2. Grid Scheduling Scenarios

In this Section three common Grid scheduling scenarios are briefly presented. This list is neither complete nor exhaustive. However, it represents common architectures that are currently implemented in application-specific Grid systems, either in research or commercial environments.

2.1 Scenario I: Enterprise Grids

Enterprise Grids represent a scenario of commercial interest in which the available IT resources within a company are better exploited and the administrative overhead is lowered by the employment of Grid technologies. The resources are typically not owned by different providers and are therefore not part of different administrative domains. In this scenario we have a centralised scheduling architecture; i.e. a central broker is the single access point to the whole infrastructure and manages the resource manager interfaces that interact directly with the local resource managers (see Figure 1). Every user must submit jobs to this centralised entity.

2.2 Scenario II: High Performance Computing Grids

High Performance Computing Grids represent a scenario in which different computing sites, e.g. scientific research labs, collaborate for joint research. Here, compute- and/or data-intensive applications are executed on the participating HPC computing resources that are usually large parallel computers or cluster systems. In this case the resources are part of several administrative domains, with their own policies and rules. A user can submit jobs to the broker at institute or Virtual Organization [3] (VO) level. The brokers can split a

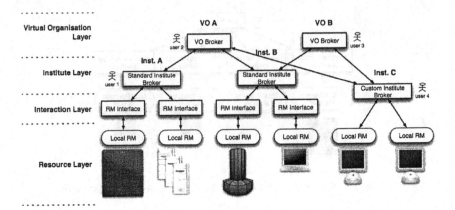

Figure 2. Example of a scheduling infrastructure for HPC Grids

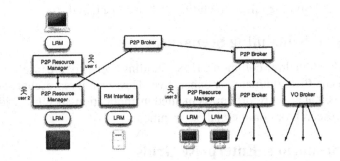

Figure 3. Example of a scheduling infrastructure for Global Grids

scheduling problem into several sub-problems, or forward the whole problem to different brokers in the same VO.

2.3   Scenario III: Global Grids

Global Grids might comprise very heterogeneous resources, from single desktop machines to large-scale HPC machines, which are connected through a global Grid network. This scenario is the most general one, covering both cases illustrated above and introducing a fully decentralised architecture. Every Peer-to-Peer broker can accept jobs to be scheduled, as Figure 3 depicts.

3.   Common functions of Grid Scheduling

The three scenarios illustrated in the previous section show several entities interacting to perform scheduling. To solve scheduling problems, these entities have to execute several tasks [4–5], often interacting with other services, both external ones and those part of the GSA implementation. Exploiting the information presented in [1, 7], it is possible to identify a detailed list of core independent functions that can be used to build specific Grid scheduling systems. In the following a list of atomic, self-contained functions is presented; these functions can be part of any complex mechanism or process implemented in a generic Grid Scheduling Architecture.

- **Naming**: Every entity in play must have a unique identifier for interaction and routing of messages. Some mechanism must be in charge of assigning and tracking the unique identifiers of the involved entities.

- **Security**: Every interaction between different un-trusted entities may need several security mechanisms. A scheduling entity may need to certify its identity when contacting another scheduling instance, when it is trying to collect sensible information about other entities (e.g. planned schedules of other instances), or to discover what interactions it is authorised to initiate. Moreover, the information flow may need secure transport and data integrity guarantees, and a user may need to be authorised to submit a problem to a scheduling system. The security functions are orthogonal to the other ones, in the sense that, depending on the configuration, every service may need security-related mechanisms.

- **Agreement**: In case Quality of Service guarantees must be considered, e.g. the execution time of a job or its price, a Service Level Agreement [8] (SLA) can be created and manipulated (e.g. accepted, rejected and modified) by the participating entities. A local resource manager can publish through its resource manager interface an SLA template which contains the capabilities of its managed resources, or a scheduling problem can include an SLA template specifying the QoS guarantees the user is looking for.

- **Problem Submission**: The entity implementing this function is responsible to receive a job from a user and submit it to a scheduling component. At this level, the definition of job is intentionally vague, because it depends on the particular job submitted (e.g. a bag of tasks, a single executable, or a workflow). The job to be scheduled is defined using a client-side language, and it may be necessary to translate this into a common description that is shared by some scheduling components. This description will therefore be exploited throughout the whole scheduling process. It should represent scheduling-related and SLA-related terms used by the scheduling instances to schedule the job.

- **Schedule Report**: An entity implementing this function must receive the answer of the scheduling instance to a previously submitted scheduling problem and translate it into a representation consumable by the user.

- **Information**: A scheduling instance must have coherent access to static and dynamic information about resources' characteristics (computational, data, networks, etc.), resource usage records, job characteristics, and, in general, services involved in the scheduling process. Moreover, it must be able to publish and update its own static and dynamic attributes to make them available to other scheduling instances. These attributes include allocation properties, local scheduling strategies, negotiation mechanisms, local agreement templates and resource information relevant to the scheduling process [5]. It can be, in addition, useful to provide the capability to cache historical information.

- **Search**: This function can be exploited to perform optimised information gathering on resources. For example, in large scale Grids is neither necessary nor efficient to collect information about every resource, but just a subset of "good" candidate resources. Several search strategies can be implemented (e.g. "best fit" searches, P2P searches with caching, iterative searches, etc.). Every search should include at least two parameters: the number of records requested in the reply and a time-out for the search procedure.

- **Monitoring:** A scheduling infrastructure can monitor different attributes to perform its functions: for instance the status of an SLA to check if it is not violated, the execution of a job to undertake scheduling or corrective actions, or the status of a scheduling description throughout its lifetime for user feedback.

- **Forecasting**: In order to calculate a schedule it can be useful to rely on forecasting services to predict the values of the quantities needed to apply a scheduling strategy. These forecasts can be based on historical records, actual and/or planned values.

- **Performance Evaluation**: The description of a job to be scheduled can miss some information needed by the system to apply a scheduling strategy. In this case it can be useful to apply performance evaluation methodologies based on the available job description in order to predict the unknown information.

- **Reservation**: To schedule complex jobs as workflows and co-allocated tasks, as well as jobs with QoS guarantees, it is in general necessary to reserve resources for particular time frames. The reservation of a resource can be obtained in several ways: automatically (because the local resource manager enforces it), on demand (only if explicitly requested from the user), etc. Moreover, the reservations can be restricted in time: for example only short-time reservations (i.e. with a finite time horizon) can be available. This function can require interaction with local resource managers, can be in charge of keeping information about allotted reservations, and reserve new time frames on the resource(s).

- **Co-allocation**: This function is in charge of the mechanisms needed to solve co-allocation scheduling problems, in which strict constraints on the time frames of several reservations must be respected (e.g. the execution at the same time of two highly interacting tasks). It can rely on a low-level clock synchronisation mechanism.

- **Planning**: When dealing with complex jobs (e.g. workflows) that need time-dependent access to and coordination of several objects like executables, data, or network paths, a planning functionality, potentially built on top of a reservation service, may provide the necessary service.

- **Negotiation**: To reach an agreement on a particular QoS, the interacting partners may need to follow particular rules to exchange partial agreements in order to reach a final decision (e.g. who is in charge of providing the initial SLA template, who may modify what, etc.). This function should include a generic mechanism to implement several negotiation rules.

- **Execution**: An execution entity is responsible to actually execute the scheduled jobs. It must interact with the local resource manager to perform the actions needed to run all the components of a job (e.g. staging, activation, execution, clean up). Usually it interacts with a monitoring system to control the status of the execution.

- **Banking**: The accounting/billing functionalities are performed by a banking system. It must provide interfaces to access accounting information, to charge for reservations or use resource usage, and to refund, e.g. in case of SLA failure or violation.

- **Translation**: The interaction with several services that can be implemented differently can force to "translate" information about the scheduling problem to map the semantics of one system to the semantics of another.

- **Data Management Access**: Data transfers can be included in the description of jobs. Although data management scheduling shows several similarities with job scheduling, it is considered a distinct, stand-alone functionality, because the former shows significant differences compared to the latter (e.g. replica management and repository information) [9]. The implementation of a scheduling system may need access to data management facilities to program data transfers with respect to planned job allocations, data availability and eligible costs. This functionality can rely on previously mentioned ones, like information management, search, agreement and negotiation.

- **Network Management Access**: Data transfers as well as job interactions may need particular network resources to achieve a certain QoS level during their execution. As in the case of data management access, due to its nature and complexity, network management is considered a stand-alone functionality that should be exploited by scheduling systems if needed [10]. This functionality can rely on previously mentioned ones, like information management, search, agreement and negotiation.

4.   Scheduling Instance

It is possible to consider the different blocks of the examples in Section 2 as particular implementations of a more general software entity called scheduling instance. In this context, a scheduling instance is defined as a software entity that exhibits a standardised behaviour with respect to the interactions with other software entities (which may be part of a GSA implementation or external services). Such scheduling entities cooperate to provide, if possible, a solution to scheduling problems submitted by users, e.g. the selection, planning and reservation of resource allocations for a job [5].

The scheduling instance is the basic building block of a scalable, modular architecture for scheduling tasks, jobs, workflows, or applications in Grids. Its main function is to find a solution to a scheduling problem that it receives via a generic input interface. To do so, the scheduling instance needs to interact with local resource management systems that typically control the access to the resources. If a scheduling instance can find a solution for a submitted scheduling problem, the generated schedule is returned via a generic output interface.

From the examples depicted above it is possible to derive a high-level model of operations that a scheduling instance can exploit to provide a solution to a scheduling problem:

- The scheduling instance can try to solve the whole problem by itself interacting with local resource managers it has access to.

- If it can partition the problem into several *scheduling sub-problems*. With respect to the different sub-problems it can

    – try to solve some of the sub-problems,

    – negotiate with other scheduling instances to transfer unsolved sub-problems to them,

    – wait for potential solutions coming from other scheduling instances, or

- aggregate localised solutions to find a global solution for the original problem.

■ If the partition of the problem is impossible or no solution can be found by aggregating sub-problem solutions, the scheduling instance can perform one of the following actions:

- It can report back to the entity that submitted the scheduling problem that it cannot find a solution, or

- it can

* negotiate with other scheduling instances to forward the whole problem, or

* wait for a solution to be delivered by the scheduling instance the problem has been forwarded to.

A generic Grid Scheduling Architecture will need to provide these operations, but actual implementations do not need to implement all of them. As this model of operations is modular it permits to implement several different scheduling infrastructures, like the ones depicted in the Grid scheduling scenarios.

Apart from the operations a generic architecture should support we can infer from the scenarios that a generic scheduling instance should be able to:

■ interact with local resource managers;

■ interact with external services that are not defined in the Grid Scheduling Architecture, like information, forecasting, submission, security or execution services;

■ receive a scheduling problem (from other scheduling instances or external submission services), calculate a schedule, and return a scheduling decision;

■ split a problem in sub-problems, receive scheduling decisions, and merge them into a new one;

■ forward problems to other scheduling instances.

However, an instance might exhibit only a subset of such abilities, which depends on its modus operandi and the objectives of its provider. If a scheduling instance is able to cooperate with other instances, it must exhibit the ability to send problems or sub-problems, and receive scheduling results. Looking at such an instance in relation to others, we call *higher-level scheduling instances* the ones that are able to directly forward a problem to that instance, and *lower-level scheduling instances* the ones that are able to directly accept a scheduling problem from that instance. A single instance must act as a decoupling entity

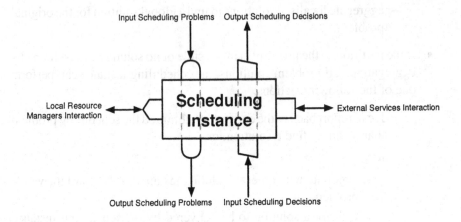

Figure 4.   Functional interfaces of a scheduling instance

between the actions performed at higher and lower levels: it is neither concerned with the instances which previously dealt with the problem (i.e. it has been submitted by an external service or forwarded by other instances as a whole problem or as a sub-problem), nor with the actions that the following instances will undertake to solve the problem. Every instance will need to know solely the problem it has to solve and the source of the original scheduling problem to avoid or resolve potential forwarding issues.

From a component point of view the abilities described above are expressed as interfaces. In general, the interfaces of a scheduling instance can be divided into two main categories: functional interfaces and non-functional interfaces. The former are necessary to enable the main behaviours of the scheduling instance, while the latter are exploited to manage the instance itself (creation, destruction, status notification, etc.).

With respect to this paper we only took the functional interfaces into account. These are essential for a scheduling instance to support the creation of a Grid Scheduling Architecture. Security services, for instance, are from a functional point of view not strictly needed to schedule a job, therefore they are considered as external services or non-functional interfaces.

In Figure 4 the following functional interfaces that a scheduling instance can expose are depicted:

Input Scheduling Problems Interface The methods of this interface are responsible to receive a description of a scheduling problem that must be solved, and start the scheduling process. This interface is not intended to accept jobs directly from users; rather an external submission service (e.g. portal or command line interface) can collect the scheduling problems, validate them and produce a neutral representation accepted as input by this interface. In this way, this interface is fully decoupled from external interactions and can be exploited to compose several scheduling instances, where an instance can forward a problem or submit a sub-problem to other instances using this interface.

Every scheduling instance must implement this interface.

Output Scheduling Decisions Interface The methods of this interface are responsible to communicate the results of the scheduling process started earlier with a scheduling problem submission. Like the previous one, this interface is not intended to communicate the results directly to a user, rather to a visualisation or reporting service. Again, we can exploit this decoupling in a modular way: if an instance receives a submission from another one, it must use this interface to communicate the results to the submitting instance.

Every scheduling instance must implement this interface.

Output Scheduling Problems Interface If an instance is able to forward a whole problem or partial sub-problems to other scheduling instances, it needs the methods of this interface to submit the problem to lower level instances.

Input Scheduling Decisions Interface If an instance is able to submit problems to other instances, it must wait until a scheduling decision is produced from the one to which the problem was submitted. The methods of this interface are responsible for the communication of the scheduling results from lower level instances.

Local Resource Managers Interface The final goal of a scheduling process is to find an allocation of the jobs to the resources. This implies that sooner or later during the process it is necessary for a scheduling instance to interact with local resource managers. While some scheduling instances can be dedicated to the "routing" of the problems, others interact directly with local resource managers to find suitable schedules, and propagate the answers in a neutral representation back to the entity that submitted the scheduling problem. Different local resource managers can require different interaction interfaces.

External Services Interaction Interfaces If an instance must interact with an entity that is neither a local resource manager nor another scheduling instance, it needs an interface that permits to communicate with that external service. For example, some instances may need to gain access to information, billing, security and/or performance predictor services.

Different external services can require different interaction interfaces.

5.   Conclusion

In this paper we discuss a general model for Grid scheduling. This model is based on a basic, modular component we call scheduling instance. Several scheduling instance implementations can be composed to build existing scheduling scenarios as well as new ones. The proposed model has no claim to be the most general one, but the authors consider this definition a good starting point to build a general Grid Scheduling Architecture that supports cooperation between different scheduling entities for arbitrary Grid resources. Future work aims at the specification of the interaction of the Grid scheduling instance to other scheduling instances as well as to other middleware services. This work will be carried out by GGF's Grid Scheduling Architecture Research Group [11] and the Virtual Institute on Resource Management and Scheduling [12] within the CoreGRID project. The outcome of this activity should yield a common Grid scheduling architecture that allows the integration of several different scheduling instances that can interact with each other as well as be exchanged with domain-specific implementations.

References

[1] R. Yahyapour and Ph. Wieder (eds.).   Grid Scheduling Use Cases. Grid Forum Document, GFD.64, Global Grid Forum, March 26, 2006. <http://www.ggf.org/documents/GFD.64.pdf>.

[2] Global Grid Forum. Web site. 1 July 2006 <http://www.ggf.org>.

[3] I. Foster, C. Kesselman, and S. Tuecke. The anatomy of the Grid – Enabling Scalable Virtual Organizations. In *Grid Computing – Making the Global Infrastructure a Reality*, F. Berman, G. C. Fox, and A. J. G. Hey (eds.), pp. 171–197. John Wiley & Sons Ltd., 2003.

[4] J. M. Schopf. Ten Actions When Grid Scheduling – The User as a Grid Scheduler. In *Grid Resource Management – State of the Art and Future Trends*, J. Nabrzyski, J. Schopf, and J. Weglarz (eds.), pp. 15–23. Kluwer Academic Publishers, 2004.

[5] U. Schwiegelshohn and R. Yahyapour. Attributes for Communication between Scheduling Instances. Grid Forum Document, GFD.6, Global Grid Forum, December, 2001. <http://www.ggf.org/documents/GFD.6.pdf>.

[6] V. Sander (ed.).   Networking Issues for Grid Infrastructure.   Grid Forum Document, GFD.37, Global Grid Forum, November 22, 2004. <http://www.ggf.org/documents/GFD.37.pdf>.

[7] U. Schwiegelshohn, R. Yahyapour, and Ph. Wieder. Resource management for Future Generation Grids. In *Future Generation Grids, Proceedings of the Workshop on Future Generation Grids*, V. Getov, D. Laforenza, and A. Reinefeld (eds.), pp. 99-112. Springer, 2004. ISBN: 0-387-27935-0.

[8] J. Bouman, J. Trienekens, and M. van der Zwan. Specification of Service Level Agreements, Clarifying Concepts on the Basis of Practical Research. In *Proc. of Software Technology and Engineering Practice 1999 (STEP '99)*, pp. 169–178, 1999.

[9] R. W. Moore. Operations for Access, Management, and Transport at Remote Sites. Grid Forum Document, GFD.46, Global Grid Forum, May 4, 2005. <http://www.ggf.org/documents/GFD.46.pdf>.

[10] D. Simeonidou and R. Nejabati (eds.). Optical Network Infrastructure for Grid. Grid Forum Document, GFD.36, Global Grid Forum, August, 2004. <http://www.ggf.org/documents/GFD.36.pdf>.

[11] Grid Scheduling Architecture Research Group (GSA-RG). Web site. 1 July 2006 <https://forge.gridforum.org/sf/sfmain/do/viewProject/projects.gsa-rg>.

[12] CoreGRID Virtual Institute on Resource Management and Scheduling. Web site. 1 July 2006 <http://www.coregrid.net/mambo/content/category/3/16/30/>.

GRID SUPERSCALAR ENABLED
P-GRADE PORTAL

Róbert Lovas, Gergely Sipos and Péter Kacsuk
Computer and Automation Research Institute, Hungarian Academy of Sciences (MTA-SZTAKI)
rlovas@sztaki.hu
sipos@sztaki.hu
kacsuk@sztaki.hu

Raül Sirvent, Josep M. Pérez and Rosa M. Badia
Barcelona Supercomputing Center and UPC, SPAIN
rsirvent@ac.upc.edu
perez@ac.upc.edu
rosab@ac.upc.edu

Abstract   One of the current challenges of the Grid scientific community is to provide efficient and user-friendly programming tools. GRID superscalar allows programmers to write their Grid applications as sequential programs. However, on execution, a task-dependence graph is built and the inherent concurrency of the task is exploited and executed in a Grid. P-GRADE Portal is a workflow-oriented grid portal with the main goal to cover the whole lifecycle of workflow-oriented computational grid applications. In this paper the authors discuss the different options taken into account to integrate these two frameworks.

Keywords: Grid computing, Grid programming models, Grid workflows, Grid portals

1.   Introduction

One of the issues that raises current interest in the Grid community and in the scientific community in general is the application programming in Grids. While more and more scientific groups aims to use the power of the Grids, the difficulty of porting applications to the Grid (what sometimes is called application *"gridification"* may be an obstacle to the adaptation of this technology.

Examples of efforts for provide Grid programming models are ProActive, Ibis, or ICENI. ProActive [15] is a Java library for parallel, distributed and concurrent computing, also featuring mobility and security in a uniform framework. With a reduced set of simple primitives, ProActive provides a comprehensive API masking the specific underlying tools and protocols used, and allowing to simplify the programming of applications that are distributed on a LAN, on a cluster of PCs, or on Internet Grids. The library is based on an active object pattern, on top of which a component-oriented view is provided.

The Ibis Grid programming environment [16] has been developed to provide parallel applications with highly efficient communication API's. Ibis is based on the Java programming language and environment, using the "write once, run anywhere" property of Java to achieve portability across a wide range of Grid platforms. Ibis aims at Grid-unaware applications. As such, it provides rather high-level communication API's that hide Grid properties and fit into Java's object model.

ICENI [17] is a grid middleware framework with an added value to the lower-level grid services. It is a system of structured information that allows to match applications with heterogeneous resources and services, in order to maximize utilization of the grid fabric. Applications are encapsulated in a component-based manner, which clearly separates the provided abstraction and its possibly multiple implementations. Implementations are selected at runtime, so as to take advantage of dynamic information, and are selected in the context of the application, rather than a single component. This yields to an execution plan specifying the implementation selection and the resources upon which they are to be deployed. Overall, the burden of code modification for specific grid services is shifted from the application designer to the middleware itself.

Tools, as the P-GRADE Portal or GRID superscalar, aims to ease the utilization of the Grid but cover different areas from an end-user's point of view. While P-GRADE Portal is a graphical-based tool, GRID superscalar is based on imperative language programs. Although there is some overlap in functionality, both tools show a lot of complementarities and it is very challenging to make them inter-operable. The integration of these tools may be a step towards achieving the idea of the "invisible" Grid for the end-user.

This work has been developed in the context of the NoE CoreGRID. More specifically, in the virtual institute "Systems, Tools and Environments" (WP7) and aims to contribute to the task 7.3 "Integrated Toolkit". The "Integrated Toolkit" will provide means to develop Grid-unaware applications, for execution in the Grid in a way transparent to the user and increasing the performance of the application.

In this paper the integration of the P-GRADE Portal and the GRID superscalar is discussed. In Section 2 the P-GRADE Portal is presented and Section 3 covers the description of the GRID superscalar framework. Then in Section 4 a comparison between both tools is given. Following that, Section 5 discusses an integration solution, and at the end of this paper Section 6 presents some conclusions, related work and future work.

2.   P-GRADE Portal

The P-GRADE Portal [1] is a workflow-oriented grid portal with the main goal to cover the whole lifecycle of workflow-oriented computational grid applications. It enables the graphical development of workflows consisting of various types of executable components (sequential, MPI or PVM programs), executing these workflows in Globus-based grids relying on user credentials, and finally analyzing the correctness and performance of applications by the built-in visualization facilities.

A P-GRADE Portal workflow is an acyclic dependency graph that connects sequential and parallel programs into an interoperating set of jobs. The nodes of such a graph are jobs, while the arc connections define the execution order of the jobs and the data dependencies between them that must be resolved by the workflow manager during the execution. An ultra-short range weather forecast (so-called *nowcasting*) grid application [2] is shown in Fig. 1 as an example for a P-GRADE Portal workflow.

Nodes (labelled as *delta, cummu, visib, satel,* and *ready* in Fig. 1 'Workflow editor') represent jobs while rectangles (labelled by numbers) around the nodes are called ports and represent data files that the corresponding jobs expect or produce. Directed arcs interconnect pairs of input and output files if an output file of a job serves as an input file for another job. The semantics of the workflow execution means that a job (a node of the workflow) can be executed, if and only if all of its input files are available, i.e. all the jobs that produce input files for the job have successfully terminated, and all the user-defined input files are available either on the portal server and at the pre-defined grid storage providers. Therefore, the workflow describes both the control-flow and the data-flow of the application. If all the necessary input files are available for a job, then DAGMan [3], the workflow manager used in the Portal transfers these files (together with the binary executable) to the site where the job has been allocated by the developer for execution. Managing the transfer of files and

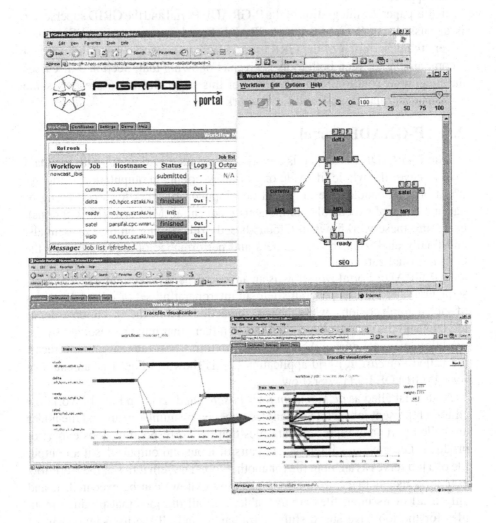

Figure 1.   Meteorological application in P-GRADE Portal; workflow manager and workflow description with status information, multi-level visualization of a successful execution

recognition of the availability of the necessary files is the task of the workflow manager subsystem.

To achieve high portability among the different grids, the P-GRADE Portal has been built onto the GridSphere portal framework [14], and the Globus middleware, and particularly those tools of the Globus Toolkit that are generally accepted and widely used in production grids today. GridFTP, GRAM, MDS and GSI [4] have been chosen as the basic underlying toolset for the Portal.

GridFTP services are used by the workflow manager subsystem to transfer input, output and executable files among computational resources, among computational and storage resources and between the portal server and the different grid sites. GRAM is applied by the workflow manager to start up jobs on computational resources. An optional element of the Portal, the information system portlet, queries MDS servers to help developers map workflow components (jobs) onto computational resources. GSI is the security architecture that guarantees authentication, authorization and message-level encryption facilities for GridFTP, GRAM and MDS sites.

The choice of this infrastructure has been justified by connecting the P-GRADE Portal to several grid systems like the GridLab test-bed, the UK National Grid Service, and two VOs of the LCG-2 Grid (See-Grid and HunGrid VOs). Notice, that most of these grid systems use some extended versions of the GT-2 middleware. The point is that if the compulsory GRAM, GridFTP and GSI middleware set is available in a VO, then the P-GRADE Portal can be immediately connected to that particular system.

Currently, the main drawback of P-GRADE portal is the usage of Condor DAGMAN as the core of workflow manager, which cannot allow the user to create cyclic graphs.

3. GRID superscalar

The aim of GRID superscalar [5] is to reduce the development complexity of Grid applications to the minimum, in such a way that writing an application for a computational Grid may be as easy as writing a sequential application [6]. It is a new programming paradigm for Grid-enabling applications, composed of an interface, a run-time and a deployment center. With GRID superscalar a sequential application composed of tasks of a certain granularity is automatically converted into a parallel application where the tasks are executed in different servers of a computational Grid.

Figure 2 outlines GRID superscalar behavior: from a sequential application code, a task dependence graph is automatically generated, and from this graph the runtime is able to detect the inherent parallelism and submit the tasks for execution to resources in a grid.

The interface is composed by calls offered by the run-time itself and by calls defined by the user. The main program that the user writes for a GRID superscalar application is basically identical to the one that would be written for a sequential version of the application. The differences would be that at some points of the code, some primitives of the GRID superscalar API are called. For instance, *GS_On* and *GS_Off* are respectively called at the beginning and at the end of the application. Other changes would be necessary for those parts of the program where files are read or written. Since the files are the objects that define the data dependences, the run-time needs to be aware of any operation performed on them. The current version offers four primitives for handling files: *GS_Open*, *GS_Close*, *GS_FOpen* and *GS_FClose*. Those primitives implement the same behavior as the standard open, close, fopen and fclose functions. In addition, the *GS_Barrier* function has been defined to allow the programmers to explicitly control the tasks' flow. This function waits until all Grid tasks have finished. Also the *GS_Speculative_End* function allows an easy way to implement parameter studies by dealing with notifications from the workers in order to stop the computation when an objective has been reached. It is important to point that several languages can be used when programming with GRID superscalar (currently C/C++, Perl, Java and Shell script are supported).

Besides these changes in the main program, the rest of the code (including the user functions) does not require any further modification.

The interface defined by the user is described with an IDL file where the functions that should be executed in the Grid are included. For each of these functions, the type and direction of the parameters must be specified (where direction means if it is an input, output or input/output parameter). Parameters can be files or scalars, but in the current version data dependencies will only be considered in the case of files.

The basic set of files that a programmer provides for a GRID superscalar application are a file with the main program, a file with the user functions code and the IDL file. From the IDL file another set of files are automatically generated by the code generation tool *gsstubgen*. This second set of files consists of stubs and skeletons that convert the original application into a grid application that calls the run-time instead of calling the original functions. Finally, binaries for the master and workers are generated and the best way to do this it by using the GS *deployment center*.

The GS *deployment center* is a Java based Graphical User Interface. Is able to check the grid configuration and also performs an automatic compilation of the main program in the *localhost* and worker programs in the server hosts.

GRID superscalar provides an underlying run-time that is able to detect the inherent parallelism of the sequential application and performs concurrent task submission. The components of the application that are objective of this concurrency exploitation are the functions listed in the IDL file. Each time one

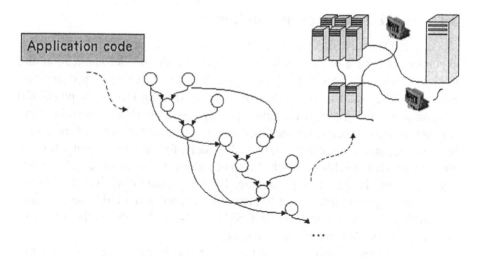

Figure 2. GRID superscalar behaviour

of these functions is called, the runtime system is called instead of the original function. A node in a data-dependence graph is added, and file dependencies between this function and functions called previously are detected. From this data-dependence graph, the runtime can submit for concurrent execution those functions that do not have any dependence between them. In addition to a data-dependence analysis based on those input/output task parameters which are files, techniques such as file renaming, file locality, disk sharing, checkpointing or constraints specification with ClassAds [7] are applied to increase the application performance, save computation time or select resources in the Grid. The run-time has been ported to different grid middlewares and the versions currently offered are: GT 2.4 [8], GT 4 [8], ssh/scp and Ninf-G2 [9].

Some possible limitations in current version of GRID superscalar are that only give support to a single certificate per user at execution. Regarding resource brokering, the selection is performed inside the run-time, but resource discovery is not supported, and machines are specified statically by the user using the GS *deployment center*. During the execution of the application the user can change the machine's information (add, remove or modify hosts parameters). Performance analysis of the application and the run-time has been done using Paraver [11], but is not currently integrated in the runtime in such a way that end-users can take benefit from it.

3.1   GRID superscalar monitor

The GRID superscalar monitor (GSM) visualizes the task dependence graph
at runtime, so the user can study the structure of his parallel application and
track the progress of execution by knowing in which machine all task are executing, and their status. The GSM is implemented using UDrawGraph (UDG)
[10], an interactive graph visualization package from the University of Bremen.
Just as the GRID superscalar, the GSM assumes that the Grid consists of a master machine, and worker machines. Additionally, for monitoring purposes, we
identify another machine, which does not belong to either of the aforementioned groups, the monitoring machine. By design, the GSM should be run in
the monitoring machine, as not to disturb or influence the Grid computation.
Although this is not mandatory, the GSM can also be located on the master or
on one of the worker machines, if desired.

Figure 3, shows an example of a GSM window, in which the user can work
manually with the graph resizing it or even changing the order of the nodes for a
better understanding of the dependencies between tasks. This is an easy way to
find out the degree of parallelism of the algorithm previously programmed with
GRID superscalar. As the graph can grow easily for more complex programs,
options for stopping the graph generation or for automatically scale / reorder
the graph are provided. The rest of the functionalities offered include saving
the graph for later reference, print the graph or export the graph to a graphical
format file (more precisely GIF, TIFF, JPEG or PNG formats).

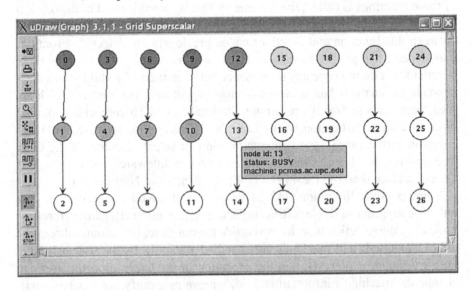

Figure 3.   GRID superscalar monitor window

The nodes representing the tasks in the GSM graph area are coloured in order to visually show the current state of the task, as well as the machine that computes the task. With this colour configuration, a user can easily see which tasks have dependencies, which ones have their dependencies resolved, the tasks currently running, and the tasks that have already finished their computation. This is very important not only to monitor the execution of the GRID superscalar application, but also allowing the user to understand why his application cannot be executed with more parallelism.

4.   Comparison of P-GRADE Portal and GRID superscalar

Table 1.   Comparison table between GRID superscalar and P-GRADE.

Products / Functionalities	GRID superscalar	P-GRADE
Support for data parallelism (graph generation)	**Advanced** automatic detection of data parallelism	**Manual** user has to express explicitly
Support for acyclic/conditional dataflows	**YES** using C or PERL	**NO** based DAGMAN/Condor
Compilation & staging of executables	**YES** Deployment Center	**Limited** only run-time staging is supported
Thin client concept	**NO** Globus client and full GS installation are needed	**YES** only a Java-enabled browser required
Monitoring & performance visualization	**Limited** Monitoring only	**YES** multi-level visualization: workflow/job/processes
Multi-Grid support	**NO** only one certificate	**YES** several certificates are handled at the same time using myproxy server
Multi-Grid support	**Limited** by using "wrapper" technology	**YES** MPI/PVM jobs or GEMCLA services

The aim of both the P-GRADE Portal and the GRID superscalar systems is to ease the programming of grid systems, by providing high-level environments on top of the Globus middleware. While the P-GRADE Portal is a graphical interface that integrates a workflow developer tool with the DAGMan workflow manager systems, the GRID superscalar is a programming API and a toolset that provide automatic code generation, as well as configuration and deployment facilities. Table 1 outlines the differences between both systems.

5.   Overview of the solution

The main purpose of the integration of the GRADE Portal – GRID superscalar system is to create a high level, graphical grid programming, deployment and execution environment that combines the workflow-oriented thin client concept of the P-GRADE Portal with the automatic deployment and application parallelisation capabilities of GRID superscalar. This integration work can be realised in three different ways:

- *Scenario 1*: A new job type can be introduced in P-GRADE workflow for a complete GRID superscalar application.

- *Scenario 2*: A sub-graph of P-GRADE workflow can be interpreted as a GRID superscalar application.

- *Scenario 3*: A GRID superscalar application can be generated based on the entire P-GRADE workflow description.

In case of the first two scenarios, the interoperability between the existing P-GRADE workflow applications and GRID superscalar applications would be provided by the system. On the other hand, Scenario 2 and 3 would enable the introduction of new language elements into P-GRADE workflow description for steering the data/control flow in a more sophisticated way; e.g. using conditional or loop constructs similarly to UNICORE [13]. Scenario 3 was selected as the most promising one and in this paper is discussed in detail.

Before the design and implementation issues, it is important to distinguish the main roles of the site administrators, developers, and end-users which are often mixed and misunderstood in academic grid solutions. The new integrated system will support the following actors (see Fig. 4);

1 The *site administrator*, who is responsible for the installation and configuration of the system components such as P-GRADE portal, GRID superscalar, and the other required grid-related software packages.

2 The Grid *application developer and deployer*, who develops the workflow application with the editor of P-GRADE portal, configures the access to the Grid resources, and deploys the jobs with GS deployment center, and finally optimizes the performance of the application using Mercury Grid monitor and the visualisation facilities of P-GRADE portal.

3 The *end-user*, who runs and interprets the results of the executions with P-GRADE portal and its application-specific portlets from any thin client machine.

Therefore, there are several benefits of the integrated solution from the end-users' points of view; they do not have to tackle the grid related issues.

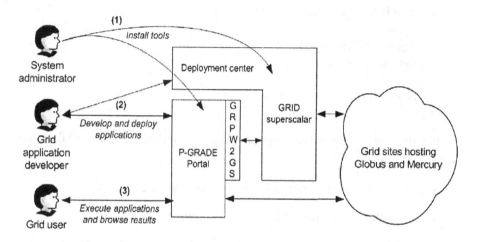

Figure 4. The roles in the integrated P-GRADE Portal – GRID superscalar system

In order to achieve these goals a new code generator GRPW2GS is integrated in P-GRADE portal. It is responsible for the generation of a GRID superscalar-compliant application from a workflow description (GRPW): an IDL file, a main program file, and a functions file.

In the *IDL file*, each job of the actual workflow is listed as a *function* declaration within the interface declaration. An example of generated GRID super-scalar IDL file is shown in next lines:

```
interface workflowname {
    void jobname (dirtype File filename, ...);
    ...
}
```

where *workflowname* and *jobname* are unique identifiers, and inherited from the workflow description. The *dirtype* can be *in* or *out* depending to the direction of the type of the actual file. The actual value of *filename* must depend on the dependencies of the file. If it is a file without dependencies (i.e. input or output of the entire workflow application), the *filename* can be the original name. On the other hand, if the file is an input of another job, a unique file identifier is generated since in P-GRADE descriptions the filenames are not unique at workflow level.

The following lines shows the structure of a main program file generated based from a workflow.

```
#include "GS_master.h"
void main(int argc, char **argv) {
    GS_On();
    jobname1('filename1', ...);
    jobname2('filename2', ...);
    ...
    GS_Off(0);
}
```

For the generation of the functions file, two options have been taken into consideration;

- using a simple wrapper technique for legacy code, or

- generating the entire application from source.

In the first case, the executable must be provided and up-loaded to the portal server by the developer similarly to the existing P-GRADE portal solution. The definitions of function calls (corresponding to the jobs) in the functions file contain only system calls to invoke these executables, which are staged by the P-GRADE portal to the appropriate site (selected by the resource broker).

In the second case, the application developer uploads the corresponding C code as the 'body' of the function using the job properties dialogue window of P-GRADE portal. In this case, the developer gets a more flexible and architecture-independent solution, since the GS deployment center can assist to create the appropriate executables on Globus sites with various architectures.

After the automatic generation of code, the application developer can deploy the code by GS deployment center, and the performance analysis phase can be started. For this purpose, the execution manager of GRID superscalar has to generate a Prove-compliant trace file to visualise the workflow-level execution. It means the instrumentation of its code fragments by GRM, which are dealing with the resource selection, job submission and file transfers. In order to get a more detailed view, the parallel MPI code can be also instrumented by a PROVE-compliant MPICH instrumentation library developed by SZTAKI.

Concerning the resource broker; the job requirement (defined in the job attributes dialog window for each jobs) can be also passed to the GS broker from the workflow editor in case of GT-2 grids, or the LCG-2 based resource broker can be also used in P-GRADE portal.

6. Conclusions, related and future work

The paper presented an initial solution for the integration of P-GRADE portal and GRID superscalar. The solution is based on the generation of a GRID superscalar application from a P-GRADE workflow. The GS deployment center is also used to automatically deploy the application in the local and server hosts.

Concerning the future work, the prototype must be finalized, and then the addition of conditional and loop constructs, and support for parameter study applications at workflow level can be started in order to get high-level control mechanisms, similar to UNICORE [13].

Therefore, we will get closer a new toolset that can assist to system administrators, programmers, and end-users at each stage of software development, deployment and usage of complex workflow based applications on the Grid.

The integrated GRID superscalar – P-GRADE Portal system shows many similarities with the GEMLCA [12] architecture. The aim of GEMLCA is to make pre-deployed, legacy applications available as unified Grid services. Using the GS deployment center, components of P-GRADE Portal workflows can be published in the Grid for execution as well. However, while GEMLCA expects compiled and already tested executables, GRID superscalar is capable to publish components from source code.

Acknowledgments

This word has been partially supported by NoE CoreGRID (FP6-004265) and by the Ministry of Science and Technology of Spain under contract TIN2004-07739-C02-01.

References

[1] G. Sipos, P. Kacsuk. *Classification and Implementations of Workflow-Oriented Grid Portals* Proc. of High Performance Computing and Communications (HPCC 2005), Lecture Notes in Computer Science 3726, pp. 684–693, 2005.

[2] R. Lovas, et al. *Application of P-GRADE Development Environment in Meteorology*. Proc. of DAPSYS'2002, Linz,, pp. 30-37, 2002.

[3] T. Tannenbaum, D. Wright, K. Miller, M. Livny. *Condor - A Distributed Job Scheduler.* Beowulf Cluster Computing with Linux. The MIT Press, MA, USA, 2002.

[4] I. Foster, C. Kesselman. *Globus: A Toolkit-Based Grid Architecture*. In I. Foster, C. Kesselmann (eds.) The Grid: Blueprint for a New Computing Infrastructure, Morgan Kaufmann, 1999, pp. 259-278.

[5] *GRID superscalar Home Page*. http://www.bsc.es/grid/

[6] R. M. Badia, J. Labarta, R. Sirvent, J. M. Pérez, J. M. Cela, R. Grima. *Programming Grid Applications with GRID Superscalar*. Journal of Grid Computing, 1(2):151-170, 2003.

[7] R. Raman, M. Livny, M. Solomon. *Matchmaking: Distributed Resource Management for High Throughput Computing*. Proceedings of the Seventh IEEE International Symposium on High Performance Distributed Computing, July 28-31, 1998, Chicago, IL.

[8] I. Foster, C. Kesselman. *Globus: A Metacomputing Infrastructure Toolkit*. Int. Journal of Supercomputer Applications, 11(2):115-12

[9] Y. Tanaka, H. Nakada, S. Sekiguchi, T. Suzumura, S. Matsuoka. *Ninf-G: A Reference Implementation of RPC-based Programming Middleware for Grid Computing*. Journal of Grid Computing, 1(1):41-51, 2003.

[10] *uDraw(Graph)*. http://www.informatik.uni-bremen.de/ davinci/

[11] *PARAVER*. http://www.cepba.upc.edu/paraver/

[12] T. Delaittre, T. Kiss, A. Goyeneche, G. Terstyanszky, S.Winter, P. Kacsuk. *GEMLCA: "Running Legacy Code Applications as Grid Services"*. Journal of Grid Computing, Vol. 3., No. 1-2, pp. 75 – 90, 2005.

[13] Dietmar W. Erwin. *"UNICORE - A Grid Computing Environment"*. Concurrency and Computation: Practice and Experience Vol. 14, Grid Computing environments Special Issue 13-14, 2002.

[14] Jason Novotny, Michael Russell, Oliver Wehrens. *GridSphere: a portal framework for building collaborations*. Concurrency and Computation: Practice and Experience, Volume 16, Issue 5 , pp. 503–513, 2004.

[15] Baude F., Baduel L., Caromel D., Contes A., Huet F., Morel M., Quilici R. *Programming, Composing, Deploying for the Grid*. In "GRID COMPUTING: Software Environments and Tools", Jose C. Cunha and Omer F. Rana (Eds), Springer Verlag, January 2006.

[16] Rob V. van Nieuwpoort, Jason Maassen, Gosia Wrzesinska, Rutger Hofman, Ceriel Jacobs, Thilo Kielmann, Henri E. Bal. *Ibis: a Flexible and Efficient Java-based Grid Programming Environment*. Concurrency and Computation: Practice and Experience, Vol. 17, No. 7-8, pp. 1079-1107, 2005.

[17] N. Furmento, A. Mayer, S. McGough, S. Newhouse, T . Field, J. Darlington. *ICENI: Optimisation of Component Applications within a Grid Environment*. Parallel Computing, 28(12), 2002.

REDESIGNING THE SEGL PROBLEM SOLVING ENVIRONMENT: A CASE STUDY OF USING MEDIATOR COMPONENTS

Thilo Kielmann and Gosia Wrzesińska
Dept. of Computer Science
Vrije Universiteit
Amsterdam, The Netherlands
kielmann@cs.vu.nl
gosia@cs.vu.nl

Natalia Currle-Linde and Michael Resch
High Performance Computing Center (HLRS)
University of Stuttgart
Germany
linde@hlrs.de
resch@hlrs.de

Abstract   The Science Experimental Grid Laboratory (SEGL) problem solving environment allows users to describe and execute complex parameter study workflows in Grid environments. Its current implementation provides much high-level functionality for executing complex parameter-study workflows. Alternatively, using a toolkit of mediator components that integrate system-component capabilities into application code would allow to build a system like SEGL from existing, more generally applicable components, simplifying its implementation and maintenance. In this paper, we present the given design of the SEGL PSE, analyze the provided functionality, and identify a set of mediator components that can generalize the functionality required by this challenging application category.

Keywords: Grid component model, mediator components, SEGL

1. Introduction

The SEGL problem solving environment [9] allows end-user programming of complex, computation-intensive simulation and modeling *experiments* for science and engineering. Experiments are complex workflows, consisting of domain-specific or general purpose simulation codes, referred to as *tasks*. For each experiment, the tasks are invoked with input parameters, that are varied over given parameter spaces, together describing individual parameter studies.

SEGL allows users to program so-called *applications* using a graphical user interface. An application consists of several tasks, the *control flow* of their invocation, and the *data flow* of input parameters and results. For the parameters, the user can describe iterations for parameter sweeps; also, conditional dependencies on result values can be part of the control flow. Using such a user application program, SEGL can execute the tasks, provide them with their respective input parameters, and collect the individual results in an experiment-specific database.

SEGL's current implementation allows executing complex parameter study workflows, involving a GUI-based frontend, an execution engine that schedules and monitors the progress of the experiment, as well as a data base server using an experiment-specific schema. By following this design, much high-level functionality has been implemented on top of existing Grid middleware, however in a way that is specific to SEGL.

Alternatively, using a toolkit of mediator components that integrate system-component capabilities into application code would allow to build a system like SEGL from existing, more generally applicable components, simplifying its implementation and maintenance. In this paper, we propose a redesign of SEGL based on such mediator components. Important insights are *(a)* the necessity to integrate components with (legacy) Web-service based middleware, and *(b)* the requirement of a persistent application-execution service.

In the following, we revisit our view of component-based Grid application environments (Section 2), present SEGL's current architecture and functionality (Section 3), and identify a set of mediator components that can generalize the functionality required by this challenging application category (Section 4). Ongoing work related to the development of such mediator components is presented in Section 5.

2. Component-based Grid application environments

A technological vision is to build Grid software such that applications and middleware will be united to a single system of components [7]. This can be accomplished by designing a toolkit of components that mediate between both applications and system components. The goal is to integrate system-component capabilities into application code, achieving both steering of the application and performance adaptation by the application to achieve the most efficient execution on the available resources offered by the Grid.

By introducing such a set of components, resources and services in the Grid get integrated into one overall system with homogeneous component interfaces. The advantage of such a component system is that it abstracts from the many software architectures and technologies used underneath. Both the strength and the challenge of such a component-based approach is that it provides a homogeneous set of well-defined (component-level) interfaces to and between all software systems in a Grid platform, ranging from portals and applications, via mediator components to the underlying middleware and system software.

As outlined in [16], both components and Web services parallel traditional objects by encapsulating state from their clients behind well-defined interfaces. They differ, however, in their applicability within given environments. Objects allow client/server communication within a single application process. With components, client and server can be distributed across different processes, however, they have to share the same execution environment which is the component model and one or more *interoperable* implementations of this model. Web services, finally, allow the distribution of client and server across different processes and execution environments, allowing the loosely-coupled integration of heterogeneous clients, resources, and services.

Components are to be preferred over Web services as they provide higher execution performance, however, at the price of reduced interoperability. Besides better performance, components also allow reflective behavior and re-composition of application software at run time, opening the path to fault-tolerant and behavior-adaptive Grid applications [8]. The limitation to a single execution environment, however, contradicts the idea of Grid computing where interoperability plays a central role for the integration of independently created and maintained resources and services. In consequence, we have to treat existing, Web-service based middleware as legacy systems that have to be integrated into a component-based Grid software platform.

A possible rendering of the envisioned mediator components along with their embedding into a generic component platform is shown in Figure 1. This diagram is based on our previous work described in [6]. Boxes in grey are examples of external services that are integrated into the overall platform.

The upper part of Figure 1 outlines a component-based Grid application, where we distinguish between three layers. The lowest layer, the runtime environment, provides the interface of the application with external (Web-service based) resources and services. The middle layer in the application stack consists of an extensible set of mediator components that provide higher-level functionality to the application. The topmost layer consists of the application components themselves, possibly enriched by a so-called *Integrated Toolkit*

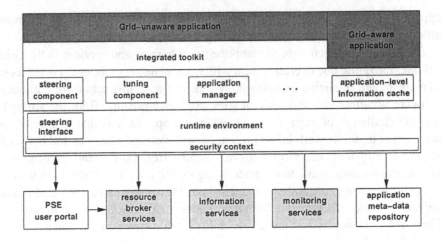

Figure 1.   Envisioned generic component platform

that provides Grid-unaware programming abstractions to the application. In the following, we present the envisioned components individually.

Runtime Environment The runtime environment implements a set of component interfaces to various kinds of Grid services and resources, like job schedulers, file systems, etc. It implements a delegation mechanism that forwards invocations to service providers. Doing so, the runtime environment provides an interface layer between application components and both system components and middleware services. Examples of such runtime environments are the GAT [2], or GGF's SAGA [12]. By providing dynamic bindings to the various service providers, the runtime environment bridges the gap between components and services, and allows to use system services with either type of interface, next to each other at the same time.

Security Context As the runtime environment implements the application's interface to services and resources outside its own scope, care has to be taken of authentication and authorization mechanisms each time external entities are getting involved. For this purpose, the security context forms an integral part of the runtime environment.

Steering Interface A dedicated part of the runtime environment is the steering interface. It is supposed to make applications accessible by system entities and user-interfaces (like portals or PSE's) like any other component in the system. This interface at the border of component-based applications and external services and components is supposed to relay to (and protect) internal component interfaces. Access control to the steering interface is subject to the security context.

Application-level meta-data repository This repository is supposed to store meta data about a specific application, storing, e.g., timing or resource requirements from previous, related runs. The collected information will be used by other components to support resource management (location and selection) and to optimize further runs of the applications automatically.

Application-level information cache

This component is supposed to provide a unified interface to deliver all kinds of meta-data (e.g., from a Grid information service (GIS), a monitoring system, or from application-level meta data) to the application. Its purpose is twofold. First, it is supposed to provide a unifying component interface to all data (independent of its actual storage), including mechanisms for service and information discovery. Second, this application-level cache is supposed to deliver the information really fast, cutting access times of current implementations like Globus GIS (up to multiple seconds) down to the order of a single method invocation.

Steering Components Controlling and steering of applications by the user, e.g., via application managers, user portals, and PSE's, requires a component level interface to give external entities access to the application. From outside the application, the steering components will be accessible via the steering interface. For example, we envision steering components with the following kinds of interfaces:

steering controller – for modifying application parameters

persistence controller – for externally triggering checkpoints

distribution strategy controller – for changing the data distribution

component explorer – for exploring (and modifying) the current component composition

Tuning Components Tuning components can be used to optimize the application's runtime behavior, based on observed behavior of the application itself and on external status information, as provided by the application-level information cache component. Tuning components can be either passive, or active, in the latter case carrying their own threads of activity.

Application Manager An application manager establishes a pro-active user interface, in charge of tracking an application from submission to successful completion. It will be in charge of guaranteeing such successful completion in spite of temporary error conditions or performance limitations. A persistent service will become an integral part of this functionality.

3.   The SEGL system architecture

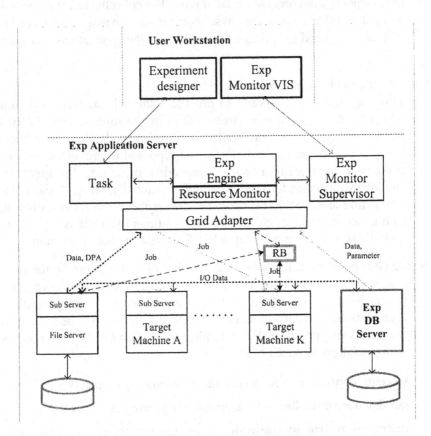

Figure 2.   Current SEGL architecture

Figure 2 shows the current system architecture of SEGL. It consists of three main components: the User Workstation (Client), the Experiment Application Server (ExpApplicationServer), and the Experiment database server (ExpDB-Server). Client and ExpApplicationServer communicate with each other using a traditional client/server architecture, based on J2EE middleware. The interaction between ExpApplicationServer and the Grid resources is done through a Grid Adaptor, interfacing to Globus [11] and UNICORE [15] middleware.

   The client on the user's workstation is composed of the graphical experiment designer tool (ExpDesigner) and the experiment process monitoring and visualization tool (ExpMonitorVIS). The ExpDesigner is used to design, verify and generate the experiment's program, organize the data repository and prepare the initial data, using a simple graphical language.

Each experiment is described at three levels: control flow, data flow and the data repository. The control flow level describes which code blocks will be executed in which order, possibly augmented by parameter iterations and conditional branches. Each block can be represented as a simple parameter study. An example is shown in Fig. 3. The data flow level describes the flow of parameter data between the individual code blocks. On the data repository level, a common description of the metadata repository is created for the given experiment. The repository is an aggregation of data from the blocks at the data flow level.

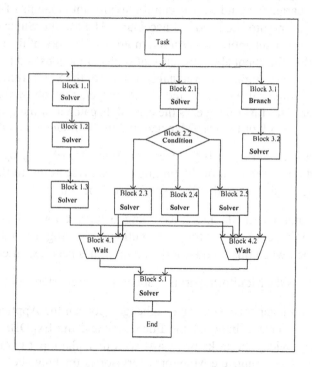

Figure 3.   Example experiment control flow

After completing the graphical design of the experiment program, it is "compiled" to the *container application*. This creates the experiment-specifc parts for the ExpApplicationServer as well as the experiment's data base schema. The container application of the experiment is transferred to the ExpApplicationServer and the schema descriptions are transferred to the server data base. Here, the meta data repository is created.

The ExpApplicationServer consists of the experiment engine (ExpEngine), the container application (Task), the controller component (ExpMonitorSupervisor) and the ResourceMonitor. The ResourceMonitor holds information about the available resources in the Grid environment. The MonitorSupervisor controls the work of the runtime system and informs the Client about the current status of the jobs and the individual processes. The ExpEngine is executing the application Task, so it is responsible for actual data transfers and program executions on and between server machine in the Grid.

The final component of SEGL is the data base server (ExpDBServer). The automatic creation of the experiment is done according to the structure designed by the user. All data produced during the experiment such as input data for the parameter study, parameterization rules etc are kept in the ExpDBServer.

As SEGL parameter studies may run for significant amounts of time, application progress monitoring becomes necessary. The MonitorSupervisor, being part of the experiment application server, monitors the work of the runtime system and notifies the client about the current status of the jobs and the individual processes. The ExpEngine is the actual controller of the SEGL runtime system. It consists of three sub systems: the TaskManager, the JobManager and the DataManager. The TaskManager is the central dispatcher of the ExpEngine. It coordinates the work of the DataManager and the JobManager as follows:

1 It organizes and controls the execution sequence of the program blocks. It starts the execution of the program blocks according to the task flow and the conditions within the experiment program.

2 It activates a particular block according to the task flow, selects the necessary computer resources for the execution of the program and deactivates the block when this section of the program has been executed.

3 It informs the MonitorSupervisor about the current status of the program.

The DataManager organizes data exchange between the ApplicationServer and the FileServer and between the FileServer and the ExpDBServer. Furthermore, it provides the tasks processes with their the input parameter data. For progress monitoring, the MonitorSupervisor is tracking the status of the ExpEngine and its sub components. It forwards status update events to the ExpMonitorVIS, closing the loop to the user. SEGL's progress monitoring is currently split in to parts:

1 The experiment monitoring and visualization on the client side (ExpMonitor VIS). It is designed for visualizing the execution of the experiment and its computation processes. The ExpMontitorVis allows the user to start, stop, the experiment, and to change the input data and to subsequently re-start the experiment or some part of it.

2 The MonitorSupervisor within the application server controls and ob-
serves the work of the runtime system (Exp Engine). It sends continuous
messages to the ExpMonitorVis on the client workstation.

This subdivision allows the user to disconnect from its running experiment.
In this case, all status update messages will be stored with the application server
for delivery to the client as soon as it will become reconnected.

4. Extracting mediator components from the SEGL functionality

The SEGL system constitutes an interesting use case for component-based
Grid systems as it comprises all functionality required for complex task-flow
applications. In this section, we try to identify, within the existing SEGL
implementation, generic functionality that could be implemented in individual,
re-usable or exchangable components.

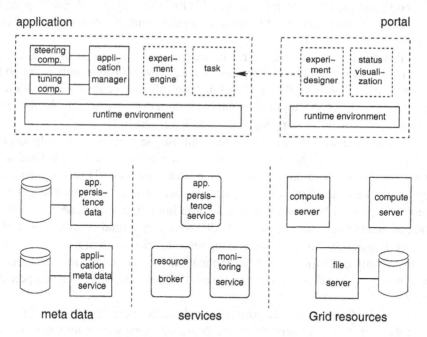

Figure 4.   SEGL redesigned using mediator components

In the current SEGL architecture, as shown in Fig. 2, there is a subdivision to
three major areas: the user interface, the experiment application server, and the
Grid resources and services. the latter consist of file servers for the experiment's
data, compute servers for experiment tasks, and additionally the experiment
database, storing all experiment-specific status information. The user interface

consists of the experiment programming environment (the "designer") and the application execution visualization component.

The most interesting element of SEGL is the experiment application server. It concentrates the application logic (implemented via the *experiment engine* and the experiment-specific *task*), a Grid middleware interface layer (called *adaptor*), as well as progress monitoring functionality. Less visible in Fig. 2 is the fact that the experiment application server is a persistently running service. It has been designed as such to decouple the user interface from possibly long-running experiment codes.

Having such a persistently running service is certainly necessary to guarantee application completion in spite of transient error conditions, without user involvement. However, adding such a domain-specific, permanent service to the pre-installed middleware may be causing administrative and security-related concerns.

Based on this analysis, we propose the following re-design based on mediator components, trying to refactor SEGL's functionality into domain-specific components, complemented by general-purpose, reusable components. This redesign is shown in Fig. 4.

In this design, the software Grid infrastructure is organized in three tiers: resources, services, and meta data. For SEGL, relevant Grid resources are both compute and file servers, the machines that are able to execute experimentation tasks and providing the application data. These servers are accessible via Grid middleware, whichever happens to be installed on each resource.

Relevant Grid services are a resource monitoring service, like e.g. Delphoi [14] and a resource broker that matches tasks to compute servers. For the Grid services, we also propose an *application persistence service*. This is a persistent service that keeps track of a given application and ensures it runs until successful completion, possibly restarting it in case of failures. Beeing a general-purpose, domain-independent service, it can be deployed in a virtual organization without overly administrative efforts, relying on a security concept that needs to be deployed only once for all kinds of applications. In a component-based architecture, we assume these services to have interfaces that fit into the component model.

The final infrastructure category is meta data. For persistent storage of such meta data, one or more servers can be deployed. One such component is the application meta data repository, equivalent to SEGL's current experiment data base. In addition, a meta data storage component is needed for the status information of the application persistence service.

The Grid infrastructure is used by two programs, the SEGL *application* and a user *portal*. Within these programs, Fig. 4 shows general-purpose components as solid boxes and domain-specific components as dashed boxes. Both programs are using the runtime environment for comunication with the Grid infrastructure. The portal is implementing both the experiment designer as well as the experiment status visualization.

SEGL's monitoring and steering facilities are divided across *application* and *portal*. Within the portal, the status visualization provides the user interface. Within the application, the *steering component* handles change requests for the parameter data. To allow the user to disconnect and later re-connect to his or her application, also the progress monitoring needs storage for its events that is persistent, at least until completion of the overall experiment. For this purpose, the *application meta data service* provides the appropriate storage facilities. The actual progress monitoring then takes place within the *application manager* component, but possibly a dedicated application monitoring and event handling component could be added.

The SEGL application is composed of components only. The experiment engine implements the SEGL-specific application logic, while the task component is created by the experiment designer within the SEGL portal. The experiment engine is accompanied by the generic application manager component which is responsible for both runtime optimization, using dedicated tuning and steering components, and for registering the SEGL application with the application persistence service. In the proposed combination, the experiment engine is responsible for the SEGL-specific control flow, while the application manager is in charge of all Grid-related control aspects, leading to a clear separation of concerns.

5. Related Work and Ongoing Developments

The work presented here is embedded in a larger scope of developments, both in a wider context and directly regarding the development of mediator components.

5.1 Related Work

Whereas notions and models for *components* are still diverse [1, 5, 8, 17, 18], there is a trend towards building Grid application environments from entities that can be selected and dynamically loaded at runtime [13].

Ibis [20] is a runtime environment for executing parallel Java applications in Grid environments. It uses Java's dynamic byte code loading for matching application needs to the given network environments and protocols, such as TCP/IP or local Myrinet clusters. The work in [10] extends this concept to configuring whole protocol stacks from runtime components.

The Grid Application Toolkit (GAT) [2] provides a simple and uniform API to various Grid middleware, like Globus [11] or Unicore [15]. The GAT API is implemented via a so-called engine that uses dynamically linked *adaptors* to bind Grid applications to the actual Grid environment. The Commodity Grid

Kits (CoG kits) [21] similarly provide simplified API's to Globus, and more recently also to ssh-based environments.

ProActive [4] is another Java-based execution environment for parallel Grid applications. Unlike Ibis, it uses the Fractal [5] component model for providing the units of dynamic composition. Assist [1] is another component-based execution environment for parallel Grid applications. Both ProActive and Assist are using components for deployment and runtime adaptation. Neither of them, however, is proposing a comprehensive component toolkit for mediating between application needs and middleware services. The proposed lightweight, generic grid platform [19] aims in this direction by building a component-based Grid middleware infrastructure, on top of which mediator components could be implemented with ease.

5.2　　Ongoing Developments of Mediator Components

Several efforts are currently undertaken to investigate the feasibility of building the envisioned set of mediator components. These efforts are explorative, aiming at gaining early experiences. Completeness and production quality code, however, are beyond our current scope.

Grid Component Model A suitable model for Grid components (GCM) [8] is vital for developing mediator components, too. Currently, our group at Vrije Universiteit is experimenting with the Fractal component model [5] which is considered a starting point for developing the GCM. First results of this work have lead to the refinements of the generic Grid component platform, as shown in Fig. 1.

Runtime Environment We are currently using the Grid Application Toolkit (GAT) [2] as runtime environment. We are designing component-level (wrapper) interfaces to its provided functionality. The design alternative of redesigning the whole runtime environment based on components has been ruled out, due to the requirement of integrating legacy services and resources, as outlined in Section 2.

Application-level Information Cache The functionality of such a cache component is currently being developed that can integrate various kinds information providers [3]. The design of a proper (Fractal) component interface is subject to ongoing work.

Application Manager The design of an application manager, in combination with an application persistence service and data repository, as shown in Fig. 4, is also currently being investigated within our group at Vrije Universiteit.

6. Conclusions

The SEGL problem solving environment allows end-user programming of complex, computation-intensive simulation and modeling *experiments* for science and engineering. As such, it constitutes an interesting use case for component based Grid systems as it comprises all functionality required for complex task-flow applications.

In this paper, we have identified, within the existing SEGL implementation, generic functionality that can be implemented in individual, reusable components. We have proposed a three-tier Grid middleware architecture, consisting of the resources themselves, persistent services, and meta data. Important insights are *(a)* the necessity to integrate components with (legacy) Web-service based middleware, and *(b)* the requirement of a persistent application-execution service.

Based on this architecture, we were able to compose a SEGL experiment execution application from mostly general-purpose components, augmented only by a SEGL-specific experiment engine and the dynamically created experiment task description. With this architecture we tried to refactor a system like SEGL such that general-purpose functionality is implemented in reusable components while a minimal set of domain-specific components can be added to compose the overall application.

With currently available technology, such components do not exist yet, as suitable component models, and especially generally accepted and standardized interfaces, are subject to ongoing work, as outlined in Section 5. Once such components become available and mature [6], refactoring SEGL's implementation will be an interesting excercise.

Acknowledgements

This research work is carried out under the FP6 Network of Excellence CoreGRID funded by the European Commission (Contract IST-2002-004265). We would like to thank Urszula Herman-Izycka and Michal Ejdys for their valuable contributions to refining the generic component platform.

References

[1] M. Aldinucci, M. Coppola, M. Danelutto, M. Vanneschi, and C. Z. occolo. Assist as a research framework for high-performance grid programming en vironments. In J. C. Cunha and O. F. Rana, editors, *Grid Computing: Software environments and Tools*. Springer-Verlag, 2004.

[2] G. Allen, K. Davis, T. Goodale, A. Hutanu, H. Kaiser, T. Kielmann, A. Merzky, R. van Nieuwpoort, A. Reinefeld, F. Schintke, T. Schütt, E. Seidel, and B. Ullmer. The Grid Application Toolkit: Towards Generic and Easy Application Programming Interfaces for the Grid. *Proceedings of the IEEE*, 93(3):534–550, 2005.

[3] G. Aloisio, Z. Balaton, P. Boon, M. Cafaro, I. Epicoco, G. Gombas, P. Kacsuk, T. Kielmann, and D. Lezzi. Integrating Resource and Service Discovery in the CoreGRID Information Cache Mediator Component. In *CoreGRID Integration Workshop*, Pisa, Italy, 2005.

[4] F. Baude, D. Caromel, and M. Morel. From distributed objects to hierarchical grid components. In *International Symposium on Distributed Objects and Applications (DOA)*, *Catania, Sicily, Italy, 3-7 November*, Springer Verlag, 2003. Lecture Notes in Computer Science, LNCS.

[5] E. Bruneton, T. Coupaye, and J. B. Stefani. Recursive and Dynamic Software Composition with Sharing. In *Seventh International Workshop on Component-Oriented Programming (WCOP02)*, Malaga, Spain, 2002. Held at ECOOP 2002.

[6] CoreGRID Institute on Problem Solving Environments, Tools, and GRID Systems. Proposal for mediator component toolkit. CoreGRID deliverable D.ETS.02, 2005.

[7] CoreGRID Institute on Problem Solving Environments, Tools, and GRID Systems. Roadmap version 1 on Problem Solving Environments, Tools, and GRID Systems. CoreGRID deliverable D.ETS.01, 2005.

[8] CoreGRID Institute on Programming Models. Proposal for a Common Component Model for GRID. CoreGRID deliverable D.PM.02, 2005.

[9] N. Currle-Linde, U. Küster, M. Resch, and B. Risio. Science Experimental Grid Laboratory (SEGL) Dynamical Parameter Study in Distributed Systems. In *ParCo 2005*, Malaga, Spain, 2005.

[10] A. Denis. Meta-communications in Component-based Communication Frameworks for Grids. In *HPC-GECO Workshop, held in conjunction with HPDC-15*, Paris, France, 2006.

[11] I. Foster and C. Kesselman. Globus: A Metacomputing Infrastructure Toolkit. *Int. Journal of Supercomputer Applications*, 11(2):115–128, 1997.

[12] Global Grid Forum (GGF). Simple API for Grid Applications (SAGA). https://forge.gridforum.org/projects/saga-rg/, 2005.

[13] T. Kielmann, A. Merzky, H. Bal, F. Baude, D. Caromel, and F. Huet. Grid Application Programming Environments. In *Future Generation Grids*, pages 283–306. Springer Verlag, 2006.

[14] J. Maassen, R. V. van Nieuwpoort, T. Kielmann, K. Verstoep, and M. den Burger. Middleware Adaptation with the Delphoi Service. *Concurrency and Computation: Practice and Experience*, 2006. Special issue on Adaptive Grid Middleware.

[15] D. Erwin (Ed.). *Joint Project Report for the BMBF Project UNICORE Plus*. UNICORE Forum e.V., 2003.

[16] R. Sessions. Fuzzy Boundaries: Objects, Components, and Web Services. *ACM Queue*, 2(9):40–47, 2005.

[17] The CCA Forum. The Common Component Architecture (CCA) Forum home page, 2005. http://www.cca-forum.org/.

[18] The Object Management Group (OMG). CORBA Component Model, V3.0. http://www.omg.org/technology/documents/formal/components.htm, 2005.

[19] J. Thiyagalingam, N. Parlavantzas, S. Isaiadis, L. Henrio, D. Caromel, and V. Getov. Proposal for a Lightweight, Generic Grid Platform Architecture. In *HPC-GECO Workshop, held in conjunction with HPDC-15*, Paris, France, 2006.

[20] R. V. van Nieuwpoort, J. Maassen, R. Hofman, T. Kielmann, and H. E. Bal. Ibis: an Efficient Java-based Grid Programming Environment. In *Joint ACM Java Grande - ISCOPE 2002 Conference*, pages 18–27, Seattle, Washington, USA, November 2002.

[21] G. von Laszewski, I. Foster, J. Gawor, and P. Lane. A Java Commodity Grid Kit. *Concurrency and Computation: Practice and Experience*, 13(8–9):643–662, 2001.

SYNTHETIC GRID WORKLOADS WITH IBIS, KOALA, AND GRENCHMARK

Alexandru Iosup and Dick H.J. Epema
Faculty of Electrical Engineering, Mathematics, and Computer Science
Delft University of Technology,
Mekelweg 4, 2628 CD, Delft, The Netherlands
A.Iosup@tudelft.nl
D.H.J.Epema@tudelft.nl

Jason Maassen and Rob van Nieuwpoort
Department of Computer Science,
Vrije Universiteit, Amsterdam, The Netherlands
Jason@cs.vu.nl
Rob@cs.vu.nl

Abstract   Grid computing is becoming the natural way to aggregate and share large sets of heterogeneous resources. However, grid development and acceptance hinge on proving that grids reliably support real applications. A step in this direction is to combine several grid components into a demonstration and testing framework. This paper presents such an integration effort, in which three research prototypes, namely a grid application development toolkit (Ibis), a grid scheduler capable of co-allocating resources (KOALA), and a synthetic grid workload generator (GRENCHMARK), are used to generate and run workloads comprising well-established and new grid applications on our DAS multi-cluster testbed.

Keywords: Grid, performance evaluation, synthetic workloads.

1.   Introduction

Grid computing's long term promise is a seamlessly shared infrastructure comprising heterogeneous resources, to be used by multiple organizations and independent users alike [12]. With the infrastructure starting to fulfill the requirements of such an ambitious promise [4], it is crucial to prove that grids can run real applications, from traditional sequential and parallel applications to new, grid-specific, applications. As a consequence, there is a clear need for generating workloads comprising of real applications, and for running them in grid environments, for demonstration and testing purposes.

A significant number of projects have tried to tackle this problem from different angles: attempting to produce a representative set of grid applications like the NAS Grid Benchmarks [13], creating synthetic applications that can assess the status of grid services like the GRASP project [7], and creating tools for launching benchmarks and reporting results like the GridBench project [21].

This work addresses the problem of generating and running synthetic grid workloads, by integrating the results of three research projects coming from CoreGRID partners, namely the grid application development toolkit Ibis [22], the grid scheduler KOALA [17], and the synthetic grid workload generator and submitter GRENCHMARK. Ibis is being developed at VU Amsterdam[1] and provides a set of generic Java-based grid applications. KOALA is being developed at TU Delft[2] and allows running generic grid applications. Finally, GRENCHMARK is being developed at TU Delft[3] and is able to generate workloads comprising typical grid applications, and to submit them to arbitrary grid environments.

2.   A Case for Synthetic Grid Workloads

There are three ways of evaluating the performance of a grid system: analytical modeling, simulation, and experimental testing. This section presents the benefits and drawbacks of each of the three, and argues for evaluating the performance of grid systems using synthetic workloads, one of the two possible approaches for experimental testing.

2.1   Analytical Modeling and Simulations

Analytical modeling is a traditional method for gaining insights into the performance of computing systems. Analytical modeling may simplify *what-if* analysis, for changes in the system, in the middleware, or in the applications.

---

[1] Ibis is available from http://www.cs.vu.nl/ibis/.
[2] KOALA is available from http://www.st.ewi.tudelft.nl/koala/.
[3] GRENCHMARK is available from http://grenchmark.st.ewi.tudelft.nl/.

However, the sheer size of grids and their heterogeneity make realistic analytical modeling hardly tractable.

Simulations may handle complex situations, sometimes very close to the real system. Furthermore, simulations allow the *replay* of real situations, greatly facilitating the discovery of appropriate solutions. However, simulated system size and diversity raises questions on the representativeness of simulating grids. Moreover, nondeterminism and other forms of hidden dynamic behavior of grids make the simulation approach even less suitable. Even if these problems are overlooked, the simulation outcome is greatly dependent on the used (synthetic) workloads [9, 11].

2.2   Experimental Testing

There are three ways to experimentally assess the performance of grid systems: *using real grid workloads*, *using synthetic grid workloads*, and *benchmarking*.

We argue that traces of real grid workloads (short, *traces*) are difficult to replay in currently existing grids: the infrastructure changes too fast, leading to incompatible resource requests when re-running old traces. This renders the potential *use of real traces* unsuitable for the moment. Synthetic grid workloads derived from one or several traces, may be used instead.

Benchmarking is typically used to understand the quantitative aspects of running grid applications and to make results readily available for comparison. A benchmarks comprises a set applications representative for a class of systems, and a set of rules for running the applications as a synthetic system workload. Therefore, a benchmark is a single instance of a synthetic workload.

Benchmarks present severe limitations, when compared to synthetic grid workloads generation. They have to be developed under the auspices of an important number of (typically competing) entities, and can only include well-studied applications. Putting aside the considerable amounts of time and resources needed for these tasks, the main problem is that grid applications are starting to develop just now, typically at the same time with the infrastructure [19], thus limiting the availability of truly representative applications for inclusion in standard benchmarks. Other limitations in using benchmarks for more than raw performance evaluation are:

- Benchmarking results are valid only for workloads truly represented by the benchmark's set of applications; moreover, the number of applications typically included in benchmarks [13, 21] is typically small, limiting even more the scope of benchmarks;

- Benchmarks include mixes of applications representative at a certain moment of time, and are notoriously resistant to include new applications;

thus, benchmarks cannot respond to the changing requirements of developing infrastructures, such as grids;

- Benchmarks measure only one particular system characteristic (low-level benchmarks), or a mix of characteristics (high-level benchmarks), but not both.

An extensible framework for *generating and submitting synthetic grid workloads* uses applications representative for today's grids, and fosters the addition of future grid applications. This approach can help overcome the aforementioned limitations of benchmarks. First, it offers better flexibility in choosing the starting applications set, when compared to benchmarks. Second, applications can be included in generated workloads, even when they are in a debug or test phase. Third, the workload generation can be easily parameterized, to allow for the evaluation of one or a mix of system characteristics.

2.3   Grid Applications Types

From the point of view of a grid scheduler, we identify two types of applications that can run in grids, and may be therefore included in synthetic grid workloads.

- *Unitary applications* This category includes single, unitary, applications. At most the job programming model must be taken into account when running in grids (e.g., launching a name server before launching an Ibis job). Typical examples include sequential and parallel (e.g., MPI, Java RMI, Ibis) applications. The tasks composing a unitary application, for instance in a parallel application, can interact with each other.

- *Composite applications* This category includes applications composed of several unitary or composite applications. The grid scheduler needs to take into account issues like task inter-dependencies, advanced reservation and extended fault-tolerance, besides the components' job programming model. Typical examples include parameter sweeps, chains of tasks, DAG-based applications, and even generic graphs.

2.4   Purposes of Synthetic Grid Workloads

We further present five reasons for using synthetic grid workloads.

- *System design and procurement* Grid architectures offer many alternatives to their designers, in the form of hardware, of operating software, of middleware (e.g., a large variety of schedulers), and of software libraries. When a new system is replacing an old one, running a synthetic workload can show whether the new configuration performs according to the expectations, before the system becomes available to users. The same procedure may be used for assessing the performance of various systems, in the selection phase of the procurement process.

- *Functionality testing and system tuning* Due to the inherent heterogeneity of grids, complicated tasks may fail in various ways, for example due to misconfiguration or unavailability of required grid middleware. Running synthetic workloads, which use the middleware in ways similar to the real application, helps testing the functionality of the grids and detecting many of the existing problems.

- *Performance testing of grid applications* With grid applications being more and more oriented toward services [15] or components [14], early performance testing is not only possible, but also required. The production cycle of traditional parallel and distributed applications must include early testing and profiling. These requirements can be satisfied with a synthetic workload generator and submitter.

- *Comparing grid components* Grid middleware comprises various components, e.g., resource schedulers, information systems, and security managers. Synthetic workloads can be used for solving the requirements of component-specific use cases, or for testing the Grid-component integration.

- *Building runtime databases* In many cases, getting accurate information about an application's runtime is critical for further optimizing its execution. For many scheduling algorithms, like backfilling, this information is useful or even critical. In addition, some applications need (dynamic) *on-site* tuning of their parameters in order to run faster. The use of historical runtime information databases can help alleviate this problem [18]. An automated workload generator and submitter would be of great help in filling the databases.

In this paper we show how GRENCHMARK can be used to generate synthetic workloads suitable for one of these goals (functionality testing and system tuning), and lay out a research roadmap that may lead to fulfilling the requirements of all five goals (see Section 6).

3. An Extensible Framework for Grid Synthetic Workloads

This section presents an extensible framework for generating and submitting synthetic grid workloads. The first implementation of the framework integrates two research prototypes, namely a grid application development toolkit (Ibis), and a synthetic grid workload generator (GRENCHMARK).

3.1   Ibis: Grid Applications

Ibis is a grid programming environment offering the user efficient execution and communication [8], and the flexibility to run on dynamically changing sets of heterogeneous processors and networks.

The Ibis distribution package comes with over 30 working applications, in the areas of physical simulations, parallel rendering, computational mathematics, state space search, bioinformatics, prime numbers factorization, data compression, cellular automata, grid methods, optimization, and generic problem solving. The Ibis applications closely resemble real-life parallel applications, as they cover a wide-range of computation/communication ratios, have different communication patterns and memory requirements, and are parameterized. Many of the Ibis applications report detailed performance results. Last but not least, all the Ibis applications have been thoroughly described and tested in various grids [8, 22]. They work on various numbers of machines, and have automatic fault tolerance and migration features, thus responding to the requirements of dynamic environments such as grids. For a complete list of publications, please visit http://www.cs.vu.nl/ibis. Therefore, the Ibis applications are representative for grid applications written in Java, and can be easily included in synthetic grid workloads.

3.2   GRENCHMARK: Synthetic Grid Workloads

GRENCHMARK is a synthetic grid workload generator and submitter. It is *extensible*, in that it allows new types of grid applications to be included in the workload generation, *parameterizable*, as it allows the user to parameterize the workloads generation and submission, and *portable*, as its reference implementation is written in Python.

The workload generator is based on the concepts of *unit generators* and of job description files (JDF) *printers*. The *unit generators* produce detailed descriptions on running a set of applications (*workload unit*), according to the workload description provided by the user. There is one unit for each type of supported application type. The *printers* take the generated workload units and create job description files suitable for grid submission. In this way, multiple unit generators can be coupled to produce a workload that can be submitted to any grid resource manager, as long as the resource manager supports that type of applications.

The grid applications currently supported by GRENCHMARK are sequential jobs, jobs which use MPI, and Ibis jobs. We use the Ibis applications included in the default Ibis distribution (see Section 3.1). We have also implemented three *synthetic applications*: sser, a sequential application with parameterizable computation and memory requirements, sserio, a sequential application with parameterizable computation and I/O requirements, and smpi1, an MPI

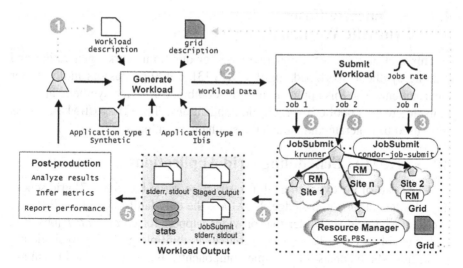

Figure 1. The GRENCHMARK process.

application with parameterizable computation, communication, memory, and I/O requirements. Currently, GRENCHMARK can submit jobs to KOALA and Globus GRAM.

The workload generation is also dependent on the applications inter-arrival time [6]. Peak job arrival rates for a grid system can also be modeled using well-known statistical distributions [6, 16]. Besides the Poisson distribution, used traditionally in queue-based systems simulation, modeling could rely on uniform, normal, exponential and hyper-exponential, Weibull, log normal, and gamma distributions. All these distributions are supported by the GRENCH-MARK generator.

The workload submitter generates detailed reports of the submission process. The reports include all job submission commands, the turnaround time of each job, including the grid overhead, the total turnaround time of the workload, and various statistical information.

3.3 Using the Framework

Figure 1 depicts the typical usage of our framework. First, the user describes the workload to be generated, as a formatted text file (1). Based on the user description, on the known application types, and on information about the grid sites, a workload is then generated by GRENCHMARK (2). A generated workload is then submitted or resubmitted to the grid (3). The grid environment is responsible for executing the jobs and returning their results (4). The results include the outcome of the jobs, and detailed submission reports. Finally, the user processes all results in a post-production step (5).

4. A Concrete Case: Synthetic Workloads for the DAS

This section presents a concrete case for our framework: generating and running synthetic workloads on the DAS [3], a 400 processors multi-cluster environment. The Ibis applications were combined with the synthetic applications, to create a pool of over 35 grid applications. The GRENCHMARK tools were used to generate and launch the synthetic workloads.

4.1 KOALA: Scheduling Grid Applications

A key part of the experimental infrastructure is the KOALA [17] grid scheduler. To the author's knowledge, KOALA is the only fault-tolerant, well-tested, and deployed grid scheduler that provides support for *co-allocated* jobs, that is, it can simultaneously allocate resources in multiple grid sites to single applications which consist of multiple components. KOALA was used to submit the generated workloads to the DAS multi-cluster. Its excellent reporting capabilities were also used for evaluating the jobs execution results.

For co-allocated jobs, KOALA gives the user the option to specify the actual execution sites, i.e., the clusters where job components should run. KOALA supports *fixed* jobs, for which users fully specify the execution sites, *non-fixed* jobs, for which the user does not specify the execution sites, leaving instead KOALA to select the best sites, and *semi-fixed* jobs, which are a mix of the previous two. KOALA may schedule different components of a non-fixed or of a semi-fixed job onto the same site. We used this feature heavily for the Ibis and the synthetic MPI applications. The structure of all used applications requires interaction between their co-allocated components.

4.2 The Workload Generation

Table 1 shows the structure of the five generated workloads, each comprising 100 jobs. To satisfy typical grid situations, jobs request resources from 1 to 15 sites. For parallel jobs, there is a preference for 2 and 4 sites. Site requests are either precise (specifying the full name of a grid site) or non-specified (leaving the scheduler to decide). For multi-site jobs, components occupy between 2 and 32 processors, with a preference for 2, 4, and 16 processors. We used combinations of parameters that would keep the run-time of the applications under 30 minutes, under optimal conditions. Each job requests resources for a time below 15 minutes. Various inter-arrival time distributions are used, but the submission time of the last job of any workload is kept under two hours.

Figure 2 shows the workload description for generating the gmark+ test, comprising 100 jobs of four different types. The first two lines are comments. The next two lines are used to generate sequential jobs of types sser and

Table 1. The experimental workloads. As the DAS has only 5 sites; jobs with more than 5 components will have several components running at the same site.

Workload	Applications types	# of Jobs	# of CPUs	Component No.	Size	Success Rate
gmark1	synthetic, sequential	100	1	1	1	97%
gmark+	synthetic, seq. & MPI	100	1-128	1-15	1-32	81%
ibis1	N Queens, Ibis	100	2-16	1-8	2-16	56%
ibis+	various, Ibis	100	2-32	1-8	2-16	53%
wl+all	all types	100	1-32	1-8	1-32	90%

```
# File-type: text/wl-spec
#ID Jobs Type    SiteType Total SiteInfo ArrivalTimeDistr  OtherInfo
?   25   sser    single   1     *:?      Poisson(120s)     StartAt=0s
?   25   sserio  single   1     *:?      Poisson(120s)     StartAt=60s
?   25   smpi1   single   1     *:?      Poisson(120s)     StartAt=30s,ExternalFile=smpi1.xin
?   25   smpi1   single   1     *:?      Poisson(120s)     StartAt=90s,ExternalFile=smpi2.xin
```

Figure 2. A GRENCHMARK workload description example.

sserio, with default parameters. The final two lines are used to generate MPI jobs of type smpi1, with parameters specified in external files smpi1.xin and smpi2.xin. All four job types assume an arrival process with Poisson distribution, with a average rate of 1 job every 120 seconds. The first job of each type starts at a time specified in the workload description with the help of the StartAt tag.

4.3 The Workload Submission

GRENCHMARK was used to submit the workloads. Each workload was submitted in the normal DAS working environment, thus being influenced by the background load generated by other DAS users. Some jobs could not finish in the time for which they requested resources, and were stopped automatically by the KOALA scheduler. This situation corresponds to users under-estimating applications' runtimes. Each workload ran between the submission start time and 20 minutes after the submission of the last job. Thus, some jobs did not run, as not enough free resources were available during the time between their submission and the end of the workload run. This situation is typical for real working environments, and being able to run and stop the workload according to the user specifications shows some of the capabilities of GRENCHMARK.

5. The Experimental Results

This section presents an overview of the experimental results, and shows that workloads generated with GRENCHMARK can cover in practice a wide-range of run characteristics.

Table 2.   A summary of time and run/success percentages for different job types.

Job name	Job type	Turnaround [s]			Runtime [s]			Run	Run+ Success
		Avg.	Min	Max	Avg.	Min	Max		
sser	sequential	129	16	926	44	1	588	100%	97%
smpi1	MPI	332	21	1078	110	1	332	80%	85%
N Queens	Ibis	99	15	1835	31	1	201	66%	85%

5.1   The Performance Results

Table 1 shows the success rate for all five workloads (column *Success Rate*). A successful job is a job that gets its resources, runs, finishes, and returns all results within the time allowed for the workload. We have selected the success rate metric to show that GRENCHMARK can be used to evaluate the arguably biggest problem of nowadays grids, i.e., the high rate of failures. The lower performance of Ibis jobs (workload ibis+) when compared to all the others, is caused by the fact that the system was very busy at the time of testing, making the resource allocation particularly difficult. This situation cannot be prevented in large-scale environments, and cannot be addressed without special resource reservation rights.

The turnaround time of an application can vary greatly (see Table 2), due to different parameter settings, or to varying system load. The variations in the application runtimes are due to different parameter settings.

As expected, the percentage of the applications that are actually run (Table 2, column *Run*) depends heavily on the job size and system load. The success rate of jobs that *did* run shows little variation (Table 2, column *Run+Success*). The ability of GRENCHMARK to report percentages such as these enables future work on comparing of the success rate of co-allocated jobs, vs. single-site jobs.

5.2   Dealing With Errors

Using the combined GRENCHMARK and KOALA reports, it was easy to identify errors at various levels in the submission and execution environment: the user, the scheduler, the local and the remote resource, and the application environment levels. For a better description of the error levels, and for a discussion about the difficulty of trapping and understanding errors, we refer the reader to the work of Thain and Livny [20].

We were able to identify bottlenecks in the grid infrastructure, and in particular in KOALA, which was one of our goals. For example, we found that for large jobs in a busy system, the percentage of unsuccessful jobs increases dramatically. The reason is twofold. First, using a single machine to submit jobs (a typical grid usage scenario) incurs a high level of memory occupancy, especially with many jobs waiting for the needed resources. A possible solution is to allow a single KOALA job submitter to support multiple job submissions. Second, there are cases when jobs attempt to claim the resources allocated by the scheduler, but fail to do so, for instance because a local request leads to resources being claimed by another user (scheduling-claiming atomicity problem). These jobs should not be re-scheduled immediately, or this could lead to a high occupancy of the system resources. A possible solution is to use an exponential back-off mechanism when scheduling such jobs.

6. Proposed Research Roadmap

In this section we present a research roadmap for creating a framework for synthetic grid workload generation, submission, and analysis. We argue that such a complex endeavor cannot be completed in one step, and, most importantly, not by a single research group. We propose instead an iterative roadmap, in which results obtained in each of the steps are significant for thoretical and practical reasons.

Step 1. Identify key modeling features for synthetic grid workloads;

Step 2. Build or extend a framework for synthetic grid workloads generation, submission, and analysis;

Step 3. Analyze grid traces and create models of them;

Step 4. *Repeat from Step 1 until the framework includes enough features*;

Step 5. Devise grid benchmarks for specific goals (see Section 2.4);

Step 6. *Repeat from Step 1 until all the important domains in Grid are covered*;

Step 7. Create a comprehensive Grid benchmark, in the flavor of SPEC [1] and TPC [2].

The work included in this paper represents an initial Step 1-3 iteration. We first identify a number of key modeling features for synthetic grid workloads, e.g., application types. We then build an extensible framework for synthetic grid workloads generation, submission, and analysis. Finally, we use the framework to test the functionality and tune the KOALA scheduler.

7. Conclusions and Ongoing Work

This work has addressed the problem of synthetic grid workload generation and submission. We have integrated three research prototypes, namely a grid application development toolkit, Ibis, a grid metascheduler, KOALA, and a synthetic grid workload generator, GRENCHMARK, and used them to generate and run workloads comprising well-established and new grid applications on a multi-cluster grid. We have run a large number of application instances, and presented overview results of the runs.

We are currently adding to GRENCHMARK the complex applications generation capabilities and an automatic results analyzer. For the future, we plan to prove the applicability of GRENCHMARK for specific grid performance evaluation, such as such as an evaluation of the DAS support for High-Energy Physics applications [10], and a performance comparison of co-allocated and single site applications, to complement our previous simulation work [5].

Acknowledgments

This research work is carried out under the FP6 Network of Excellence CoreGRID funded by the European Commission (Contract IST-2002-004265). Part of this work was also carried out in the context of the Virtual Laboratory for e-Science project (www.vl-e.nl), which is supported by a BSIK grant from the Dutch Ministry of Education, Culture and Science (OC&W), and which is part of the ICT innovation program of the Dutch Ministry of Economic Affairs (EZ). We would also like to thank our reviewers for their helpful comments, Hashim Mohamed and Wouter Lammers for their work on KOALA, and Gosia Wrzesińska, Niels Drost, and Mathijs den Burger for their work on Ibis.

References

[1] The Standard Performance Evaluation Corporation. SPEC High-Performance Computing benchmarks. [Accessed] March 2006. [Online] http://www.spec.org/.

[2] Transaction Processing Performance Council. TPC transaction processing and database benchmarks. [Accessed] March 2006. [Online] http://www.tpc.org/.

[3] Henri E. Bal et al. The distributed ASCI supercomputer project. *Operating Systems Review*, 34(4):76–96, October 2000.

[4] F. Berman, A. Hey, and G. Fox. *Grid Computing: Making The Global Infrastructure a Reality*. Wiley Publishing House, 2003. ISBN: 0-470-85319-0.

[5] Anca I. D. Bucur and Dick H. J. Epema. Trace-based simulations of processor co-allocation policies in multiclusters. In *HPDC*, pages 70–79. IEEE Computer Society, 2003.

[6] Steve J. Chapin, Walfredo Cirne, Dror G. Feitelson, James Patton Jones, Scott T. Leutenegger, Uwe Schwiegelshohn, Warren Smith, and David Talby. Benchmarks and standards for the evaluation of parallel job schedulers. In Dror G. Feitelson and Larry Rudolph, editors, *JSSPP*, volume 1659 of *Lecture Notes in Computer Science*, pages 67–90. Springer, 1999.

[7] G. Chun, H. Dail, H. Casanova, and A. Snavely. Benchmark probes for grid assessment. In *IPDPS*. IEEE Computer Society, 2004.

[8] Alexandre Denis, Olivier Aumage, Rutger F. H. Hofman, Kees Verstoep, Thilo Kielmann, and Henri E. Bal. Wide-area communication for grids: An integrated solution to connectivity, performance and security problems. In *HPDC*, pages 97–106. IEEE Computer Society, 2004.

[9] Carsten Ernemann, Baiyi Song, and Ramin Yahyapour. Scaling of workload traces. In Dror G. Feitelson, Larry Rudolph, and Uwe Schwiegelshohn, editors, *JSSPP*, volume 2862 of *Lecture Notes in Computer Science*, pages 166–182. Springer, 2003.

[10] D. Barberis et al. Common use cases for a high-energy physics common application layer for analysis. Report LHC-SC2-20-2002, LHC Grid Computing Project, October 2003.

[11] Dror G. Feitelson and Larry Rudolph. Metrics and benchmarking for parallel job scheduling. In Dror G. Feitelson and Larry Rudolph, editors, *JSSPP*, volume 1459 of *Lecture Notes in Computer Science*, pages 1–24. Springer, 1998.

[12] Ian Foster, Carl Kesselman, and Steve Tuecke. The Anatomy of the Grid: Enabling Scalable Virtual Organizations. *International Journal of Supercomputing Applications*, 15(3), 2002.

[13] Michael Frumkin and Rob F. Van der Wijngaart. Nas grid benchmarks: A tool for grid space exploration. *Cluster Computing*, 5(3):247–255, 2002.

[14] Vladimir Getov and Thilo Kielmann, editors. *Component Models and Systems for Grid Applications*, volume 1 of *CoreGRID series*. Springer Verlag, June 2004. Proceedings of the Workshop on Component Models and Systems for Grid Applications held June 26, 2004 in Saint Malo, France.

[15] M. Humphrey et al. State and events for web services: A comparison of five WS-Resource Framework and WS-Notification implementations. In *Proc. of the 14th IEEE HPDC*, Research Triangle Park, NC, USA, July 2005.

[16] Uri Lublin and Dror G. Feitelson. The workload on parallel supercomputers: Modeling the characteristics of rigid jobs. *Journal of Parallel & Distributed Computing*, 63(11):1105–1122, Nov 2003.

[17] H.H. Mohamed and D.H.J. Epema. Experiences with the koala co-allocating scheduler in multiclusters. In *Proc. of the 5th IEEE/ACM Int'l Symp. on Cluster Computing and the GRID (CCGrid2005)*, Cardiff, UK, May 2005.

[18] Warren Smith, Ian T. Foster, and Valerie E. Taylor. Predicting application run times with historical information. *J. Parallel Distrib. Comput.*, 64(9):1007–1016, 2004.

[19] Allan Snavely, Greg Chun, Henri Casanova, Rob F. Van der Wijngaart, and Michael A. Frumkin. Benchmarks for grid computing: a review of ongoing efforts and future directions. *SIGMETRICS Perform. Eval. Rev.*, 30(4):27–32, 2003.

[20] Douglas Thain and Miron Livny. Error scope on a computational grid: Theory and practice. In *HPDC*, pages 199–208. IEEE Computer Society, 2002.

[21] G. Tsouloupas and M. D. Dikaiakos. GridBench: A workbench for grid benchmarking. In P. M. A. Sloot, A. G. Hoekstra, T. Priol, A. Reinefeld, and M. Bubak, editors, *EGC*, volume 3470 of *Lecture Notes in Computer Science*, pages 211–225. Springer, 2005.

[22] Rob V. van Nieuwpoort, J. Maassen, G. Wrzesinska, R. Hofman, C. Jacobs, T. Kielmann, and H. E. Bal. Ibis: a flexible and efficient java-based grid programming environment. *Concurrency & Computation: Practice & Experience.*, 17(7-8):1079–1107, June-July 2005.

Author Index